D1478232

Escape from Dubai

Hervé Jaubert

Headline Books, Inc.
Terra Alta, West Virginia

Escape from Dubai
by Hervé Jaubert

Helen Jaubert, co-author

To order additional copies of this book:

Headline Books, Inc.
P.O. Box 52
Terra Alta, WV 26764

Tel/Fax: 800-570-5951
Email: mybook@headlinebooks.com
www.headlinebooks.com
www.escapefromdubai.com

ISBN: 0-929915-94-1
ISBN 13: 978-0-929915-94-4

Library of Congress Control Number: 2009936710

PRINTED IN THE UNITED STATES OF AMERICA

A Personal Note

After escaping from Dubai and reflecting on my situation from the safety of my home, I decided to write my story. It has taken a year of intensive work and focus to complete it. I had to face two challenges: first, as a French national, writing a book in English was as tough as eating a stale baguette; second, I had to lay out the contradictions and the two faces of Emiratis without generalizing, for I do have very devoted and true friends who are of Middle-Eastern origin.

This would not have been a noteworthy story without my devoted wife Helen, who is herself a writer. Her skills were paramount in transcribing my less than perfect English and then editing my manuscript. But even more, this book would not be what it is without her keen perception of the Emirati society, her witness of what happened to me, and her own victimization on my account.

Helen, through these fifteen years, only you have courageously journeyed alongside me from the gardens of Versailles and the beaches of Puerto Rico to the very deserts of Dubai. We touched the sky. You are the support on which my ruins rest. If I am still anyone, it is your entire gift… *Je t'aime pour toujours.*

My children were too young to even understand what happened, but I took these extreme and risky escape measures to keep my children from being fatherless and my wife a widow. My situation was complex and arduous, to say the least. There were so many convoluted details to this story that it would take more than one sitting to tell you everything, and I do mean *everything.*

I'm overflowing with gratitude to my valuable friends, whom I cannot name, but whose risks were instrumental to bringing this to life.

Table of Contents

Chapter 11—Dubai—The Fraud 219

Conclusion 299

Preface

No doubt that if you listen to the news, Dubai seems to be the cool new vacation spot for the rich and famous—or the new place to become rich and famous.

Unlike its neighbors Riyadh or Teheran, Dubai is associated with glitz and glamour. It shows the world astonishing images of its ultimate constructions—beautiful beaches and extreme nouveau-riche lifestyles. It presents itself as a safe, progressive and cosmopolitan city with a liberal outlook mixed with Middle Eastern traditions. This modern city, stretched between the Persian Gulf and the desert, attracts investors, celebrities, and politicians from all over the world. It is frequently referred to as the City of Gold, and its desert landscapes and palatial resorts are said to mix the *One Thousand and One Arabian Nights* with Western atmosphere.

Who wouldn't want to live there? And why would anyone ever want to escape from this paradise?

To lure tourists and investors, the Dubai government and its family of Royals have spent billions to skillfully craft an image of a safe, tourist-friendly, tax-free haven that gladly welcomes entrepreneurship. Favorable news reports are the result of bribed experts. Reporters and other media practice self-censorship so they may remain in the country where they can make money and not be fined or imprisoned for printing stories that damage the royal family or the Emirate's reputations.

My story will tell you why I escaped from Dubai. It sheds light on the true faces of Dubai—one of corruption and lies at the highest levels of government—another of greed, lawlessness, and hypocrisy used by officials to lure tourists, workers and investors. Often foreign nationals uproot their families to set up house and office only to later discover their newly built assets have been stolen—along with their intellectual properties.

No one will ever tell you the *truth*. Like me, many will arrive at DBX with lots of hope and curiosity for the new and different, looking forward to building a happier life than what they've left behind. After a few years, Westerners start to realize they have unknowingly become disposable instruments in building the vision of Sheikh Mohammed bin Rashid al-Maktoum—the absolute ruler of Dubai.

With all of this international buy-in and media puffery, I don't expect you to believe, beneath all the glitter, there are insidious and sinister secrets the government and ruling families of the UAE do not want the rest of the world to know; but the truth will slowly seep out.

Escape from Dubai is based on true events of my life from 2004 to the spring of 2008.

With nothing held back, I tell you how I went from glitter to bitter, from becoming a prominent, publically-recognized CEO to scapegoat. It is how I discovered that my silver-lined cloud was turning dark gray and was about to run into severe weather—all in the space of four years. This story also serves as a warning for anyone already living there or wanting to go.

In 2004, I was invited to go to Dubai to create and become the CEO of a multi-million dollar submarine manufacturing company for Dubai World—one of the largest holding companies in the United Arab Emirates. I was contracted to design and build one-of-a-kind personal submarines and custom boats. But after only two years serving in that capacity, I became the victim of extortion, threats, and harassment from the police and government—mobsters posing as auditors, board members, and company executives.

Fortunately, my good physical and stable mental condition, along with the skills I developed during my years of service as an intelligence officer and a good dose of motivation, allowed me to get out of the trap in which I was caught. Hundreds of other people are held in the UAE, tangled in the same web that threatened to destroy me—with no passports, no resources, and no clue of what they can do. They remain ensnared—financially destitute or imprisoned—until the *Emiratis* holding them get what they want—money, confessions, coerced statements, admissions to crimes they didn't commit, or testimonies to be used against other innocent victims.

In order to save my family and myself, I had to come up with a plan for what was to be the escape of my life. I did escape and lived to tell about it. Now, I intend to expose the *too-good-to-be true* picture of Dubai—luxury cars, self-rated seven-star hotels, ski slope malls, and exclusive beaches—by pointing directly at the cracks in its façade, exposing the hidden truths that have already begun to seep from the foundations of its society, built on the backs of modern-day slaves.

This is a story the government of Dubai and its ruling families have tried to prevent me from publishing. Because once you know what's really behind the red velvet curtain, you will think twice about going to Dubai and getting bushwhacked by the well-set trap that has netted the Emirates billions of dollars and landed hundreds of foreign victims in jail without charges, without legal representation, and without the rights we take for granted in our countries.

I invite you to read the story of my escape and learn the inconvenient truths of Dubai.

Chapter 1

My Life as a Spy

Amazingly my story in Dubai started years before I even knew this place existed. The only reason I am able to tell about it now is because of who I was before. Twenty years ago, I was a Navy officer on special assignment for the DGSE—in other words, I was a spy. DGSE stands for Direction Générale de la Sécurité Extérieure, France's foreign intelligence agency—the equivalent of the CIA in the United States. The DGSE's motto is *"Partout où nécessité fait loi,"* which translates, "Wherever necessity makes law," and symbolizes my line of duty while in Service and my life line while trying to save myself from Dubai.

I received formal training in the Navy as a marine engineer, specifically mechanical, electrical, and electronics. Then I joined the DGSE where I was in charge of the high-tech covert operations division. I designed, built, and modified devices, robots or vehicles for use in my missions. My catalogue of devices covered areas including eavesdropping, covert communications, concealed photography, chemistry, locksmithing, special weapons, vehicles, and sometimes submersibles.

A career of spying is the best school in the world. This is where I had the opportunity to learn the unconventional ways to win a war without a fight and how to survive perilous situations. This kind of knowledge is not something I could have learned at any university. In the end, my covert training and operative experience at the DGSE definitely paid off during my escape from Dubai.

The extensive program designed to bring a Military Officer to a fully trained multi response secret agent would take too long to describe here, there is just no area left uncovered. It includes physical training for combat and survival—psychological training for resilience and for the art of manipulation—technical for the ability to conduct surveillance, use of weapons, explosives, chemicals and other special devices—mobility training for the ability to get in and out of places despite the difficulty, whether by driving a car, sky diving, scuba diving, sailing a boat or flying a single engine aircraft.

My missions were most often assigned to me with a "you are on your own—we don't know you." But, thanks to the high level of preparation I put into them (as a rule in the French Service), I never felt fear—even during risky operations—not even once—nor did I ever fear the bad guys I worked against.

In fact, I never experienced fear at all before I lived in Dubai. During my career as an "intelligence officer" (spy is actually a dirty word we used for the bad guys working for the other side), hell yes, I had been scared, many times. I jumped out of an airplane at night and found myself above a foreign city, not knowing where to land. I was scared that I would get hurt, hitting some pole or power line and not be able to get away—but I managed to land on a grassy area in the street, unseen and without a scratch, cursing the pilot who dropped me off the planned course.

I once swam underwater in a foreign port to board a yacht at night, and I became entangled in a net in pitch-black waters. I was scared that I could not get out, but I managed to cut my way out unharmed and again, unseen.

I got scared when hunted by counter-espionage police in the former Soviet Republics and when I was chased by armed militants in Lebanon. I was scared to death when stopped at gunpoint in Africa—an AK47 against my stomach, held by a young boy who could not have been older than fourteen and for whom killing a European was a score.

I liked the challenges the Service brought me. This career had me working in dangerous environments with no back up and no one but myself to rely on. It brought me a tremendous knowledge about myself and gave me a different perspective on life. Being scared was a normal part of my life—more like a tool than a parasite. So I knew what being scared meant, but I didn't know the difference between being scared and true fear. Being scared is a feeling you have in the head and in the chest; it is a temporary survival mode, a set of mental and physical reactions to put you in a better position to respond to an immediate threat. The heart pounds, pumping more blood, and adrenaline boosts the brain and muscle response. I always managed to control my body's reactions to being scared. I knew what to do—go back to square one and follow the procedures I had practiced. Make choices quickly and eliminate any bad solutions. Think, and remember the training.

Fear is visceral and permanent. You cannot control it. It is triggered by expected events. There is no adrenaline rush, no pounding heart—fear mines your spirit and your body. It is a psycho-physiological state generated by excessive pressure coming from your living and working environments or an ongoing conflict with a partner, employer, or relative. I experienced fear for the first time in Dubai, as a result of the relentless harassment I endured from Dubai World agents and from the very real risk I faced of being jailed indefinitely.

The mission of an intelligence service is to guarantee national security. To achieve this, it seeks information that adversaries want to keep secret. Then it conducts covert actions to disrupt their plans and preempt threats in matters of politics, economics, and national security—and in such a way that the government can say it knows nothing about it.

Intelligence services get most of their information from informants and through the interception of broadcasted communications such as phone calls and emails. Sometimes, they require unlawful action from their most secretive agents to acquire first-hand information, to manipulate an objective or group of people into doing things they would normally never do, or to neutralize threats before they become a crime and make victims. Although conducted by government agencies and for a just cause, these operations are illegal and never attributable to the government who authorized them. They violate domestic and international laws and treaties. They are straight-up stealing of information, breaches of privacy, coercion, manipulation, disinformation, influence and effective neutralization of individuals. When the decision is made, these actions do not take place over night with shootings or poisonings like in the movies. They are highly elaborate operations, where deceit and fabricated scenarios dramatically break off the course of the lives of the individuals who have been targeted, often without them knowing what is really going on.

This was my line of duty, my day-to-day job, so to speak. I was one of the secret agents who were called in to neutralize threats to national security or get information when other assets would not do the trick.

Most people wonder what the personal life of a secret agent is like. Well, the truth is, it's difficult to have a personal life at all. I didn't have one. It was like being a ghost. My IDs showed that I was born in an African colony where birth records had been destroyed in a fire long ago. I officially didn't exist, which served the purposes of my job perfectly. During my missions, the targeted parties never knew I was there, so they would not know what to look for.

Despite what you may believe, I only carried a weapon on rare occasions. I had a permit to carry one, but only under my real identity, so it was totally useless during covert operations. There is no such thing as a license to kill, even when the "neutralization" of dangerous individuals is sought by the government. I was trained to use all types of guns, but I found my best protection to be the guise of a nobody—someone easily ignored and just as easily forgotten. A nobody does not carry a gun, so I organized my assignments in such a way that I didn't need one. If I carried one, it only meant that I would use it, like the Medieval Samurai who only drew his blade to strike.

However, if an "elimination" was an absolute necessity to save lives, I would rather manipulate the situation so that someone else would be doing the shooting for me, and taking the blame at the same time.

How does one do that, you might wonder? Of course, it's more difficult than a direct hit, and requires some work to pull off. But think of it this way: when a bomb maker is blown up by his own bomb, or when a bad guy is shot by another thug, it does not surprise or bother anyone. It looks more like a job-related accident. In my case, I would fabricate a scenario where eventually the mark is gunned by another bad guy of his own group—an accomplice, so to speak. I would spread acute paranoia and conspiracy theories among them like a disease. We called it *bleuite* in French spy slang. It means figuratively that people start seeing blue rats or imaginary moles everywhere and they no longer trust one another.

During one assignment, I created a situation where the mark, who happened to be a murderer and a bomb maker, was found by his accomplices with a tape recording in his raincoat. They discovered the tape held a recording of phone conversations of the group's leader. Even under torture, he didn't tell them anything about the recording because he could not tell what he didn't know, so he appeared to be a liar and a traitor. I was the one pulling the strings; I was the one who had intercepted the group leader's phone conversations with a phone tap. In truth, I knew when I installed it there would be nothing useful on the tapes. The guy was always talking with codes, and therefore, the content was mostly incomprehensible. But, if I could not use the tapes for their content, I could use the tapes for what they were—intercepted conversations from the leader's phone. I knew that if my mark were to be found with these tapes, he would be seen as a snitch and a threat to their organization.

On a late evening in a restaurant in Warsaw, I slipped the tape into the mark's raincoat as my colleague simulated a violent stomachache nearby, puking all over and screaming in pain and knocking the dishes off the table to draw everyone's attention. It was very dramatic and effective for our purposes. Later, after he walked out the restaurant, my mark put his hand into his pocket and pulled out the tape in front of his highly paranoid friends, like I expected he would when finding something that had not been there before. His fate was sealed—he was found a few days later with two shotgun wounds in the chest. I'd rid the world of a dangerous terrorist, and their organization was pretty messed up, yet I didn't carry a gun, and I didn't pull the trigger. No one even knew I was involved. I was a ghost.

The life of a spy is highly glamorized, and it appears to be the perfect calling for someone who thrives on adrenaline rushes and danger around every corner. Yet it is not a job I would recommend to anyone. A spy's world is lonely, cynical, dark, and cold. You cannot have friends outside the Agency, and you cannot have a social life and meet people. There is nothing you can talk about with others regarding yourself or what you do for living, because it can only harm you later. As a result, to the rest of the world, you appear to be person who is either antisocial or uninteresting.

As the years wore on, I realized that I wanted to do something else with my life, something that would be more constructive. I wanted to have a social life like everyone else. I knew that I had to get out of this secret, lonely shell in which I lived for a very long time, so in 1993, I resigned from the DGSE with the Navy rank of Commandant. Unlike many intelligence officers, when I quit, I quit for good. I never looked back, never considered continuing in that line of work. I broke off all relationships with the Service. I made a complete change of direction and never considered working for any intelligence agencies ever again.

It sounds simple, but it wasn't. As you can imagine, the Service doesn't like loose cannons walking around with secrets and special skills. I left my life as a secret agent—yet I never forgot the special techniques I learned on the job. These were skills and techniques I used again in Dubai, beginning in April 2007, against the person who had betrayed me—His Excellency, Sultan Bin Sulayem.

Chapter 2

New Opportunities

After I cut all ties with the Service, I relocated to another continent to start a new life in a completely different professional environment. I moved from France to the United States, to its Caribbean island of Puerto Rico—going from the murky waters of secret service to the crystal-clear ones of the Caribbean Sea.

No, I didn't throw a dart on the map; the woman who would become my wife and future mother of my two children is Puerto Rican. She caught my eye in Baltimore at a Covert Operations Expo where she worked as a hostess. Just two weeks away from retiring, this four-day stint was my last run for collecting info and buying spy goods for the Service. As my luck would have it, I met her on the very last day of my visit. What happened next and how I seduced her, ahhh — that's another book.

While in Navy training, I performed my first dives in the 1980s in the atolls of the Pacific Ocean. It was a stunningly beautiful introduction to scuba diving. The enjoyment of the sport was short-lived, however, because the sea quickly became a place to hide and conduct covert actions—no time to observe the underwater beauty.

After a fifteen year commitment to the service, I rediscovered scuba diving in the tropic waters of Vieques and Isla Verde in a more peaceful way. When diving for leisure and business, I could see it from a completely different perspective. I came to realize how so many people would be willing to go under the water if only they had a cool way to do it.

The underwater world, although beautiful, is a hostile environment that can only be explored with a life support system. Most people don't want to get wet or put on bulky equipment so they can enjoy all the sea has to offer below its surface.

It is from the basis of this observation that I developed a unique submarine technology specifically designed to take the public in shallow water excursions right from their resorts. I designed recreational submarines for shallow water leisure operations with three criteria in mind—they had to comply with the laws of physics, provide 100 percent safety, and be user friendly. They were built with an equalization pressure system, pressurizing the inside of the cabin to counter the pressure from the water outside. This meant that I didn't have to build a strong hull to resist the external water pressure. This gave me a lot of freedom in designing the shape of my subs, and since they were not going to operate in deep water, the air pressure inside was moderate. This technology allowed me to build recreational submarines faster and for less money than the pressure-resisting hulls. These new submarines didn't need to comply with all of the requirements of other submarines that made deep-water dives because they were only meant for shallow water use.

Lending further credence to the viability of my idea was my belief that the general public doesn't want to dive deep anyway—and for good reason. It is cold and dark below 150 feet. There is little to see, and it's out of reach of normal rescue divers. If a submarine has a problem at this depth, the rescue operation turns into an international event. Diving in shallow water is much safer, requires less surface support, and the majority of underwater life lives within the first thirty feet of water.

Submarine design was not new to me. I built my first submarine when I was fourteen years old. It was a remote-controlled, six-foot long, wooden submarine. Later, during my career with the French Navy, my submarine knowledge and design work was only intended for military or covert operations. When I began designing submarines in the Caribbean, I left the black ops subs for the yellow submarines, so to speak.

Submarines are not currently a popular means of transportation; at least, not until humans develop underwater habitats. So, besides the scientific communities, the only markets left for my subs were the leisure and military markets. Subs for this niche are still expensive, and, with the necessary life support systems onboard, their operation requires special training for their crew.

Tourist submarines attract a lot of attention and generate huge interest in their underwater tours. I conducted a market study that confirmed diving in a submarine, if available, was the first pick for a vacation activity. It ranked ahead of jet skis, helicopter rides, or fishing tours. I used to joke with people, asking them, "When was the last time you took a ride in a submarine?"

I operated a small tourist submarine for two years. My sub had the capacity to carry two passengers at a time for half-hour rides. I was located only a few minutes away from the beach and nearby hotels. Unlike bigger tourist subs, there was no need for a ferry to transport my passengers to the diving site. A small submarine is much more maneuverable than a large one and can approach reefs much closer and more safely. I would compare large submarines to a big bus packed with strangers and my personal submarines to a four-by-four all-terrain vehicle allowing safe rides with friends or relatives. All the small tourist submarines available on the market that I knew of had limited range and speed—they were merely elevators to take people in one direction. My subs could literally fly between reefs and had a ten-mile range.

I not only built submarines to use in my underwater tour business, I also custom built subs. I had a handful of customers every year. I didn't really know what they were doing with them, and that was a concern since submarines have a dual use—they can be used for leisure but also for evading police or committing crimes. I would never know for sure if my submarines were used for family members as declared on the end user agreement or for smuggling illegal cargo.

How could I know whether those potential buyers or those visiting the facility were really committed or just pretending? Once, I had a visitor who came to the company on a bicycle to inquire about purchasing a submarine. As he peddled away, I thought to myself that there was no way this guy would buy a submarine. Well, I was wrong. He did come back to buy a submarine, and he paid with a briefcase packed full of twenty-dollar bills. I learned two things from this event. One: never judge a book by its cover. Two: never look for signs of disposable income to determine if somebody can afford a submarine.

There were only a handful of submarine manufacturers worldwide, and nobody was building specially-designed shallow water submarines, so I was confident that with this niche market it would just be a matter of time before my designs would become successful.

Eventually, I moved my submarine business to Florida, where I had ready access to materials, labor, and clear testing waters. My small company was called Seahorse Submarines, and it had a dozen employees. As word got around, buyers showed up at my door. Three years passed, and I was getting offers from New Zealand, China, and the Caribbean, but it was Dubai that got all my attention.

It started in December 2003 with a visit to my factory in Florida from His Excellency, Sultan Ahmed Bin Sulayem, the Executive Chairman of Dubai World and Dubai Ports Authority of the United Arab Emirates, or UAE. He was accompanied by a tall chap named James Miller, or Jim, an American who was working for Sultan as a personal assistant. At the time, I didn't know where to put this tiny country on a map, and I had no idea who His Excellency was. He appeared to me more like King of the Hill rather than some Sultan of Dubai. I subsequently learned that Sultan is his first name and not a title—although he is one of the elite of Dubai.

Sultan is not a Sheikh, nor a member of the ruling family of Dubai, but he comes from the same tribe, and is very, very close to the Ruler of Dubai and Vice President of the United Arab Emirates, His Highness Sheikh Mohammed Bin Rashid Al Maktoum. Regardless, he is one of the most important decision-makers and executives of the Dubai government.

When I met Sultan, he seemed to be an extremely busy man, constantly on the phone—three phones to be exact—making him appear detached and not paying attention to my presentation. He was dressed casually in jeans and Adidas sneakers with no jewelry or other signs of wealth other than a gold watch. But the wealth of this fifty-three-year-old businessman was magnanimous. He showed up in Stuart, Florida, in a chartered jet. He left his private plane parked on a New York Airport tarmac because it was too big to land on the Stuart runway.

Sultan explained that he was interested in buying submarines for his artificial islands off the coast of Dubai. I didn't realize he was talking about the largest man-made islands in the world. He definitely had a vision for the mass use of recreational submarines and he had obviously done some research into other submarine manufacturers. But I could not visualize the coasts of Dubai as a location of choice for submarine recreational diving. Dubai was not on the list of the top fifty worldwide diving locations. Sultan shared with me that he wanted to bring Dubai to the top level. Knowing what I did about diving and marine ecosystems, I didn't see how he could realistically achieve that goal.

Dubai was not recognized as a place for scuba diving, like the Red Sea or the Maldives. Plus, with Dubai being in the proximity of a war zone and across the embargoed Iran with many war ships cruising in the vicinity of the strategic Strait of Hormuz, I thought my submarines would make every government body nervous knowing that people could be running around somewhere under the water without notice and virtually undetectable. Because of the context, I was not sure if Sultan really intended to purchase my submarines or if he was just curious.

I shared my skepticism at the viability of a personal submarine industry off the coast of Dubai with Jim, hoping that as an American, he could appreciate my concerns and share them with Sultan. I suspect he did because two months after his visit, Sultan wired a deposit to order one submarine—the Goby. He invited me to Dubai for an introductory tour and to convince me of the potential business there.

Before I traveled to Dubai, I needed to learn more about this tiny state in the Middle East. I did some research and learned some basic and historical information. Many people see the Middle East as a cradle for Islamic militants and a region torn with conflicts, inherently violent where freedom is a demon to fight. Regardless, today, the Middle East is certainly one of the world's most economically, politically, strategically, and culturally sensitive areas.

Dubai is a member of the United Arab Emirates, a federation of seven states created thirty-seven years ago after the British withdrew from the region. It was inhabited by primitive tribes living a simple life in poverty on open land—fishermen working in pearl trading or Bedouins living a nomadic life searching for water and resources. Farmers settled deeper in the desert in villages close to oases. The lawlessness of the region favored pirates who cruised the Persian Gulf waters to find their bounty and smugglers who transported contraband, which was anything from gold to slaves.

In the early 1800s, Great Britain imposed a truce on all parties and divided the region into seven Sheikhdoms, which became the Trucial Coast, referencing the British-imposed truce upon the local tribes. The seven current ruling families snatched power in their respective regions of influence. The British truce further reinforced the leading role of the ruling families and created a political status quo between the Sheikdoms.

After the discovery of oil in the 1960s, the economy changed dramatically. Oil became the major source of income for the country. With the construction of oil fields, oil companies provided settlements and logistics for their workers and families and opened exchanges with the rest of the world. Oil-generated wealth in the UAE created a demand for a commercial deep-water port, and services increased. Dubai invested its oil share revenues to dredge and build the Jebel Ali Port and achieved what is now the world's largest man-made port— strategically located to channel goods to the rapidly growing UAE and neighboring countries.

Sheikh Mohammed Bin Rashid Al Maktoum is the current ruler of Dubai. He was born in 1949, and is the third of four sons of Sheikh Rashid. He was privately tutored before beginning his formal education, eventually attending the Bell School of Languages at Cambridge University in 1966. He is known to many expatriates as Sheikh Mo. He married his senior wife (his first cousin), Sheikha Hind bint Maktoum bin Juma Al Maktoum, in 1979. His junior wife is Her Royal Highness Princess Haya bint Al-Hussein, daughter of Hussein of Jordan.

In 1995, Sheikh Mohammed was appointed Crown Prince of Dubai and started transforming Dubai into the world's most luxurious resort and business destination. He initiated the development of the man-made Palm Islands, the Dubai trademark Burj al-Arab hotel, the Burj Dubai skyscraper, the Dubai World Cup, Emirates Airline, and the Godolphin Stables. Sheikh Mohammed was named Ruler of Dubai and Prime Minister and Vice President of the UAE in 2006 after the death at age sixty-five of his elder brother, Sheikh Maktoum, who had been the ruler of Dubai since 1958.

During the last twenty-five years, massive changes have rapidly taken place. Local and federal government offices were established in all the Emirates, providing jobs and incentives for its citizens. Emiratis abandoned the countryside and migrated to cities in an effort to achieve a stable monthly income and better living conditions. Dubai initiated formidable construction projects using advanced technology and laborers imported from abroad, building a huge city in the desert in a very short period of time.

Sheikh Mohammed wanted Dubai to emerge as a trading center for the whole region, so he opened its domain to all who wanted to trade, invest, and work there, along with all the necessary facilities and logistics. As a result, today Dubai is one of the most cosmopolitan cities in the world, host to dozens of major international firms.

Once I became acquainted with all this information, I was eager to travel to Dubai. I had lived in, worked in, and traveled to other parts of the Middle East, but that was nothing compared to what I was soon to discover.

In March 2004, I flew to Dubai for a week's introductory trip. The first thing that hit me when I left the airport was the heat. It felt like I had opened an oven door. Warm summery temperatures were familiar to me after living in the Caribbean and Florida, but the heat in Dubai is way beyond anything I had felt before. I wasn't prepared for scorching sun and sweltering weather at least nine months out of year. Most of the rest of the world has rainy seasons, but Dubai has none, and when it happens to rain on a rare occasion, it does not get better with the water quickly flooding the streets. The average temperature from April through August was 125 degrees Fahrenheit; for the other months of the year it was seventy to ninety degrees Fahrenheit.

I was surprised by the numerous and vast construction sites. The whole place was a supercolossal structure in the making—erections of buildings at an unprecedented rate. The entire city was a beehive of activity. Thousands Asian workers milled about in pale blue jumpsuits waiting for their busses, within walking distance of the lots full of trucks and cranes. The roads were jammed with buses, cars, SUV's, Bentleys and Ferraris in stark contrast to the endless lines of workers

On the human side of things, it was impossible to miss the formidable mélange of culture in Dubai. Most of the 1.5 million people living on this thirty five mile long piece of land along the Persian Gulf, came from somewhere else to visit and work. Nowhere else in the world have I ever seen such a concentration of different nationalities in one small place.

On my second day in Dubai, I met with Sultan, who took me to visit as many of his projects and real estate developments as time would allow. He shared with me that he was the chairman of more than 250 companies. At a later date, I think it became more like 1,000. I never asked him how one person could be the chairman of 250 companies and remember all of them.

My first stay in Dubai was also an opportunity to take a glimpse of the DIBS, the Dubai International Boat Show, and see how my subs would fit into the market. Sultan gave me my first taste of chaos and pressure when he asked me to set up a booth to introduce my submarines days away from the opening. Thanks to his powerful connections, the last minute preparations and the submarine set-up was completed and ready seconds before the public rushed into the Show.

At the time, Dubai was a burgeoning presence in the international boat arena, but there was yet to be a strong local market for boats or submarines. The boat show had little to compare with the Cannes or Fort Lauderdale Boat Shows, but Sultan intended to make DIBS competitive. He showed me the potential sales from all the wealthy Middle Eastern buyers who were present and ready to spend their money on personal watercrafts.

Everywhere we went, I was treated like a VIP. Sultan was opening all the doors of opportunity for me, and with all of this unlimited money flowing into the UAE, I could visualize a formidable submarine marketing strategy for the region. Sultan explained that with the low cost and plentiful labor available in Dubai, building submarines would be cheap. While I trusted and bought into a lot of what Sultan said to me, this was one concept I didn't agree with because submarines cannot be built cheaply. Building a submarine is not like piling up concrete blocks to make a building. It's a high-tech vessel that requires the skills and knowledge of highly trained individuals to design and assemble. Nobody wants to dive in a cheaply built sub, just like nobody wants to fly in a cheaply built airplane.

During one visit, Sultan took me on his yacht with his closest and long-time Emirati friends for a two-day trip off the coast of the Emirates. His 154-foot boat has three decks, and no expense was spared in its design. There wasn't much to see, other than two pretty Russian girls dancing around in bikinis. When I first saw them, I thought they were girlfriends of someone on the boat, but then I saw them going from one guy to another, feeling up one of Sultan's friends, kissing and massaging feet. I understood they were onboard for those who wanted to be entertained. I was surprised these Emirati men exposed their willing participation in the use of prostitutes in front of a stranger. Either this was normal in Dubai, or they were simply arrogant, or it was to bait me into doing something they could use against me later. Regardless, I minded my own business. This was my first of many experiences observing Emiratis taking pleasure in wide-open spaces with paid sex.

On this occasion, I saw that Sultan was not participating at all, but that did not make me trust him more. I just thought he might be more discreet than his guests. He had a playful side he shared with me while fooling around with a new toy he had just purchased—a small thermal camera. We holed up in a dark cabin, trying to figure out how the camera worked. This high-tech camera cost around $50,000, and he played with it like it was a disposable.

I discovered a rare quality in Sultan during this boat trip. He noticed that one of the boat's propeller shafts was making an unusual noise. In the middle of the night, he jumped into the water wearing scuba equipment and carrying a flashlight to inspect underneath the hull. He came back to tell his captain that a four-inch bushing had come off its seat. The captain reduced speed, and we returned to port on one engine. I don't know many boat owners or businessmen who would jump into the darkness of the ocean in the middle of the night to check the propellers. I found this quality valiant, and it drew me close to him.

A few days later at the marina during a dinner onboard his yacht, I discovered a somewhat ruthless facet of Sultan's personality. A German guest was bragging about his level of knowledge regarding hot sauces— he knew them all and none were strong enough to take a smile off his face. Sultan didn't openly challenge him. Quietly, he just pulled a small bottle out of a cabinet and invited this guy with a nod to put a few drops of its contents onto his Chicken Biryani.

The hotness of a chili pepper is measured by the Scoville scale by the amount of capsaicin (a chemical compound that stimulates nerve endings in the skin) present in the chili pepper or the chili sauce. Instead of the average 80,000 Scovilles chili hot sauce, Sultan gave this guy a 15,000,000 Scovilles pepper sauce out of his special collection.

I know a bit about hot sauce myself. Sultan would not have tricked me on that one, which was more like weapons-grade chemical warfare, not a sauce. The German guy took a mouthful and then jumped to his feet, tears pouring out of his eyes. His face turned purple, and he ran for the bathroom half-blind. I couldn't see him, but I could hear him— he sounded like a squealing pig. The surrounding white robes continued to make fun of him, but I am not sure his bragging deserved the pain he must have been in. When he returned, he had the humble look of someone whose mouth and tongue have been paralyzed from surviving 'the sauce.' His silence after the incident showed me that he had learned his lesson—*don't ever try to sell a pair of shoes to someone without first knowing what size he is.* It was a lesson I needed to learn for myself as well.

I observed in silence, but there was one time on a trip on Sultan's boat when I made a comment. I am by nature very observant with a sharp technical eye that comes from being a mechanical engineer with extensive experience in reverse engineering. I noticed a slight angle in the attitude of his ship that was not normal. The bow was dipping a little bit, indicating there might be a bigger problem somewhere else in the boat's arrangement to cause this shift with the center of gravity. I thought Sultan would appreciate me pointing out a potential problem with his valuable yacht.

I knew what I was talking about, unlike the German guest, but it didn't matter. Sultan didn't like my observation at all. He gave me an explanation that made no sense, brushing off the importance of what I noticed. I saw from his reaction and his attitude afterwards that whatever the truth, he didn't want to hear it if it didn't correspond with his view. I resolved that it was not my problem anyway—after all, I was just his guest. I later learned that to get along with Emiratis you can't tell them anything that might be a negative reflection on them or their personal properties. It must be excellent, beautiful, and fantastic or be quiet.

During this trip, we also went scuba diving with Jim around Palm Island, checking the underwater conditions—a key element for the development of tourist submarines in the area. For the first time in my life, I had three assistants to help me put on my scuba gear. Scuba diving was comfortable there without the need to carry the tank, the weights, and everything else. Jim even had a personal Sherpa just to carry his towel. The water was too hot; even a three millimeter wetsuit was unbearable, and there was no visibility. The terribly salty water blurred my vision. Sultan spent $50,000 to buy a night vision camera just to play on his boat. But when it came to diving, he dove with a Chinese underwater scooter he bought for $100—pure junk that didn't work, not even for one full dive. He ended up dropping it to the bottom of the ocean because of its dead weight. Later he sent a diver to try and recover it—fat chance of that happening. I didn't get to look at it.

Sultan had plans to develop a major scuba diving center on Palm Island, recreating dive sites on a three-mile crescent-shaped area. He wanted to reproduce the best diving sites of the world in one place: the Great Barrier Reef, the Caribbean reefs, the Pacific Atolls, the Red Sea reefs, and the Indian Ocean reefs. He had a complete showroom at Nakheel's headquarters (Nakheel was the real estate development company under Dubai World and the creator of the artificial Palm Islands) with scale models and video animations. It looked like a movie set out of a modern *20,000 Leagues under the Sea*. It must have a cost millions just for the display, and I guessed it would cost hundreds of millions of dollars to actually build the project.

We also dove in an area where, to create a wreck diving site, he had sunk several planes—three F100 Super saber jets and three Tupolev commercial airplanes. The fighter jets were still intact, but two of the three airliners had just disappeared or had been reduced to pieces on the seabed fifty feet below the surface. I thought it was insane, but in Dubai, if somebody wants to dump forty tons of junk aircraft in fifty feet of water, they just do it. They don't even bother to update the marine charts, either. Too bad for the unfortunate guy who later trashes his boat on the wreck.

The lack of visibility under the water was a real concern for me. With only five feet of visibility, I could not see any submarine development or even scuba diving activities in the future unless there was a drastic change in the water quality. When I shared my concerns with Sultan, he told me the turbidity was created by ongoing real estate development around the Palm Islands, and when the projects would be completed the sediment would settle down. I didn't believe this was the only explanation for the poor condition of the water. There was no marine life and nothing to filter the seawater—only algae and suspended particles in water that was too warm. It would take decades before the water quality could improve enough to welcome divers, but I had already seen what happened to people who tried to tell Sultan what he didn't want to hear, so I kept my opinions to myself.

In order to create the demand for diving next to his artificial islands, Sultan told me that he would throw one kilogram of gold bullion into the water every day of the year to attract divers from everywhere for treasure hunting. Three hundred sixty-five kilos of gold dumped in the water every year is at least $10 million annually. It sounds like a lot, but I came to find that it was pocket change for Emiratis—and this was only the beginning of my comprehension of what wealth meant to them. As far as I knew, this ambitious gold bullion project never became a reality, and there were still no divers diving around the islands. No one can bribe Mother Nature.

Sultan had so many projects to show me there wouldn't be fifteen minutes of the day when I was not visiting something he was developing. He drove so fast, weaving in and out of gridlock to get from one project location to the next, that I was afraid we were going to have an accident in the insane traffic. We weren't the only ones rushing to get where we needed to be. Dubai was an extraordinarily busy city where everybody was pressured to cope with deadlines.

Sultan had a boat manufacturing company he wanted me to see called Palm Marine, which he felt could be the start up for a submarine manufacturing company. Palm Marine was managed by an Indian gentleman named Sanil Mohammed Subair. I met him for the first time during my tour of the Palm Marine facility. Sultan had several yachts under construction or being recommissioned there. After the visit, I was not interested in being involved with this company because I saw so many blatant construction flaws and copyright infringements right in front of my eyes—though I didn't want to comment about it. I knew better than to be the one bringing Sultan bad news.

Sultan did have some other interesting projects on the Palm Marine back lot that caught my attention. There were two boats, inventions of Sultan, already built and being tested. One was what he called the Boat on Wheels, and the other the Car Boat. The Boat on Wheels was a twenty-five-foot boat with retractable wheels like the landing gear on an airplane. The boat was designed to get out of the water on its own power and drive on the beach. Its problem was that it had an over-designed landing gear and an underpowered engine.

The Car Boat looked like half of a car installed on top of half of a boat. I watched it almost capsize every time Sultan made a sharp turn during sea trials. His crew was scared they might not make it back alive.

Both boats were technological nightmares—totally unstable, unmarketable, and useless. However, I considered them good efforts that showed me Sultan had an interest in research and development, innovation, and new technologies. With the vast funding available through Dubai World and Sultan's interest in innovation, I saw opportunities to develop and market more of my inventions. Sultan had already asked me to think about designing a submersible fishing yacht, a custom jet ski, a flying boat, and a boat on wheels that would actually work. I had the proven creativity to accomplish what he was asking of me. As long as I had engineering staff to work with me, the funding, the materials, and sufficient time, I could meet his expectations. I left Dubai with a lot to think about. I had a growing business in Stuart but a very attractive offer coming from Dubai. The time to make a decision was coming soon.

Three months later I returned to Dubai on Sultan's request. I noticed the long open space of Sheikh Zayed Road beginning to look more like the Las Vegas strip. Buildings were popping up at an astounding rate. The unprecedented pace of new construction was unthinkable. Changes in road grids and buildings were so significant that maps and GPS devices were rendered useless because they could not be updated fast enough.

In July 2004, Sultan came back to my factory with Jim and Hamed Kazim, the CFO of Dubai World. They made me an offer to purchase everything I had in my Florida company, both equipment and intellectual property, and move to Dubai to set up a 50/50 joint venture between Sultan and myself. He also proposed that I design special submarines for him in Dubai, a type that had never been built before. In the meantime, he ordered two more subs to be built: a six passenger and a one-man personal sub, which I started constructing straight away in order to deliver them to Sultan before moving to Dubai. Inevitably, I would have to expand the business and hire more employees to respond to the growing demand for personal submarines, but I didn't want to initiate an expansion in the U.S. if I was going to move to Dubai.

Dubai was undoubtedly the city of superlatives—the city of an unmatched cultural mélange, the city of the highest, the biggest, the most expensive, and the need to be first in everything. With the wealth, the support of high ranking and well-funded sponsors with innovative and visionary thinking, I could easily see my submarines on the list of superlatives that people would talk about before, during and after their visit to Dubai.

The answer to my dilemma to stay in the U.S. or to go to Dubai came during the summer of 2004, when three Category IV hurricanes trashed South Florida with two directs hits on my hometown in one month. The area was declared a disaster. The monster storms tore off roofs, telephone poles were snapped like tooth picks and trees were uprooted. The county was left without power, gas pumps, phone service, Internet, and water for weeks. My staff was not able to show up to work, and although my building didn't suffer any significant damages, my company was idling without its workforce, power, supplies or deliveries.

With deadlines for the delivery of the submarines to Dubai looming, Sultan told me I had no other choice but to stop production, close the business, move to Dubai, and complete the constructions of the current submarines over there.

I am an innovator and designer. I thought the opportunity being presented to me would allow me to focus all of my efforts on building submarines and watercrafts on a large scale, which would have been difficult if not impossible without the funding provided by Sultan. And it was being offered to me by a man who I thought had the same goals that I did, with a vision for the future.

But it was not an easy choice—relocating to another country never is, especially to the Middle East. My wife, a professional radio personality, was concerned with the way women are treated, cultural problems in general, and media censorship issues. But it was a business opportunity that was difficult to ignore. We decided to take Sultan's offer and move our family to Dubai.

Jim, Sanil, and I discussed the details via phone, email and fax almost every day. It was a major move—my wife and two very young children, all of our furniture, my tools, and seven forty-foot shipping containers.

Sultan didn't waste any time. I was not yet there when he directed Sanil and Jim to assist me on designing and building the new factory. They had the approval and the budget from Sultan to fund a complete facility in the Jebel Ali Free Zone south of Dubai. I was told by Sultan to "spare no expense." He wanted the very best facility money could buy. I designed the first unit on a 40,000 square foot plot that was allocated to me, just next to the beach and a UAE Navy base. The factory had to be a state-of-the-art manufacturing facility that could handle the construction of vessels up to ninety feet in length.

I prepared the drawings and sent them with the bill of materials to Sanil so that he could initiate the purchase orders and building permits. Around the time I was completing this process, I received notice from the U.S. Small Business Administration that loans I had applied for to expand my factory in Florida were finally approved. It was with irony that I turned them down. I had been asking for so many years, and now that I had the funding, I no longer needed it.

By November 2004, I had shipped everything in containers: partially built submarines, various parts, fifty tons of lead bricks for ballast, and other technical equipment; and I was with my family on a plane to Dubai for what I thought would be a promising new life.

Believe it or not, I actually moved to Dubai on a handshake deal with Sultan. I had no joint venture or any signed contracts yet, nor had I received any advance payments. Sultan paid for the tickets and the moving costs, but I took the risk of moving on his word, thinking the word of a top Dubai official was a serious and legal guarantee. Little did I know how wrong I was. It took three years for the fallout from my misplaced trust to reach me. But at the time, I had no way of knowing that Sultan's word was not something I could rely on for anything.

I still go over it in my head and wonder if there were signs I missed, but back in 2004 when this all started, the news and information about Dubai was scarce and much of it censored to be skewed in favor of Dubai and its governments. I wasn't too concerned at the lack of information at the time because I felt my background had prepared me for anything.

During my years as a spy, I faced intense technical challenges when I had to come up with quick solutions in counter-terrorism situations. I faced and witnessed the worst of human tragedies. I dealt with the ugliest side of human nature, when people made decisions fueled by the vilest motivations, willing to go to the worst extremes to get what they wanted. Because I survived many complex and dangerous situations, I felt confident I could manage a Dubai endeavor, despite warnings from my well-meaning friends who had read some negative anecdotes online about Dubai.

After a twenty-hour flight, I arrived in Dubai on a tourist visa. It was only after I arrived that my employer, Dubai Ports Authority, applied on my behalf for a work permit and resident visa. Sultan, as the Executive Chairman of the Dubai Ports Authority, facilitated everything to help me get in position as quickly as possible—leaving little time for any second thoughts I might have had. Sultan's assistants, Sanil and Jim, took care of every administrative step on my behalf. Everything I could see moved quickly, but the trap I couldn't see slowly built around me. By the time I figured out that I should *not* have placed so much trust in these people, it was too late.

Anyone who wants to work or live in Dubai needs a visa endorsed by an employer or sponsor, so I was officially hired as the general manager of Palm Marine, the boat building company. The 50/50 joint venture with Sultan turned out to be a renewable five-year employment contract and agreement for twenty percent share of profits. But the promises contained in those documents were about as worthless as the paper on which they were printed. I was now just an employee in top management—with an army of middle men and bureaucrats.

Once I received my visa, I sponsored the residency visas for my wife and children. Sanil processed the entire procedure on my behalf. The government expedited my visa applications and bypassed several procedures under Sultan's pressure to finish them quickly.

I discovered soon after that the visa situation in Dubai is quite unique. Visas are granted to accommodate the Emiratis, not the foreigner. Furthermore, the immigration laws tend to change about every six months. I have traveled to over thirty countries, and I've found that hidden rules or changes to visa requirements without notice only exist in Dubai.

A residency visa in the UAE is much more than just a stamp in your passport. It is a permission granted by a local sponsor, a company or an Emirati, to whom you have to surrender your passport, your freedom, and most of your rights. The government hides behind the law and says it is illegal to retain foreigners' passports, yet my company, like other government companies, held the passports of all employees—clearly illustrating their motto, "Do as I say, not as I do." When confronted, the government says it is a conservative measure to help the employee by making sure he doesn't lose his passport, as if all foreigners were little children or imbeciles.

The resident visa is not only an entry visa—it is also an exit visa. Every time a person wants to exit the country for any reason, he must ask permission from his sponsor to get his passport returned. If the sponsor denies the request, the person cannot leave the country regardless of his situation and the reasons he may have. Emirati sponsors are absolutely ruthless. I have seen people miss funerals, births, and weddings because their exits from the country were not authorized for the silliest reasons.

The residency visa to the expatriate is like water is to a plant—the 'thread of Life.' Without it you can't function in the society—and to live in Dubai, you must work. For slightly higher salaries in an exotic country, expatriates are willing to make big sacrifices and adapt to an unconventional culture. The resident visa is required to rent an apartment, register a car or a boat, get a driver's license, apply for utilities and phone service, run a business, hire employees, open a bank account, register children at school, and dozens of other basic day-to-day activities. You even need it to purchase and possess alcohol for personal consumption in the privacy of your home. Oh, you are limited to how much alcohol you can buy per month, too.

If you get fired or find yourself in trouble with the law, employers and/or authorities will cancel your visa on the spot. Then you'll have thirty days to exit the country or try your luck at finding another job.

Sultan made me feel like I was privileged to get my visa not just for myself, but also for my family. Indeed, I was privileged, because getting visas for family members was not granted for a majority of people—and I also didn't have to exit the country with my tourist visa and return with my work visa like everybody else.

Sultan knew I would not have come or stayed if I was unable to bring my family. Upon my arrival in Dubai, we lodged at the Emirates Twin Towers hotel for two months. One of the twin towers houses a five-star hotel, and the other tower is an office building with the headquarters of Dubai World and Sultan's office. We had no home to move into yet, and our furniture was still in transit. Throughout our two months in the Twin Towers, we were given the VIP treatment, though it was difficult keeping our two young children entertained in the business-oriented hotel.

A major move like this overseas was exhausting, intrusive and extremely stressful. I would *not* recommend it to anyone—especially now, due to ever-changing laws and restrictions that complicate the process tenfold. Also, you may not be able to ship your stuff back. You see, I was in this for the long haul, so this was to be my new job and my family's new home. My wife and I had been both driving a Hummer in Florida for some time, and I thought they would be the best four-wheel options for a desert-like area. Nowadays, to ship those cars would be a bad idea because of the newer UAE laws which have become stricter on vehicle imports.

During a previous trip to Dubai, I was invited to visit the gun range to check on the facilities and to shoot a few rounds. It was no surprise to anyone I owned a rifle I used for sport shooting and that I would bring it with me. I made a *huge* mistake when I moved to Dubai, a mistake I came to deeply regret in the end. Even after my wife argued with me numerous times *not* to, I decided to bring my fifty caliber rifle. It sounds ludicrous that someone would even own a sixty-pound canon sniper rifle, let alone travel with it to the Middle East. Looking back, I think bringing it was completely daft too. I had been using guns for sport shooting and shooting competitions all of my adult life. I shipped everything else I owned; for me, it didn't make sense to leave my rifle behind.

Before I left Florida, Sanil sent me the Customs approval for the import of my gun and ammunitions, and after I arrived, Sultan himself endorsed my license application with a copy of his passport. I claimed the rifle on my customs documents and with the airline as well. For safety purposes and to comply with international regulations, I shipped the ammunition separately. I put three cases of 150 rounds in the containers that were shipped to Dubai with all of my work equipment inside. I declared them on the content list of everything in the containers. There was no problem when I arrived at the Dubai airport with the rifle, and as planned, the police kept my rifle until I received the final license. I never did regain possession of my gun. I should have listened to my wife.

I didn't sneak the rifle or my ammunitions into the country or otherwise hide its presence in my belongings. But had I known what would eventually happen with that gun, I never would have brought it, regardless of the permissions I secured.

After my containers finally arrived in Jebel Ali, we moved into a house provided by Sultan. My stuff was delivered and unpacked by unskilled personnel—at least fifteen Indian nationals with no belts or caddies, not a single hand truck or lifting equipment— nothing but bare hands. They chanted in a bizarre sounding language, establishing a rhythm to help them rock, lift and move the furniture two feet at a time. It was like watching a scene from *Mr. Bean* meets *The Gods Must Be Crazy*.

The house we moved into was located in Jebel Ali on the outskirts of the desert, in an upscale village of 300 vacant villas. It was built by Nakheel, a good example of the engineered housing development wasting away, and exacerbated by stupidity. We were alone with five other families in a ghost village while hundreds of thousands of other individuals and families had to shack up in crowded housing conditions. I have never seen anything like it before. What kind of contractor or developer can afford the construction of 300 villas with no buyers, no tenants and not even renters? Sultan must have had at least $100 million up front in the cost of construction of this entire project with no concern about realizing a return on his money, even years later. It was astounding to me the many examples of wealth and waste I saw there.

With only six villas housing privileged government executive tenants like me, we rarely saw any neighbors. This was aided by the fact that everyone was so busy working all the time we didn't have opportunities to gather for neighborly BBQs. It took two years before we finally saw new faces moving into the villas around us, and had our first gathering. One of our neighbors, a nosy and funny Italian guy four villas down from us, was making fun of a new tenant across the way. He thought the guy was a real jerk to live such a meager life in such a nice house with no furniture while driving a Lamborghini. He explained that he once peeped through the windows, but he couldn't see any curtains, chairs, tables or anything else. I realized he was talking about my collector car, so I told him there was no cheap monk tenant living there—it was just me using the empty house parking spot.

My wife was not working. It was quite a challenge for her to go from a professional and high-paced position to being a housewife in a Muslim country with no friends. Used to doing her own house cleaning, it was even harder for her to adjust to a housemaid living with us; she saw it as intrusive. Eventually, she did get a job with *Gulf News* doing radio journalism again. She became busy like I was, and we hired more helpers to assist us with running our household.

I didn't have much time to stay at home. I had to build an entire submarine company from the ground up. I started the company from a trailer, under the name Palm Submarines. I wasn't partial to the name, but I was told it had to begin with the word *Palm* because of the Palm Islands branding.

Sultan never gave me a time frame within which I had to develop the company, other than "do it as quickly as you can," but we had an understanding the company should be in full production within three years. We had a long way to go and no time to waste. Not only did I have to build the company—I also had to be present at exhibitions and make demonstrations at boat shows in order to start building the brand for our submarines and developing interest in our products. I had three months before the coming Dubai boat show.

My first order of business was to raise from the sands a modern manufacturing facility. Besides giving it a better name, I had to build it, hire and train the personnel, do the engineering, resume the construction of submarines and boats, get all the required permits and certifications, and start the branding and marketing for the entire operation. Before the factory was even complete, I already had a dozen vessels around the free zone under construction in separate buildings and sheds.

Like any other foreign executive working for a Dubai Government Company, I didn't have direct access to funds—not a single penny. Sultan had to approve all vessel constructions and all expenditure requests I made to purchase equipment or any other asset or material for the company. Every financial issue that arose and every payment for the company was controlled by one of the executive chairman's financial officers and a handful of financial managers. Every project I undertook for the company, I did so at the direction and wishes of Sultan himself. This strict Emirati control of the company's finances and projects was a key component of my later troubles. One that I could never reconcile with the accusations that were later leveled against me.

But unlike my requested expenditures, I only had to mention Sultan's name to expedite administrative or payment issues once they were approved. Many people in the group were jealous because they had to struggle for months to get things done. Even though this made running the company easier for me than it could have been, I never took advantage of it. I turned down lots of perks in the interests of the company's financial well being. For example, in a city where every other CEO was allocated a new car to use for free, I drove my own.

After being in Dubai for only one month, I registered the company to attend the IDEX, the International Defense Exhibition & Conference of Abu Dhabi, and the most important exhibition of security and military equipment of the Middle East. Although I had only actively marketed the leisure submarines, I still received many inquiries from government agencies to provide their military with specialty mini submarines—this was, after all, my area of expertise. Attending this exhibition was a must and a perfect opportunity for the company to show the models I had designed for law enforcement. It was a last-minute booking, but I managed to put on display scale models of the new designs and an old complete and working submarine that I had previously built in the U.S. I also had a video presentation on a flat screen.

The model getting the most attention at the exhibition was the Submersible Patrol Vessel (SPV). It was an immediate success. Military buyers are not like resort owners—they know and understand the need for and applications of underwater vehicles right away, without too much of an explanation. And one country, Indonesia, initiated a $150 million order for the SPV.

One month after the IDEX came the 2005 DIBS, the Dubai International Boat Show. We were used to the organized chaos of the last-minute preparation of IDEX, so we just continued on our momentum for the boat show. I had three subs and one boat in the water and a static presentation with two other submarines to officially launch the company supported by a large-scale advertising. The magic and uniqueness of the submarines I created drew mass attention from the international media and public alike. The Emirati ego considers itself supreme and will not accept expats overshadowing it, taking credit for innovative developments on 'their' turf. Temper tantrums are traditionally the end result of that situation.

Once the boat show, the after parties, and the interviews were over, I became the subject of many TV shows, international newspapers, magazines, and online and broadcast media articles. Due to the nature of my inventions, the press hailed both the opportunity I had been given and the one Dubai had received as a result of Sultan convincing me to come onboard with his exciting plans. The innovations and novel aspect of what I was developing there—personal submarines and high-speed boats—fit right in with the Dubai allure.

But not all of the articles about me were lauding my opportunities—some were controversial, even foreboding. One of them was written by Lena Luteau in the French newspaper *Le Figaro*. It was all about the Frenchman spearheading this company—a former French spy now building extreme watercrafts in the midst of strained living conditions in Dubai—among human exploitation and surrounded by barbed wire and the obnoxious security in the so-called *Free Trade Zone*.

Lena was a proven talent in investigative reporting, especially in presenting the dark sides of stories. She caught me by surprise when she revealed I used to be an intelligence officer. I also thought she was exaggerating and talking out of turn when she painted me surrounded by barbed wire and guards—but I was wrong. I ignored the premonitions in her article, and I disregarded her assertions that there was something not quite right about this too-perfect picture of Dubai.

Before I moved to Dubai, few people, myself included, had read anything about Dubai. I ignored the rare articles that held warnings or showed the not-very-nice sides of this booming Arab city. I didn't just brush off stories written by talented journalists. I also shrugged off warnings from friends who told me to be careful. I played deaf to the whole idea of the warnings. I fell for the propaganda generated by Dubai. Little did I know that three years later I would find myself on the wrong side of the barbed wires, discovering that the fences around Dubai were designed not to keep people out—but to keep anyone from leaving.

Hervé Jaubert

Chapter 3

Exomos

It took me six months to complete the first phase 20,000 square foot building. Something of that scale usually takes two years. We moved in the new facility and relocated all equipment, vessels and other assets that were scattered in the free zone.

It was a five-star factory, years ahead of its time. It was divided into different zones and workshops to optimize the production flow. It had everything from fifteen-ton overhead cranes to a video conference meeting room and a studio for producing videos for the company's marketing and TV productions.

I wanted the best quality manufacturing and the cleanest environment, free from fiberglass dust and resin smell. To reach the goals set by Sultan and me, we had to have the best facility for molding and fabricating fiberglass hulls, so I built the fully air-conditioned facility with the latest technologies, including a central dust vacuum system and resin infusion system. All interior and exterior areas were monitored by a closed circuit television and surveillance system. I even included a system to recover the condensed water from the air conditioning to use for general purposes and to water the lawn. It produced 200 gallons of fresh water that didn't need treatment every day. It wasn't much, but it was free water that would have otherwise been wasted.

Six months after the completion of the first phase, I opened the second phase—a 20,000 square foot building on the same plot with more production bays, labs and a cafeteria, so that employees could have their lunch on the company campus. I included a mosque, because the majority of my employees were Muslims. Being a government-owned company, with no separation between religion and government, it was mandatory to provide a place of worship for them. The whole office area had glass walls, stainless steel stairs, and décor reminiscent of the sea. I put a 1,500 gallon tropical fish aquarium in the lobby, designed to appear as an invitation to the underwater world. Even the carpet was custom, with coral reef patterns. The company flag was a twenty-five-foot, yellow, three-passenger submarine mockup installed at the top of a pole outside the entrance. It was an unmistakable landmark for visitors to Palm Submarine and the Jebel Ali free zone.

I extended the facility on another 20,000 square foot plot across the street and brought in five mobile offices for the operations and training department, a briefing room, and storage for diving equipment and the compressors to refill the air tanks. A hyperbaric chamber completed the whole set-up for testing purposes and hyperbaric treatment if required.

The third phase was already approved by Sultan: a two-million dollar testing facility on the beach, housing a forty-five foot deep test pool with direct access to the ocean. But it would take two years before we could use it, so in the meantime, I built a temporary above ground testing pool on the plot across the street with an overhead gantry crane. I contracted with a trucking company to fill the pool with seawater for the testing of small submarines and the training of pilots and engineers. I watched as they pumped dirty seawater from the port into the tank truck that said "DRINKING WATER" on its sides with no concern at all for the risk of contaminating the fresh water of the next customers who might get gastroenteritis and suffer numerous trips to the toilet as a result.

We also built a submersible submarine cabin mockup to simulate catastrophic flooding of a submarine so that we could practice ditching, or emergency evacuations. During training, the mockup sub with three passengers was lowered into the test pool, and then a diver would retract one of the viewports to provoke a fast flooding. It was always a thrilling experience for the three passengers, but with the preparation, a person had enough time to ditch the sub safely. It was better for a pilot to practice in a pool under controlled circumstances, than having to learn how to ditch during an emergency in the ocean. Every engineer and pilot had to go through and pass the same ditching test.

The *Palm Submarine Company* name was temporary. Sultan had given me carte blanche to change the name to one I felt was more appropriate. He understood that to be on the international scene, an Emirati name for a submarine manufacturing company would not be the best choice. I needed a new name that would become a trademark—a name people could remember and pronounce in any language, not another name with the word *Palm* in it. I wanted a name with a Latin-like base for an exotic touch. I was inspired by *Nostromo*, the gigantic spaceship in the movie *Alien*. I contracted a major branding company out of New York, and together we came up with the name Exomos. It means second skin, or outer skin—like the hull of a submarine would be for its passengers. It was perfect. I brushed aside a proposal from Sultan's assistants to name the company after myself, Hervé. To have used my name for a company that didn't belong to me would have been a mistake.

The image of the company was instrumental for its successful development and marketing. When you build submarines, it is easy to have an exotic image without much effort because the subs themselves attract a lot of attention. But there is a lot to explain about a submarine before people feel confident enough to buy one or to take a ride in one.

I had several years of experience dealing with the public behind me, so I knew how to pass the message pretty well—and with Sultan's support, I had the budget to build a powerful marketing strategy. The communications company in New York did fantastic work. The website for Exomos was awesome—vivid, with action and character. It promoted a true invitation to go for underwater exploration. I immediately received tremendous exposure with inquiries coming in from all over the world full of cheering messages.

I registered the name Exomos as a trademark—this was important, as I was targeting a worldwide market. The logo represented two interlaced waves—simple and memorable.

In March 2005, Sultan appointed me as the CEO of Exomos when I officially launched the company at the DIBS. Exomos was a Dubai Port Authority member of the Dubai World Company owned by the Dubai government with Sultan as Executive Chairman. Exomos was one of Sultan's special projects, and I didn't realize it at the time, but I was sitting on a barrel of gunpowder. Many powerful people were envious of my situation and the media attention I was receiving— jealousy grew into anger about the freedoms I had, my ability to get things done so quickly with Sultan's support, and my popularity with the outside world.

Even with Sultan's resources at my disposal, branding and marketing submarines was no easy task. I needed to popularize the concept, make subs accessible to the public and create a new trend. I was selling dreams—traveling in slow motion under water, discovering marine life, and enjoying unforgettable experiences. I had to pass that message along, worldwide. Being in Dubai helped in that sense—it was another extravagant and unique project from the tiny Middle Eastern city, so I felt I could just catch the train that was already rolling and release news about my submarines too. It became a domino effect—one article would generate other interviews. And the word continued to spread like wildfire about my "one-of-a-kind" water rides.

I spent close to 100 hours doing live demonstrations with the submarines, many times with a reporter inside the cabin. It was an adventure every time. None of them had ever experienced a flight under water. For me, it meant even more focus because I wanted to make sure that everything would run smoothly. I knew that any failures or technical problems under the surface would not look good—and these reporters carried expensive cameras and sound recording systems with them that didn't mix well with seawater.

One day a young Australian reporter showed up for a ride in one of our submarines wearing a tiny bikini. I didn't want to say anything that would offend her, she was not shy, but with twenty male Indian employees on the accompanying boat, and all of them just gawking at her I was thinking it would be more appropriate for her to put on one of my jump suits. I spent two hours with her inside the submarine cruising under the water. Actually, I didn't pay much attention to her. Because of poor visibility, I had to fly very close to the reefs so we could see them, focus on my controls, and be very careful not to hit anything. When we came back to the surface, everybody was looking at us with raised eyebrows. Nobody said anything, but they probably thought we had plenty of time for a romantic underwater tour. It was nothing like that—far from it. Dubai may seem to be a little more liberal than Saudi Arabia, but it is just a façade, as proven by the obnoxious stares she received.

Interviews were a good way to inform the public about the submarines because the interviewers were normal people, not submarine engineers. So they asked questions the average consumer would want to know. Sometimes when you work in a very specialized environment, you lose track of what people really want to know. Interviews gave me that insight into people's minds—to see how they viewed the submarine business so I could adjust my marketing strategy to better explain and better advertise, focusing the product to better address their questions.

A reporter once wrote the company looked like the lair of the bad guy in a James Bond movie. It was not my intention to create that image, but with all these exotic faces in yellow jumpsuits around weird underwater crafts—and because of my background—I found it amusing.

During the first two years, I saw articles about Exomos in more than twenty languages, and television reports were broadcast in fifty countries. In 2006, there was not a week that went by without a press release or a show on television about the company. Today, there are still hundreds of pages on the Internet and links to Exomos or its creator. The website got thousands of hits every day from all over the world, and hundreds of inquiries every week. The difficulty for the marketing team was to identify who the real buyers were and not to waste time with kids fooling around or people who would have liked to buy a submarine but could never afford one.

Although the marketing and advertising looked like we were offering yellow submarines for leisure, the greatest demand came from the military market. Only ten percent of the prospective buyers wanted personal or tourist submarines; the other ninety percent wanted them for military applications. But it would take a long time before orders would be placed.

The communication, the advertising, the website, the logo, the products, and the name—I set up everything. With time, Exomos would become a trademark in the submarine industry and generate income. Word was getting out about our products. We did not have submarines entirely 'made in Dubai' yet, so I made live demonstrations and started to train my employees with four subs I had built in the U.S. and brought with me. These submarines gave me platforms for people to experience a real submarine and to show my production staff the systems and how to put them together. It was sort of like reverse engineering. Only after they understood how this sub technology worked could we move forward to draft new designs and build more underwater machines.

Most of the submarine trial sessions that we conducted were documented and filmed. Jim hired a professional videographer from South Africa, a really talented guy who had our state-of-the-art media room at his disposal to put together movies and demos for training and marketing purposes. He edited more than 100 hours of video footage of our submarine operations.

I organized the company into four departments that constituted the backbone of the company—Management, Production, Operations and Marketing/Communications. The Management Department was headed by Sanil, the Indian manager from Palm Marine who became my general manager. He was in charge of human resources, security, facility management, and accounting.

I hired a gentleman named Mark Rego, an experienced production engineer from India, to supervise the production department—the largest department of the four, with more than 150 laborers, technicians, and engineers. It included the different workshops, quality control services, and the testing of submarines. He proved himself to be a very efficient and valuable foreman.

The Operations Department was headed by Jim Miller. Since Jim had been Sultan's consultant for years and had been involved in having me come to Dubai and assisted me in setting up the company, I put him in charge of the company operations. According to his resume, he was an aircraft pilot and a scuba diver, so it made sense to make him responsible for pilot training on the submarines. Although a full-time employee, I soon realized half of the time he was not even there, working and traveling with Sultan, my boss, so I saw it a bit tricky to complain about it.

My first submarine test pilot was a great guy from Nepal, Thapa. He was an experienced self made diver who got really motivated to test my prototypes and piloting subs. I had been scuba diving with him and taught him how to pilot a sub. He may not have had all the western credentials, but I felt I could dive with him anywhere...or in anything.

The marketing and communications department was headed by Mohammed Amin, a Yemeni national who liked to pretend to be an Emirati by dressing the part. This proved to be a useful habit to oversee public relations between the company and various government agencies. It was an essential role in Dubai. In addition, he had the responsibility of popularizing the submarines and selling them along with other custom-built vessels.

Once the departments were set up and things were beginning to run, I asked Jim to secure the $150 million contract for the ten police versions of the submersible patrol vessel that the Indonesian Navy had ordered from us at the IDEX. I saw it as a vote of confidence from the market that we were doing everything right. Jim traveled to Indonesia with Amin to finalize the contract and make arrangements with the local authorities for the down payment.

After two months over there on the company dime, they came back with nothing. Jim apologized to me, and Sultan curiously never blamed me for losing this deal. Still to this day I don't know exactly why this deal was never finalized and fell through, but I do know there were unidentified players with their own agendas pulling strings backstage—players who didn't want me or Sultan to succeed. Jim and Amin may have had personal plans as well that sidelined business concerns.

For the first two years, I built or had in construction a dozen vessels, four of which were working submarines and two that had been partially built in the U.S. and then shipped to Dubai for final completion. Two other large submarines, the *Nautilus* and the *Submersible Yacht,* were being entirely built in the UAE. I arranged the construction and designs to be reviewed by Bureau Veritas for certifications, but top management didn't want to pay for it. I later found out the certifications were considered an annoyance by my Emirati partners who wanted to go around them. They could get away with buying off a cheap certificate for pleasure yachts, but they didn't understand the certification is mandatory and expensive for tourist submarines.

Other vessels were custom orders for Sultan—surface vessels and other boats that were all amazing and unique with no equivalents anywhere in the world.

A submarine is a unique vehicle—like a living machine that breathes and interacts in harmony with its environment. It can take you to a fascinating world not too far from your doorstep. I used for my designs the latest technology including ion lithium batteries to power my submarines so they could go faster and farther. With their specialized cabin pressurization, the hulls didn't have to be designed to resist outside water pressure like other subs. So I was able to build submarines with flat walls and flat windows, for instance. Other submarines are built out of spheres or cylinders, which restrict the space inside the cabin and the size of the viewports, making passengers feel like they are locked up in a can.

An Emirati told me my submarines were more expensive than a car. I asked him, "Why don't you go down to the beach and try to drive your car under the water?" He didn't like my humor.

I also made my subs safer. Even in the worst-case scenario, the special cabin pressurization would allow passengers to exit and swim back to the surface safely. In most other submarines the passengers cannot escape unaided and require assistance from the surface. All my subs had no less than three backup safety systems, including over-sized air bags to gradually climb the submarine to the surface in the event of any loss of buoyancy, guaranteeing that the passengers would never even get wet, regardless of the emergency.

One problem I faced when I started in Dubai was the stereotype skepticism toward the company from visitors and potential foreign buyers. No one could believe that my submarines were actually built by the UAE. Everyone assumed that Exomos was selling submarines under a license from some company in Europe or in the U.S. This left me, early on, to understand it would take years and consistent marketing to demonstrate our high quality and reliable products before the company would be able to build credibility and sell to private and foreign buyers. I explained this to Sultan and the executives at Dubai World. But, as with everything else, they remained adamant they could buy recognition, and the daunting idea of earning it was unacceptable. This lack of understanding was just one of many problems yet to surface. The biggest drag on my business was the petulant childlike nature of the Emiratis; they wanted their new toys built yesterday.

As the chairman of such a large company and an independently wealthy man, Sultan frequently made requests that made no logical sense. He could be cheap for no reason, looking to pinch pennies on critical equipment and devices, potentially putting his own life at risk.

One day he came to my office with a pair of diving fins made out of carbon fiber. One was broken, and he asked if I could build or reproduce them cheaply. Carbon fiber fins are a little more than just a fin made of carbon fabric and epoxy. The fabrication process involves high technology and special ovens to process the curing and the chemical reactions.

I knew Sultan was a daredevil diver, and I knew he sometimes went deep free diving, so I explained to him that the last thing I wanted was to see him fifty feet down and not able to swim back to the surface because of a cheap, poorly built fin. He got my point and threw them away, and I stayed out of the carbon fiber fins business.

Sultan was like a rich child, eager to buy toys to quench his thirst for thrills, this translated into him coming to me with challenges and ideas that turned out later to be my downfall because I accepted them. He may have had the means, but he sorely lacked the perception to know what it takes to design an actual prototype in terms of time and human resources. I designed submarines before I went to Dubai, Emiratis brought me there for the innovation of my creations without thinking about what it takes to achieve them. So after they funded the start up and realized it was too expensive, they dropped the ball.

Here's the perfect example: an innovative, matchless design, the first ever submersible yacht. The inspiration was based on a concept Sultan had dreamed up. Back in the U.S., even before my first trip to the UAE, he asked me to design a fishing boat that could submerge and travel under the water—so people could go fishing and then dive to look at the fish through the windows. Given his size and feature requirements plus all of the other mechanical compartments that would be necessary to accommodate, the submarine would have a gross weight of at least seventy-five tons.

At the time, I was not sure if he understood where this would take me in terms of cost and delivery time, and I didn't really understand why he would want a submersible boat to go fishing anyway. They are two opposite applications—fishing boats are fast, submarines are slow—fishermen catch fish, while a submarine passenger observes them. After I gave him the details and conceptual drawings for the design, he said that was exactly what he wanted. So I went ahead and I designed the Submersible Yacht and started to build her as soon as I moved to Dubai.

From the Submersible Yacht, I designed the SPV (Submersible Patrol Vessel), a much more realistic application, but not his. I was aware of piracy and smuggling in the south Asian and African waters. Thousands of islands between straights made it difficult to control and almost impossible to catch criminals because police boats could be spotted from so far away giving criminals time to jump to another island and disappear. So I came up with the idea for the SPV. A police boat that could patrol on the surface and submerge under water to gather intelligence about marine activity, including the traffic and routes of suspect boats. It could also approach the shoreline or the pirate boats undetected and surface to apprehend these criminals with a guaranteed surprise effect. Once publicly known, these submarine police boats would also be a deterrent because the criminals would never know if the police could be cruising somewhere under the water ready to surface and bust them at any time.

Cruising just below the surface in shallow water with a plastic hull would make the SPV very difficult to detect by sonar. The SPV was heavy like any submarine, but two gas turbines would provide surface top speed close to thirty miles per hour—and for a seventy five-ton boat, that is performance.

A boat like this had never been designed or built before. It was pioneering. It was not that I invented something completely unique, as the sub would have the same theory, equations and principles as the smaller ones—only bigger in size. What was new and exciting was a boat that could submerge, rather than a submarine that could surface. In this regard, the police SPV was totally innovative. People looking at her cruising on the surface would never think she was a submarine because she looked like a normal boat.

The police SPV had an added quality—not only did she have stealth, but she also had deception on her side. Deception causes criminals to look but then go ahead, deciding there is no threat. This design was much like the state of mind I had in my career with the secret service—showing itself in such a way that it appears innocuous and not what it actually is, so that she can get in close and surprise her target before the target has a chance to realize what is going on. The SPV was all that—deceptive, furtive, aggressive, powerful, and invisible. She was also very safe with several backup systems, because with ten people onboard, failure was not an option.

Sultan unjustly demanded that I build the Submersible Yacht in three months. The fabrication of the custom fuel bladders took six months alone so the request was not possible, and this was just the tip of the iceberg. Management's timeline expectations were unrealistic, and stemmed from the fact they had no clue as to the level of engineering and intricate detail work that would have to go into this project. If they had asked me to build a space portal, they would have given me a week. "Beam me up, Scotty." If it works in the movies, then it can be built—or so they think. It took a year and a half to build and launch the Proteus: prototype of the Submersible Yacht.

From a business point of view, this venture was already a success because I had a confirmed order of ten units of the military version, the SPV—worth around $150 million, even though Jim and Amin let that contract slip away for whatever reason.

I took my work very personally, putting a lot of pride into the construction of the *Proteus*. It was with deep emotions that we eventually took her into the water the first time for a test. The cabin was quite large and comfortable. As we submerged, the cabin pressurization system maintained pressure on the walls to balance the water pressure. It was quite a view to see the water rising along the panoramic windows of the cabin as we were going down. I had an impressive safety set-up around the seventy-five-ton vessel, to ensure the security of my crew and myself. Standing by were divers (who were in the water with us), cranes, emergency breathing apparatuses and so forth. The water was filthy, but the divers didn't complain too much because the excitement of the event was too overwhelming to think of their lack of comfort. There was zero visibility. I could only see the divers when they were against the viewports. The pressurization system was kicking out as designed, and I could feel the thrust of the propulsion systems beneath my feet.

Onlookers standing on the dock were shocked to see the boat sinking—they had no idea it was a submarine. I could see them in the periscope gathering and taking pictures and videos. Maybe if You Tube wasn't banned in Dubai, I would have seen it online the next day. The submarine was moving a lot of water through her propellers and making a lot of bubbling sounds while venting the ballasts. Inside the cabin, my engineers assisted me by checking the systems one after another, looking for leaks or signs of failure.

Everything went without a glitch. I expected some problems after having seen what the local employees were capable of. I was ready to grab my emergency breathing apparatus in case of catastrophic flooding. But NO such calamity took place and it was a complete success. The submarine needed to be heavier, but they never are at launches. It is always better to go too light and add weight as necessary, than to build too heavy and sink to the bottom of the ocean. This project and its launch were a world premiere—the first ever submersible yacht in the world This was a first for me, for all of us, for Dubai—a seventy-five ton "Built in Dubai" submarine's first dive test; however, it was totally ignored by top management and Sultan. As sensational as it was, it was *not* my favorite design in my portfolio.

My favorite project was the *Nautilus*. Based on the systems of the *Discovery* sub, I redesigned the hull to make the *Nautilus* a true and unmistakable resort submarine. I had been inspired all my life by Jules Verne and his creations. The most exciting one to me was the Nautilus from *20,000 Leagues under the Sea*. My *Nautilus* was inspired by Harper Goff's design in the Walt Disney movie but was different in many ways because it had to work as a real submarine and not be just a movie prop. I proposed the idea to Sultan, who found it so exciting he asked me to start it right away.

Eighteen months later, I built a submarine that looked like a metallic dinosaur fish built in the nineteenth century. The hull looked like it was shaped with metal plates and 15,000 rivets. The interior was Victorian and could accommodate up to nine passengers and the captain. But I had in mind another application that would have been a better fit with the image of Dubai. It was to arrange the interior with two tables for two, for an exclusive and unique underwater dining experience—like the Orient Express restaurant atmosphere but under the water.

I wanted to address the problem of the poor visibility and lack of marine life. I thought that if the passengers were busy chatting with each other and eating they would spend less time with their noses stuck to the windows trying to see something. It would be a memorable gift for a wife or a fiancé to take them for dinner on a one-of-a-kind submarine like this.

At the 2006 Dubai International Boat Show, I had five working submarines in the water, a jet engine airboat, a gas turbine yacht for live presentations and the *Nautilus,* featured as a static display centerpiece. It was the most photographed vessel of the exhibition. I opened the *Nautilus* submarine to the public. Hundreds of people were able to get inside and get a first impression of what it was like to be inside a machine that looked like it came from the nineteenth century—a steel monster with bulging eyes through which passengers could observe the bottom of the sea.

The other star was the *Stingray.* At night it was very impressive, skimming around under the water with its high beam lights cutting through the murky depths with Thapa at the controls. With so many people watching, the floating docks could barely support the load.

The uniqueness of the prototypes I was building brought me notoriety from the public, the wealthy, and the powerful.

I even caught the attention of Sir Richard Branson, the British entrepreneur known for his Virgin brand, when he boarded one of the high-speed boats I had just built in three months for Sultan, another crazy challenge. She had raw power—riding her would was a "G" force in itself. She had a killer look and two jet engines that rocketed my 25,000 pound boat at eighty miles an hour. I was humbled by Sir Richard's acceptance of my invitation for a ride. As the speedometer climbed towards the seventy miles per hour mark, the bold and fearless Mr. Branson stepped on the deck while my other passengers inside the cabin were glued to their shock absorbing seats. I watched my special guest enjoying the face contorting impacts of the wind—*this* is what totally impressed me.

On another occasion, Sultan came to the Dubai Marina with a group of Japanese businessmen. I was there testing the gas turbine boats, and they wanted to go to the Jebel Ali port, so this was a good opportunity to try the new high speed yacht with them. On a regular boat it takes forty minutes to get there—it took us ten minutes at seventy miles per hour. What a blast that was—a thrilling experience—but not for everyone. When we arrived at Jebel Ali Port, the businessmen had been so scared they decided to take the bus back to the Marina.

The cabin was soundproof, but standing on the deck required hearing protection because of the tremendous roaring sound of the engines. Yet, on the water 100 yards away, the boat was surprisingly silent because the sound faded away and up thanks to the vertical design of the exhaust. I thought this quiet operation combined with speed would be an interesting feature for the police or Coast Guard, who would be able to chase at high speed and approach suspect boats without advance knowledge. In comparison, offshore race boats with their twelve-cylinder piston gas engines can be heard three miles away. During a sea trial, I passed a Coast Guard boat at seventy-five miles per hour. They look so frustrated to be out matched on the water. I didn't have a registration on the hull, but they didn't even try to stop me.

Sultan visited me once a week at the factory in the evenings after seven o'clock and on weekends when nobody was around. We toured the premises and the different projects so he could see our progress and comment on anything he saw that needed to be addressed. On other occasions he came at my invitation to try my creations—riding on airboats and high-speed boats.

These projects were the reason I went to Dubai. I reveled in the challenges these ideas provided. I loved to test my engineering skills and push them to the limit. I didn't realize that enjoying the successes as I did would turn out to be the undoing of everything that I worked for at Exomos. For the Emiratis, there must only be one creator—and he is never supposed to be the foreigner. The media gave too much credit for what I had done and not enough for Sheikh Mohammed and Sultan. I was not aware this was an intolerable situation for Dubai officials and they would soon remedy it in their own way. Their supreme egos could not tolerate taking a back seat to this French expatriate.

Shakespeare once wrote, "All the world's a stage, and all the men and women merely players," but in Dubai, the only ones who are supposed to walk the red carpet are the Emiratis, not the expatriates who are expected to stay quiet backstage.

Speaking of working backstage, twice Dubai World top executives consulted with me for my intelligence officer background. The first time they asked for my opinion about mobile phone interception. They heard the U.S. was listening to ambient conversations surrounding mobile phones even if they were not in use or turned off. Somehow they wanted a confirmation from me, but I didn't give them any indications. The second time, they asked me to prepare a plan to set up a security service for Dubai World. I didn't have the time nor the intention to go back into this kind of business, so I politely declined.

One time, and one time only, did I speak with Sultan about intelligence. It was on his yacht on a weekend evening. He explained how shocked he had been when the P&O deal went down the drain; he could not understand what happened. I told him that although I did not have access to information like he did; I had predicted it, and I could have told him there was no chance in the world that such a deal would have been allowed by the U.S. On the same evening he showed me a book I would have never expected to find in his possession. It was the Koran in Hebrew. It was the first time I had ever seen such antagonistic book.

I did not hide my surprise and asked him where he got it, and why he had it. He told me a Colonel from the Mossad had given it to him, and it was all about knowing the enemy, and thinking ahead of them. I did not doubt him, but I thought there was more behind the Israeli colonel giving it to him than that. Manipulation was certainly not a skill Sultan had mastered, especially confronted with Israeli intelligence officers coming from possibly the best intelligence service in the world. So although he was very excited with the book; I suspected he was not the one pulling the strings.

Chapter 4

Chaos

One thing I can say about Dubai is that chaos reigns everywhere. Not only was there chaos from a big picture perspective—the construction, traffic and masses of people moving around the city on a day to day basis—but also on a smaller scale, inside each business and their departments. There was macro and micro chaos made worse by inconsistent laws, inequality in the ways laws are applied, and corruption in the government. It is impossible to trust or believe anything coming from the government or the media—media which is tightly controlled by the rulers. It makes a mockery of its essential purpose to inform the people of the truth. There is chaos with hiring people, chaos dealing with the government agencies, chaos with housing, and chaos with day to day life and human dramas because of the pressure Dubai can bring upon individuals.

I experienced the chaos right from the start till the end—first with the construction of the Exomos factory. I was getting so much pressure from Sultan to get the projects moving that I had to go around the administrative annoyances to avoid delays, and I started to build the factory without permits at all.

Once the building was up six months later, some Emirati government official came by to complain and ask where the building had come from, since there were no permits on records. He was not happy, to say the least, but I came up with a story of deadlines, chaos and ignorance of the laws. The problem quickly went away when he asked me the name of the owner of the building. When I told him it was Sultan bin Sulayem, the conversation ended, he walked away, and I got my permit the next day.

One morning, in July of 2005—four months after I started Exomos, my general manager and friend, Sanil, didn't show up to work nor did he answer his phone. I waited until noon to ask his whereabouts, but no one, including his wife, seemed to know where he was. That evening at six o'clock, I received a call from my operations department director, Jim. Sanil was dead! Early that morning, he had checked into the hospital alone, for what was supposed to be a checkup. He didn't tell anyone, not even his wife, that he had been having chest pains. He died that day of a massive heart attack at age thirty-nine in the lobby of the hospital waiting for medical care, leaving behind a wife and a seven-year-old son. My son was around the same age, and I was deeply saddened to think his son would probably not remember his father because he was so little when he died.

I was fifty at the time. It affected me greatly to see a close friend die this young. It angered me; I blamed Dubai for killing him with its paralyzing stress, relentless deadlines, dictatorial way of life, and for leaving him to die unattended in the so-called best hospital in town. Sanil was working sixty hours a week—also under extreme pressure from Sultan. Exercise was never on his agenda. He ate a poor diet and sported the resulting oversized waistline. His death was a jolting reminder for me to get frequent checkups and do what I could to avoid stress in my own life. It was also personal warning that Dubai was not a place where you wanted to have a medical emergency. I remember thinking about how many others like Sanil died every year, and then were just quietly replaced?

At Sanil's funeral, I realized the extent of his network—1500 people showed up, all men. That is the size of a small town—that's a lot of people to know just a manager. They were friends, professionals, relatives and people he'd helped find employment.

After Sanil's death, I was left without a general manager and had to deal with the chaos he normally handled. I left his office vacant for one month before I allowed anyone to take his seat. I took over some of his functions, and I hired an executive secretary. But word got out that I was looking for a secretary, and even months later I still had candidates for the position.

One day a Romanian girl showed up at my office. She had managed to get an appointment for an interview. I felt what could only be called a dead silence go through the building moments before she reached my office—she had a big impact on my employees. She was stunning. She had tried to dress in a businesslike way, but the Russian red lipstick on her Angelina Jolie lips only served to emphasize this raven-haired beauty's voluptuous body in a very non-businesslike way. Starting with her head and going down, my eyes ended on dainty feet in stilettos that elongated her tiny physique. I am like every other man in that I can recognize a beautiful woman—I know; I am married to one. But this lady was something else—a real head-turner. As she sat in front of my desk for her interview, everybody was watching through the glass walls, just gawking. In perfect English—aahhh—she offered me a lot more than secretarial skills. She insisted she would provide 'full service' and would be my round the clock personal assistant as well, under the condition I would overlook her lack of qualifications and promise the job to her.

I flat-out turned her down. I knew too well what 'full service' meant, and I don't operate that way. It is my personal mission not to get involved with anyone I work with. It guarantees misery and blackmail—two things that I keep away from in my position. I would never have been taken seriously with a secretary like her. Everybody would have assumed she had been hired for her other services—not to mention the fact the most important judge in my life, my wife, would think the same thing.

Like the Romanian applicant, there are a lot of girls in Dubai looking for opportunities like this. I used to call them 'CEO chasers.' They were always very aggressive, didn't care if the guy was married or not, they just wanted to sign up and move in—women looking to be kept.

When Sultan made me CEO of his company. I started with a roster of seventeen employees who were assigned, hired or transferred from Palm Marine into my operation. It quickly became apparent they were not competent and were more trouble than they were worth. They were all related and, to my dismay and anger, top management continued to send people with no qualifications whatsoever only because they were cheap and knew someone in the system. I had to put a stop to this and employ qualified people myself.

Hiring in Dubai was a lot different than it was in the other countries where I had lived. Cultural differences, government regulations, the distances involved, the reasons why people want to go to Dubai, and the high demand for employees all made it very difficult and complicated to find qualified people who would join the company. Also, I could not rely on résumés, as they were totally unverifiable.

Like everybody else I had to choose candidates from people whose only motivation was to make a quick buck and leave, or so they thought——people who didn't want to be in their home countries for economic reasons, or because they were running away from a broken life, a tragedy, the misery in India or Bangladesh, the crime rate in South Africa, the low wages in Russia and so forth. They would take any job just to stay in the UAE, even if it meant they had to sleep on a bunk at night surrounded by strangers. I met a father who had lost his son to cancer, a mother who had lost her son to murder and kidnapping in South Africa, and many who had suffered through ugly divorces and bankruptcies. Their tragedies had left them scarred and traumatized, and many of them needed a lot of handholding just so they could get to work in the morning. The best I could do was to try to understand them and address their problems so they could focus on the job.

When I hired people for Exomos or when they were transferred to the company, they would never disclose the truth about the reasons to look for a job in Dubai, but I would always find out later. I remember a German engineer who came to the company. He left behind an alcohol addiction that eventually caught up with him again in Dubai. Another engineer I hired left his country after his girlfriend had his baby but left him to then raise the baby with her long-term lesbian lover.

I met only a handful of expatriates who had the pioneering spirit that I had expected to see when I came to Dubai. These entrepreneurs invariably became disillusioned and disappointed very quickly and left after only several months' stay. Most qualified and talented engineers or experts from the West with genuine résumés and a well-established reputation would simply not accept offers in Dubai unless the compensation was a multiple of what they are earning back home— and I was not in a position to offer that.

Not everybody goes to Dubai because they are on the run from something, of course. Many go because they see it as the opportunity of a lifetime, a chance to realize career goals about which they could only dream anywhere else.

And this is where I fit in. I went to Dubai because I was offered the opportunity of a lifetime to build a concept, a chance to realize career goals I thought I could only imagine. It was a dream come true when Sultan offered me the chance to build a world-class submarine factory. I was blinded by the light reflecting off that dream.

Sultan would let me spend without concern for equipment and buildings, but I could never afford qualified human resources. I had to repeatedly explain to top management why I needed the budget to hire mechanics, workers, and highly skilled technicians from Europe or Russia and not from developing countries because they were cheap. Many Western experts would simply decline employment offers on the basis that no decent compensation or housing was provided. The lack of affordable accommodation was one of the biggest problems I had to deal with.

Executive management had no shame, offering shared apartments and bunk beds to skilled engineers, even though it was, by the letter of the law, illegal. Emiratis show a marked lack of respect for foreign workers and their basic needs of privacy and home life. They see no problem with having them shack up together or leaving their families behind.

I came to Dubai with only three engineers who had expertise in building submarines—all were my former U.S. employees. It was very difficult to convince them to move to a Middle Eastern country because the war in Iraq brought with it a negative wave of opinion about the whole area to many Americans. They signed on for one year.

At the beginning, I covered all of the design and engineering tasks with them. We taught the company's supervisors about the specifics of building submarines so they could pass the techniques on to the workers. Most of our employees were from South Asia. They lacked the basics of building modern boats, but were hard workers and willing to learn. One element remains true: the Indian carpenters clearly demonstrated themselves to be the best in craftsmanship and the most reliable workers I've seen.

Because I had to fight the salary restrictions, it took fifteen months before qualified help joined the company. It was very difficult to find submarine engineers and technicians who would leave their current position to come to Dubai. Usually, good engineers have to give a long notice to their current employers and are not just sitting at home doing nothing.

Eventually, five of the fifteen submarine engineers I contacted—two Germans, two French, and one American—responded and told me they were willing to relocate to Dubai with the package I offered. Three of them were still under contract with another company and could only be released from their responsibilities after one year. The other two were available after six months. From the beginning, getting everything off the ground was an uphill challenge. I also hired from local marine industries when I found them to be competent and honest. Nevertheless, I found many of the Indian engineers in Dubai only experienced in engineering their résumés, but I would say it was more stupid than malicious. They really try to do their best to achieve goals, and are hard workers and honest people. But when they are under-qualified, they think they can learn on the job and make it through. They also have this misplaced philanthropy to lobby for their cousins and brothers for jobs they don't even qualify for.

As the company expanded, we built more vessels at the demand of Sultan. I was able to hire only a few technicians from France, the U.S., South Africa, and Russia to supervise the workforce, but they had to share the same apartment. The company's employee roster reflected the cultural diversity found in Dubai. After two years, I had 250 people from sixteen different nations and five religions, the majority from South Asia, India and Philippines. There was no uniform salary scale. People in Dubai were paid according to where they came from rather than for their level of education. An engineer from India was paid $3,000 per month, while an American engineer was earning $9,000 per month. At first, I couldn't understand why the pay schedules were drastically different for the same positions. Sadly, I wasn't at liberty to dispute these matters since every penny paid to employees was directly approved by upper executive management. However, I was looking for employees according to their experience and not their citizenship.

I looked into high-tech local companies to see how they were hiring top engineers. Well, they weren't. For instance, Emirates Air services its airplanes at many of its destinations, and high performance car dealers such as Ferrari and Lamborghini offer only basic maintenance packages at five times what it costs in the U.S. For specialty work that requires high expertise, companies actually fly in experts and top notch mechanics just for the job. Skilled engineers wouldn't take a position to live in camps or accept to spend two thirds of their salaries on rent. For these reasons experts needed to be paid very high salaries. Top management didn't allow me to match these figures in salary expenditures for the company.

Top management wanted cheap employees they could treat like slaves. But they didn't understand what that meant—it would take a long time to train them to reach the high standards necessary to produce a high-tech product. I came across many obstacles with my employees from South Asia which affected our ability to produce quality work. I had to correct their previous teachings that were outdated and/or wrong. For instance, they insisted on wiring our vessels using twenty-year-old techniques that are no longer used today.

In 2006, although my boats were not wired to international standards, Exomos received an ISO certification because the inspectors themselves were also from South Asia and had received the same antiquated training. Now, my Emirati partners felt the certifications were worthless and unnecessary, much like sweeping dust under the rug. If nobody else sees it, why bother? In their eyes, shortcuts are cheaper, faster and no questions asked.

I also had the added headache of what is known as the Emiratisation Policy. In Dubai it is mandatory to hire a certain percentage of Emiratis as ordered by the federal government. The problem is that once an Emirati is hired, he cannot be terminated. Its purpose is to involve Emiratis directly in the economic fabric of the country, but it does not work because they are not qualified. I tried to follow the mandate of the program, but in the end the only Emirati involved in the company was Sultan. I could not find a single Emirati fiberglass technician or mechanic, let alone a submarine engineer, to hire. I interviewed a few and they were the worst candidates I had ever seen. Their attitudes were extremely arrogant, they always wanted a significantly higher salary than anybody else, they didn't want to do manual labor, and they had unverifiable and/or questionable résumés.

The lack of modern qualifications or training and inherent miscommunication, whether through language or ignorance, proved itself one day when I was launching a submarine. As it was being lowered in the water with slings, Rahshid was on the deck to remove the slings once it was afloat. Shams, the supervisor, called me over to tell me his friend manning the slings didn't know how to swim. So, here I had an individual who was ready to drown for fear of losing his job because he forgot to mention it during his job interview. On another occasion, just before the 2006 boat show, I almost lost a submarine because an electrician failed to monitor the battery charge of the *Goby* parked inside the factory. The *Goby* is a luxury 2 seater sub with veneer, leather seats, A/C...in other words—it's loaded. After five hours of over charging the lithium batteries, two of them blew up and torched the interior of the sub. The employee tried to deny any mishandling but he was caught on tape with the surveillance system.

A submarine is a life-support system. Highly skilled employees were a must for Exomos, and top management was not cooperative at all in allowing me take that route.

I asked Jim and my other managers to help find qualified people to work at Exomos. They ended up hiring totally unskilled workers with fixed résumés—friends, family, and others offering favors to my managers whose only concern was to accommodate their network of friends and relatives. Jim hired people for his own personal agenda, and at the same time he was making life very difficult for the employees I did manage to hire. He was always maneuvering and doing his best to irritate them and push them towards the door. I didn't discover the extent of his meddling until much later, after he had single-handedly disenfranchised one of my most qualified employees. Jim had the power to get away with it because he was a director of the company and was, strangely, fully supported by Sultan as well. Yet I had no clue to what extent or for what purpose his private agenda served.

The fallout from this incestuous managerial infrastructure can be catastrophic to a company. I had an Indian civil engineer who made it to Exomos because of his fake résumé and relatives in the organization, and who ended up being directly responsible for a critically failed crane structure that surely would have killed someone if I hadn't discovered his fraud.

His assignment was to hire a local contractor to build and supervise the construction of a lifting system that I designed to lift, move, and lower submarines into the pool for testing or training purposes. His job was to do the structural calculations and verify the structure met the loads and stress requirements, and to ensure it was constructed properly and safely. At this point in my tenure at Exomos, I didn't trust anyone whom I had not hired myself. So, during the construction, I took a peek at the structure and noticed the poor quality of the welding and some major defects in the load beam assemblies. I investigated further and inquired about the contractor and found out that my engineer was related to him. When I confronted him, I learned he was not capable of doing any quality control and he didn't know how to make the structural calculations. His engineering degree was a computer generated paper with a bogus university. I was infuriated; he could have killed someone.

Not only did I fire him at the speed of light, but I also made sure he would not get hired as an engineer in another company of the Dubai World group—he was a liability. A few months later, I found out he was working as a civil engineer at Nakheel. Somehow, somebody from his village had managed to overcome my recommendations. He was not an isolated case or an exception to the rule—he was just one example of hundreds, probably thousands, of people in Dubai who were faking credentials and yet put in charge of building multimillion and even billion dollar projects to be used by tourists and foreign businesses and their employees.

Another example of a Group-sponsored employee taking advantage of his position was the facility manager, who would let employees from other companies sleep and eat at the company's expense. Every time I toured the buildings I would find people I didn't know sleeping in hiding places and eating in the cafeteria. The Indian in charge would always have an excuse to cover up for his friends. It was like the factory was their dormitory and a place to eat cheap. I was never able to prove he was getting money from them as kickbacks.

Then there were the purchasing managers, all coming from the Group. The equipment and materials they purchased locally for Exomos would, more often than not, be overpriced, with any volume discounts going into the pockets of those involved in the scheme. It was difficult to catch them because Exomos was not handling any cash. Payments were processed by Dubai World through a chain of accomplices in finance. In fraudulent transactions that I did catch, merchandise was overpriced by as much as 400 percent.

I also had to deal with the day-to-day culture clashes that my Western engineers bulldozed their way into. A French engineer working for me was once lucky enough to avoid being arrested by a police officer at a gas station. He was giving a lift home to a female Syrian employee. As he stopped his car to refuel, she pulled up her shirt and asked him if her breasts looked nice. Of course, a cop just happened to be there and saw the whole thing. I don't think my employee was completely innocent of participating in or instigating the incident, and I don't know what they were up to other than fooling around. But a phone call came in from my engineer, who was in complete panic. I managed to talk the police officer out of reporting the incident and the female received a warning instead of jail time for indecent exposure.

Another employee raised the bar for insane behavior at the Dubai Boat Show in 2006. I asked my employees to email me copies of the pictures involving our submarines they had taken during the exhibition. One of them, Paul, an American engineer, gave me a memory stick instead, telling me that all of his photos were on it. Later as I was going through his files, I could not believe I was looking at pictures of a completely naked blond girl in provocative positions inside one of my submarines. I looked further to see if it was maybe something downloaded from the Internet or some Photoshop trick, but I quickly recognized the interior of the Discovery submarine, and through the windows I could see that the submarine was submerged, under the water and at night.

I demanded an explanation. He acted totally confused and explained to me that he had handed over the wrong memory stick. I didn't dispute the fact that he gave me the wrong files, but I responded that he still had a long way to go to explain how a girl turned up naked and diving in one of my submarines. He finally confessed he had invited a Russian hostess from the boat show onboard, closed the hatch, and submerged the submarine to have some privacy—then with all this excitement they got naked, took pictures, and did the nasty. If this situation had ever reached Dubai police, the officers would have given them a taste of Emirati corrections. Lucky for him, he got off with just a warning from me instead of a direct trip to jail.

With 250 people to manage plus their problems, employee management ended up overruling all my other responsibilities. Instead of focusing on the day-to-day engineering and business operations I was hired to do, I was left to deal with untimely temper tantrums and handling the mobocracy that had cruelly taken two thirds of my time in attempts to remedy dilemmas and total turmoil in order to prevent my operations from caving in. Anywhere else in the world it would have been manageable with qualified, responsible, reliable, employees. But in Dubai, this is an impossibility due to the anachronistic regulations which, in fact, create additional and greater problems.

On many occasions, these human resource problems caused the terminations of those who were inevitably found not to meet company expectations. It was always difficult because it meant deportation if the employee didn't find another job within thirty days. In the three years I was the head of Exomos, I had to terminate close to 100 employees because they had misrepresented their education, lied about experience, and/or lied about their qualifications on their résumés. In all of my professional years I have never witnessed fraud on this unimaginable scale. Because it was so bizarre, it compelled me to be a HR detective in a bid to figure out if there was any truth to the employee's documents at all. Indeed, I made a lot of enemies when I fired the incompetents, even though many of them would manage to find jobs elsewhere in another government branch—thanks to their networking.

It didn't matter the age or nationality of the employee—no one was immune from the difficulties that can unexpectedly surface in the land of the Burj. Even my director caught me by surprise when I discovered his pink room. Jim had already resigned from Exomos and he was working at Sultan's office, so I decided to check on the operations department yard and buildings he supervised. There were four big trailers—one was an office space where we used to have our meetings and briefings before and after diving. The second and third ones were for storage, diving equipment and compressors to refill the scuba tanks. There was enough equipment in there to support diving operations for the submarines and a dozen divers. The last trailer had a studio office for the videographer on one end, and a locked room on the other end—a locked room that I had never visited before as a courtesy to Jim. He told me he was using it sometimes to sleep. We worked hellishly long hours, so I assumed he used it as a place to rest instead of going home. It always puzzled me why I felt uncomfortable with that idea. It was prohibited for employees to sleep in the free zone, a rule to prevent employees from using it as a place for extracurricular activities. It wasn't fair for me to allow Jim to sleep at the factory and not allow anyone else, he had a huge company-provided villa to himself just ten minutes away. I decided to put an end to it right there and then, and went to the room to close it down.

When I asked Tajik for the key, I felt a sense of embarrassment in the air, as if there was some secret. He hesitated in giving me the key. So I insisted, and again, he was reluctant and vexed to open the door. The more he resisted, the more suspicious I became. I gave him a penetratingly rigid stare to show him that I meant business—after a few minutes he finally got the message and hesitantly opened the door.

I would have never believed if I hadn't seen it with my own eyes. The first thing that came to mind? *Oh yeah, baby! I have just invaded Ali Baba's shag shack in need of a home makeover.* There it was, a bedroom, with a transparent burgundy-colored net suspended from the ceiling. The matching bed sheets were of at least four shades of red and pink and had a silky, shantung shine. The bed was neatly topped with tethered, silvery-pink decorative pillows like those you'd find in a

Frederick's of Hollywood catalogue. Oh, let's not forget wall-to-wall flaming fuchsia carpet throughout and the wood paneling. Okay, this definitely had a feminine psychedelic touch.

Five people stood there with me, all turning the same color as the sheets. I remember wondering what on earth Jim was thinking when he set up this room. I had to take pictures to document what I saw there—no one would have believed me. I gave employees immediate instructions to dismantle everything, including the cabinets and closets in the bedroom. The assistant also avoided opening the cabinet doors. I opened them, one after another, and they were full of clothing, mostly underwear and other undergarments, nothing to be embarrassed about.

I told Tajik to arrange with Jim for the quick removal of his clothes. I felt the awkward sense of anxiety and agitation that resonated throughout the room and spewed outside as the workers whispered to each just outside the door. Tajik told me that the clothes didn't belong to Jim, that they belonged to Amin. I looked at them. Amin's underwear? In Jim's bedroom? Aahhhh—okay—*Je comprends tout.*

Finally, let's break this down—the clear display of shame and awkwardness of the employees, the concealment, Jim's stringent demands for Amin's raise on several occasions, the fact that Jim and Amin were constantly together, devoting weekends and company cell phone records indicated no less than twenty calls a day to each other, electing one another for business trips at company expense. To the rest of the world, they were hiding and living in the closet. I finally understood why Jim responded defensively to my wife a year earlier, saying, "No, I am not gay," when she asked him if she could ask him a personal question. He blurted out his answer before she could even ask him anything. It was a fairly-shocking response at the time, when all she wanted was to ask him politely how tall he was. It might also explain why Jim had a picture of me in my military jumpsuit on the screen saver of his computer—which I found inappropriate at the time.

I have no issue with people's sexual orientation, and as long as it does not affect my everyday life, I just don't care. But I strongly oppose any sexual acts taking place on my work premises and involving my employees hiding things from me. And I'm strongly against employees using company resources to support their intimate relationships. To think it was Sultan's right hand man doing this was unbelievable. In Dubai, homosexuality is absolutely taboo—a crime that carries severe punishments and long-term jail sentences. In reality there are small, hidden communities of homosexuals who dare not publicly express their sexual orientations. I am sure Sultan would have been very upset to learn all of this was going on under his nose at his expense.

Part of the package I offered to my qualified employees included accommodations to entice them to come to Dubai, so they would not have to go through the trouble finding an apartment and paying a fortune for it.

Marc, a French engineer, spent two months in a dormitory with Indians and Pakistanis because I could not find any vacant apartments. I admired his sacrifice and motivation to work in a submarine company. I don't mean to sound like I have discriminatory feelings towards people of these countries—it's just that we don't eat the same food, we don't listen to the same music, and we don't have the same ideas about hygiene. After a while, those differences can wear on a person's nerves, especially when we are all putting in long hours and feeling the stress under time constraints to get the job done. Whether it is related or not, this guy ended up at the hospital with a skin disease that took three months to cure.

Thanks to my relationship with Sultan, I was privileged to receive a pool of ten apartments from Nakheel that I could lease back to my Western employees at half the market rate. This represented new homes for twenty-five of my employees. What good does the outside beauty of an apartment building bring, if people inside them have to live like sardines in a can?

Camilla, in her late twenties and attractive, and Günter, an engineer in his fifties, were sharing a two bedroom company apartment. He was educated and rather geeky and shy. I didn't see a problem with rooming them together for a short while, as I felt it was unlikely they would do anything stupid during weekends or at nights. Günter was an expert in submarine construction, and was an asset to the company. Because they were male and female under the same roof, this arrangement was illegal. But how else was I to accommodate him without getting rid of the young woman?

The problem showed up in the form of Camilla's boyfriend one day. He was at the apartment making a scene because he thought his girlfriend was cheating on him.

I lived five minutes away from the apartment complex, and when Günter called me at ten that night telling me what was going on, I jumped in my car and went to the apartment to calm everybody down. I explained that all three of them would go to jail if the police showed up. I was able to resolve the situation, and the next day Camilla left the apartment and moved in with her boyfriend.

It did not last long, though, because a month later, she and her boyfriend were arrested at home because they were living together unmarried and therefore illegally. It was all due to a kitchen fire. They called the firemen, who put out the fire quickly, but when the police found out that they were not married, the couple was arrested, jailed for one month, and then deported.

Although these human resource complications affected the business, I had more important issues to deal with and other chaos to manage, such as the communication with government agencies.

I needed to get Exomos' vessels certified and sailing. Now, it wouldn't have been so bad if the civil servants were good at their jobs or at least efficient. But, in Dubai, efficiency and proficiency from the government sector is wishful thinking at best. Their theory seems to be the more public servants who can be involved in a process, and the longer it takes, the better. Talking to a public servant is like talking to an answering service; sometimes you have to spell the words you are saying—and it isn't because of the accent. It is even worse when the clerk is a woman fully covered with a black veil. You might as well put out an automated box with a cardboard cutout and save the expense. If you apply for something that does not fit in the books, they keep repeating the same irrelevant information to you over and over until you get frustrated and go stand in another line in the hopes that someone else will have a different book to look into.

I applied for permits to sail my submarines, but after going in circles between different administrations for three months, I sailed them without any type of registration. There were no rules about submarines or my other boats in their books. I had to face twenty public servants one after another who were nothing more than a bunch of pencil-pushers, showing up at their thankless desk jobs to fill an empty chair. The registration office told me that in order to get the registrations, I needed to have the boats or submarines inspected by the port officers. The port officers told me that prior to being inspected, the submarine had to be certified by the certification office. And the certification officers told me that the submarine had to be tested while sailing in order to be certified. Yet, without the registration, I was not even allowed to sail at all—not even for demonstration for the port officers.

So, for two years I sailed without a registration or permits. I was stopped only once, but I told the police that the boat belonged to Sultan and I got off the hook. In January 2007, after Sultan started to drift away from me, executive management told me I could no longer sail any boats at all for demonstration or testing purposes.

For two years I coped. When it comes to this type of chaos with the Arab governments you just learn not to argue—not to put yourself under unnecessary stress. So, I just lived with it and found other ingenious ways to get around it.

Chapter 5

The Betrayal

In March 2006, after the Dubai Boat Show and as the company was gaining momentum to secure orders, Sultan told me during a meeting on his yacht that he was going transfer the control of Exomos to Istithmar, the investment arm of the Dubai World group. I felt his awkwardness as he clumsily explained to me that auditors would begin to review the day to day accounting and purchasing procedures of the company. Sultan was becoming increasingly busy and traveling to manage the expansion of Dubai World, so I thought he no longer had the time to control Exomos himself and had to pass the management over to Istithmar.

Istithmar was primarily an equity company for the real estate and investment operations of Dubai World. Istithmar had no experience in production, manufacturing, or research and development. At the time, it typically invested for short term returns, not long-term industrial development. So I didn't take this change of management as good news.

During the first year at Exomos, I had already been audited two times in six months. No stones were left unturned, so I didn't understand the need for more auditing, especially since the company was not handling any money directly. I already had enough with managing the anarchy around the company. More audits meant more meetings and fruitless, time-consuming explaining. This time it was different; the previous auditors were consultants hired outside the Group. The new auditors came from the GIA, or Group Internal Audit, headed by Abdul Qader. Submarines were not these auditors' everyday type of business, and it became clear that these bureaucrats would rather eliminate what they didn't understand. My employees and I spent countless hours working with the auditors already—instead of working on the subs— and now we were going to have to go through it all over again and be under constant grueling, unnecessary pressure.

I was aware that many people in Dubai World and Istithmar had been against the submarine project from the beginning. I knew they were going to have a field day going after my operations, trying to demonstrate to Sultan that he was wrong to pursue a submarine business. The jealousy that was created when Sultan put Exomos under his direct control was taking its toll.

One year of tumultuous Emirati bureaucracy had already made my job arduous. Now, with no response to my calls and no signs of direct support from Sultan, I was dreading the possibility of facing this predicament alone. I would have to put up a fight, in order to stay the course. Jim was showing more of his true colors in the face of trouble. I saw him pretending to be my best mate on one side and sabotaging everything I did on the other.

He had been a problem for me from the very beginning. He was on Exomos' payroll and reporting to me, when he was in fact the Sultan's cabana boy all the while, playing cloak and dagger during office hours. After management shifted control over to Istithmar, Jim somehow always managed to break or damage the submarines. The result of his actions caused delays. It cost money to fix, and the blame would always be directed at the production staff and ultimately fingers would be pointed at me.

Here's an example: Jim callously decided to turn the Stingray submarine upside down. I got so infuriated that he actually ran away. He came back to apologize the next day. At the French Naval Academy, we were taught that a navy officer should allow himself only three bursts of anger per year, two of which should be simulated. This one was genuine, and I had good reasons to be angry. He said he wanted to see what would happen to the sub if it flipped over, but this explanation made no sense. By design, the Stingray could not overturn in the water. It was impossible.

So when Jim forced the submarine to flip over, acid spilled out of the battery box and ruined everything—the electronics, piping and valves. This required two months of repairs and made the submarine unavailable for demonstrations, sea trials, and pilot training. I asked him if I could flip his car onto its roof to see what happens. He had nothing to say and could not care much because the car he was driving around was a rental paid for by Sultan.

I could not fire this fumbling idiot because he was a Group Director. It would have taken a meeting of the directors and a month of paperwork for me to get him out of there, not to mention big problems with Sultan, who was already acting strange.

When Jim was traveling with Sultan, the people in his department were shy reporting to me, following his wanna be paramilitary type organization. When I was travelling, he would always take advantage and push his own agenda.

The summer of 2006, I was on vacation with my family when I received a call from my secretary telling me Jim had issued a request to accounting to increase Amin's salary. I was concerned that favoritism was at play, especially because I had been very specific that due to Amin's poor performances he was not to receive any salary increment anytime soon. Thanks to my secretary's call, I was able to stop the request before it went any further...yeah...

He would take advantage of my business trips away from the office to fire the engineers I had hired. One of them was a French submarine engineer named Marc. He had proven himself in his day-to-day work ethic and by successfully repairing and improving a submarine for the company. But while I was on a business trip to Canada, Jim fired Marc for alleged insubordination. That time I was too late and couldn't do anything to fix the situation. I lost a valuable employee, and I got the distinct impression that Jim wanted to make sure that I was not getting the help I needed to succeed.

My trip to Canada was initiated by Jim, who had put the idea into Sultan's head to buy a submarine company there. They wanted $10 million for it, which I thought was overpriced. I went there to assess the company, see its assets, and take a look at the books. I determined that even at $3 million, it would be too much, but more importantly, the purchase of this company would not be profitable for Exomos. A company like that would be impossible to relocate; their employees and experts would never, ever move to Dubai. I knew them: top notch engineers, experts in their fifties with families, wives with their own jobs, children in college, and roots deep in their country. There would be no way to convince these people to drop everything and move to Dubai on a temporary guest worker visa and submit to an unconventional way of living.

When I returned from Canada, I told Sultan that buying this company was not a good idea. I am sure Jim had a little percentage lined up on condition that I sealed this deal. Why else would he be pouting and having a temper tantrum when I got back? Yes, he wasn't happy that Sultan scrapped the idea.

In the end, Jim didn't participate as his title indicated and actively took part in sabotaging my work at every turn, even at one point suggesting that I should step down. I had to oppose every one of his decisions because they seemed to be made from the basis of self-interest rather than from the company's interests. He eventually resigned in September 2006. I also suspect he left because he knew what was coming for me, and he didn't want to be around to take any of the blame.

My real problems started in January 2007, with a visit from Ahmed Butti to the Exomos factory. From the beginning, he had advocated that the factory and Exomos should be an asset of Palm Marine, not a stand-alone company solely in place to build submarines. For two years, I had been pressured by Dubai World's top management to take over Palm Marine. I refused, because I didn't want to be involved in the yacht building business in Dubai. Palm Marine was a government boat manufacturing company trying to enter the market against competition like Ferreti, SunSeeker and other prestigious European builders. I knew they would never make it because of the poor investment in human resources and the dictatorial and inexperienced management at the helm.

Ahmed Butti was chairman of Palm Marine, director general of Dubai Customs, and a board member of Dubai World under Sultan. Every time I met him, I had to make an effort not to laugh; A. Butti almost sounds like *A bruti*. This man could not have had a more appropriate name—*Abruti* means idiot in French. He had no knowledge whatsoever of the boat building industry. He was not an engineer. He was clueless, and he was rude to everyone who was not an Emirati.

Another reason I wanted nothing to do with Palm Marine was that like many other Dubai Companies, they were copying hulls and designs from other brands to make their boats. I heard the rumors before I went there, but in their factory, I saw it firsthand. I witnessed hulls being copied from British and Italian boats.

Butti and Sultan had asked me, on separate occasions, to duplicate and modify boats and other watercraft—the Jet Ski project was one of them. They would buy used boats on the aftermarket, and then duplicate the hulls, making molds out of them. They knew it was totally wrong, but at the same time they thought it was perfectly okay since they had purchased the boat—as if ownership would allow them to do anything they wanted, even if that included copying hulls to make new boats and selling them. So, they got around the violations of other people's intellectual property rights by making the molds slightly different to avoid blatant copyright infringements.

When I visited the Palm Marine site, I didn't see any plugs on the premises. A plug is the initial step in building a boat. The plug serves to build the mold, and then the mold serves to build the hulls. Since they built their molds using other manufacturers' hulls, they didn't need to build any plugs. I also never found any proofs of purchase of plug materials in their books. Duplicating somebody else's design is a crime, and when it is done in a government company, it is even worse. Unfortunately for Butti, stealing a design is not all that goes into making a boat work well. What Butti and his ilk never understood was that there was more to building a boat than just copying it.

This is why, two years after my first visit, the five Palm Marine boats in production were either not completed or not working. They were trying to reverse engineer boats without engineers in an attempt to save even more on the cost. Reverse engineering requires an understanding of the equations used in the design and how the systems work.

Despite their demands, I always refused to duplicate someone else's technology. At the production level, because they had no clue how to build boats, they built the molds out of standard, cheaper gel coat instead of tooling gel coat. The molds were flawed from the start, hence when they pulled out the first hulls, they were all defective. Then they used cheap labor for months to try and cover up the defects and patch the holes in the hulls.

When Sultan transferred Exomos to Istithmar, the executive management merged Exomos with Palm Marine at the same time. The very same day, Butti walked into my office with a smile of victory on his face and instructed me that he was the new chairman of Exomos and that Exomos was to take over Palm Marine.

As Ahmed Butti became my new boss, the chaos I had been able to turn into a manageable annoyance was to become anarchy. I inherited the flaws in the Palm Yachts and insane human resources. Sultan essentially took the control of Exomos out of his hands and put it into the hands of Butti. I saw this move by Sultan as a harbinger of disaster, but there was nothing I could say about the changes or Butti— the man bull. It was not my place, and I knew better than to question Sultan's business decisions.

As the former chief of police, Butti ruled the companies he was in charge of like prisoner of war camps. His authority relied on the worst form of power—the power to punish and the power to terminate. He demanded respect but worried nothing about earning it. I heard the murmurs behind my back as he called me an idiot on more than one occasion. I didn't take the insults too personally. After all, he was the one supposedly qualified to manage a boat and submarine manufacturing company, yet he wasn't wise enough to know better than to purchase a boat for himself with a flawed design and a porous hull. I also didn't let it bother me because I have learned during my life that when somebody resorts to using insults, it means he has nothing else to challenge you with.

After the merger I found that Palm Marine had twenty Vietnamese workers building its yachts, yet nobody in the company spoke the language and the Vietnamese didn't speak a word of English or Arabic. Because of lack of communication, the Vietnamese employees had built the fiberglass hulls with the wrong proportions of catalysts in the resin. The resultant hulls were warped and porous once released from the molds.

I started to restructure Exomos in April 2006, dismissing the nonproductive and unskilled employees from the company, as well as those who had been hired and maintained their positions by lobbying and networking. With this merger, I let go another thirty-five people, including some influential managers and the Vietnamese workers. It caused an internal revolution and made me a lot of enemies who would later turn against me with the auditors. Everything I did to try to make the company run more smoothly, the auditors turned against me. The fact the managers and supervisors of Palm Marine didn't realize what was going on bordered on criminal negligence. They sold these boats to people who trusted they knew what they were doing. Butti, the guy in charge of all this mess, and now my boss, was hell bent on getting under my skin.

Three Palm Marine customers had purchased yachts three years earlier, and those boats were still on back order. Butti gave me a deadline to get them delivered, and I had to finish these three half-baked boats in six months or I would be fired.

The first one was a forty-two-foot fly bridge yacht for a customer in Croatia. The boat was copied from a renowned UK boat manufacturing company. I knew from the start that it would be unstable. Palm Marine copied a hull originally designed as a cabin cruiser, and built the yacht with a heavy fly bridge, which dramatically raised its center of gravity. The hull didn't have enough righting moment to compensate for the high center of gravity.

I completed her after two months. During the sea trial, as expected, the boat showed severe instability; it would roll with an angle of twenty-eight degrees on either side. My crew was face down on the deck, scared that it would tip over. I had to add 1,200 pounds of lead bricks in the bottom of the boat to make it stable and compensate for the extra weight and height of the fly bridge. The added weight dropped the top speed from thirty-five to twenty miles per hour. An experienced boat owner would have noticed the poor speed performance against the power of the engines, but Palm Marine got lucky. The buyer had never owned a boat before, so he would never know. I was commanded by Ahmed Butti never to reveal the added weight in the hull to this customer.

I had no respect for this supposedly high government official whom I had caught in a lie. He proved he was a cheat. Due to the defect, certification was sought from a low rated agency, with the added incentive of more money, against the blueprints rather than a thorough inspection of the finished boat. That particular vessel would never have been approved by highly recognized agencies such as Bureau Veritas or ABS (the American Bureau of Shipping).

The second boat was also too heavy, yet delivered on time.

The third one was a sixty-foot yacht for Ahmed Butti himself. He had ordered one of the boats built by Palm Marine three years earlier for a quarter of the list price. I went to see the partially-built boat. I told him to get his money back because she would always leak water through the faulty and porous hull. It was not that the boat would sink, but there would be moisture and water under the carpets all the time. He told me I had two months to complete his boat, or he would fire everybody.

I tried to convince the auditors they were working against the wrong person, indicating that I was being audited on issues that had been dealt with previously. Major irregularities were being deliberately overlooked in other areas of the company under Butti's direction. It became apparent the auditors had been instructed to look for anything I could be directly blamed for. They were not interested in someone else's wrongdoing.

Even Sultan himself had his share of wrongdoings. He once gave me what he thought to be an impossible task—one that I successfully completed to the frustration of Butti and executive management. It was another of Sultan's boats. She had been there before I arrived in Dubai and Palm Marine had been working on her for years without success.

A swath boat is a high performance vessel with a complex transmission and a leveling system, built in a catamaran hull, to compensate roll and pitch created by waves which keeps the boat stable at high speed. This particular swath boat was like no other that I had seen before—picture a square box sitting on two torpedo-shaped hulls, possibly the ugliest thing I ever set my eyes on. Jim had somehow convinced Sultan to purchase this sixty foot junk boat in California, without a survey, for half a million dollars. They could have known she would never be certified by any marine agencies because the aluminum hull was too thin. He had her transported to Dubai by cargo for a good chunk of money, and undoubtedly, Jim got his commission, the real winner in this deal.

Once in Dubai, Palm Marine "engineers" attempted to retrofit the boat. They added a cabin on the top of the torpedo twin hull, piling on three tons of weight in the process and raising the center of gravity— a common trend in Dubai boat building.

But they had failed miserably. The boat was not working at all. Each one of its systems broke down—it was a joke. When I saw how they refitted it, I realized how far they were from having the most basic knowledge and understanding of boat building. It really looked like they just put parts together and painted the whole thing so that no one would notice. What can you expect from a Dubai boat builder engineer when the guy who replaces the electric bulbs in an elevator is also called an engineer?

Eventually, Sultan called me and instructed me to refit his Swath Boat for a second time. I didn't have a written instruction, but since he was signing the checks, I was covered. I decided to take her out for a full check up. Sultan insisted he be onboard with some VIP's despite no work having been carried out to rectify the problems.

During the sea trial, around the Palm Islands, a hydraulic hose burst and I immediately lost control of the steering. The rudder locked itself full to port, putting the boat at full speed onto a collision course with rocks 100 yards away. My reflexes took over and I put the engines in reverse, and the boat stopped twenty feet away from the rocks. That was a close one. Sultan saw something was not right, but he down played it in front of his VIPs. I called in a patrol boat to pick up Sultan and his VIPs, and I had the boat towed back to the factory.

Because the swath boat was too heavy by three tons, she sat too deep in the water and the swath effect was nullified. It created so much drag and stress on all the systems that it caused the ruptures. Before I got this boat into the Exomos yard, the Palm Marine refit had already cost $1,000,000. It cost me another $500,000 and ten months to properly retrofit her and make her sea worthy. I could not remove the cabin or make it lighter, so I lengthened the torpedo hulls to create more flotation. I replaced the complex mechanical transmission with a hydraulic transmission, which saved almost a ton of weight in junk and metal parts. In the end, I succeeded in making the boat work. She was still ugly, but more functional and practical—and more importantly, she was running stable.

During the final sea trial in four-foot waves, I drove the boat with a glass full of water on the table and not a drop was spilled. But when she was all done and ready for delivery, Sultan didn't want her and ignored my calls. Nakheel didn't want her either, and Butti looked the other way. Instead, they sent a surveyor to analyze the welding my staff had performed on the hull. I saw the back-stabbing maneuver and ordered the surveyor to analyze all the welding, not just mine. The result was a blow to Sultan. My welding met all requirements, while the original welding didn't pass. Now they were all embarrassed because they had all bet that I would not be make her work, and their plan to use it as an excuse to blame me for it, failed.

Not only did I fix the boat, but I was also instructed to fix the books. I was ordered by executive management to take Palm Marine's million dollar expenditure onto Exomos' balance sheet while the accountants cooked the books of Exomos and Palm Marine to hide the mess they had created—and all the while, the auditors had the audacity to look the other way and question me about my operation.

As no one in the group wanted her, I proposed selling her at cost, and I got the green light. They only agreed because they thought I would never find a buyer for a boat like that, but against all odds, I found somebody oversees who was willing to pay twenty-five percent under and use her as a dive support vessel; granted, it was a bit less than cost, but it was better than a total loss. Sultan and Butti refused to sell her. The message was loud and clear. They were on a mission to make sure I would not succeed with anything. Today the boat is still rotting under the scorching sun.

Other projects were total failures due to Sultan's hasty decisions. Some of them were good ideas in the beginning, but either Sultan's mind changed partway through the process, or changed when the project made it to production towards the end.

At one point Sultan said he wanted me to build three airboats for a local Sheikh. An airboat is a flat-bottomed boat with an aircraft propeller; they are also known as swamp boats. They can trek in the mud, shallow waters, sand bars and over vegetation because they don't have a propeller in the water. I was very familiar with these types of boats—I drove many in the Everglades of Florida.

On my airboats, I installed gas turbines—the engine produced the same amount of power and was four times smaller than a piston engine, with the added bonus of burning diesel fuel instead of gasoline. These airboats were thirty-five feet long—and thanks to Gordon, my gas turbine engineer from Zimbabwe, we made them the Rolls Royces of airboats. They were remarkably powerful vessels capable of carrying twelve people at fifty miles per hour in one inch of water. Riding on one was an incredibly hair-blowing experience—and loud.

I cautioned Sultan these airboats were not for the casual boater, and that they required training, gas turbine qualification and responsible behavior, or someone could get killed. I think my warnings scared him. He gave up on the idea after they were completed—another total waste of time and money. It's no secret that many rich, spoiled Emiratis feel compelled to flaunt their new toys, but callously mishandling these boats at high speeds, they could wind up killing themselves in the process. I would have liked to bring one back to the U.S. for business, but management didn't let me buy anything I could be successful with somewhere else.

We moved from one wasted project to another. Sultan had a fishing boat he had owned for a long time. It was one of his first boats—the *Little Ocean Star*, named after his yacht, the *Ocean Star*. The boat was old and was only going about twenty-seven miles per hour tops. So one day Sultan asked me to retrofit it. He wanted it to go at least forty-five miles per hour. I accepted, and a week later I received the boat at Exomos and started working on it right away.

To limit the cost of the transformation, I recovered two powerful engines from another boat Palm Marine had trashed. With two 440 horsepower engines instead of two 275 horsepower engines, I was confident the boat would exceed the forty-five miles per hour mark.

While working on my notes, I noticed there was a problem with the boat itself; it was too heavy for its size. My calculations didn't add up, and I could not understand why. I found no trapped seawater anywhere or anything hidden in the hull. To reduce drag and improve the hydrodynamics, I needed to lengthen the hull at least four feet, so I sliced off the rear of the boat to extend the hull. That's when I discovered the reason why the boat was too heavy. The fiberglass hull was four inches thick, of solid fiberglass. Insane. It should have been one inch at the most and with a sandwich material. I saw this too many times to recite in the UAE; it is a constant pattern where workers overbuild hulls, making them too heavy. Regardless of the precautions you take, if you don't have a qualified supervisor permanently watching over their shoulders, the workers will manage to overbuild the hulls or somehow put on too much material.

The hull of the *Little Ocean Star* was too thick, and there was nothing I could do about it, but I knew I could still make it work. According to my calculations, even with too much weight, the boat would exceed the forty five miles per hour mark with the new installed power. I went ahead and extended the hull and redesigned the swim platform and the ladder. In the end, it became a much more functional boat, it was more comfortable, and it exceeded Sultan's speed target. He was very happy with the retrofit.

Along with the modifications, I installed a much stronger and double tow eye, because Sultan told me the boat was to be towed behind Sheikh Mohammed's supply ship the *Shadow* on her way to the Maldives. Sultan has a hotel there and he needed a dive boat, so *Little Ocean Star* would be given the job. I voiced against the towing of the boat in high seas on a 2,500 mile voyage, but no one cared to listen. I delivered the boat to Sultan's captain and he signed off after the sea trials. I demonstrated the boat's performance and everything went well.

Three days later, Sultan called me in the middle of the night to announce the *Little Ocean Star* had sunk on her way to the Maldives. He sounded as if I had done something wrong when refitting the boat to make it sink. Because the *Shadow* had cranes, winches and lines, they were able to fish the boat out of the water and bring it back to Exomos. The crew onboard the *Shadow* and the people at Nakheel were quick to point fingers at me, so I decided to conduct and document a full and thorough survey to determine the cause of the accident.

There was evidence of amateurism and negligence throughout. I learned they were not just towing the *Little Ocean Star*, but in all there were three boats in a row. The Captain was no fool; either he was instructed to do so or he didn't check what his crews were doing. I could not believe they could be so irresponsible. The ocean is not a lake. There are waves and motion and splashing walls of water hitting the boats.

They hadn't even put wrap covers on the boats, so under tow, waves had come in, one after another, filling the boats, and with no pumps running, they started to sink. As they were watching the last boat sinking and pulling down the second one and then *Little Ocean Star* attached to the same line, a deck mate jumped in the *Little Ocean Star* to start the engine to run the pumps and get her to speed.

They didn't want to cut the two other boats loose, and assumed with the tow speed they could save the boats. This would not have worked anyway, but to make it worse someone shut the cooling water valves prior to the journey. Of course the guy who jumped into the boat forgot to open them before running the engines. They were still closed when I inspected the boat. With these valves closed and no cooling water running through the system, one engine didn't start, and the other burned out in a cloud of black smoke. With no power and no pumps, all three boats went down hanging on the tow line.

This was another failure, waste of money and time, and embarrassing for Sultan. The insurance didn't cover the accident for some reason. My report included the reconstruction of events and evidence of the negligence of the captain and his crew. I made it loud and clear that he bore the responsibility for this accident and I would not take the blame for it.

But, as others were accumulating mistakes, the auditors were still harassing me. Obviously they wanted to blame me for something—even if I couldn't possibly have caused the events. I felt it was important I stand up for myself and keep record and evidence of my activities. At least from a technical point of view, I eliminated the possibility of being accused of any wrongdoing. I remember, for instance, when the auditors accused me of buying equipment that did not fit into submarines. They mentioned 25 pumps I returned to the supplier with the notation, "Do not meet the requirements for submarine use." Like always, the auditors blamed me for their mistake. I ordered these pumps in the U.S. When they arrived at Dubai Customs for clearance, it was as if the devil himself had come up out of the box. The pumps were made in Israel, and this created such embarrassment and rage at top management they asked me to repack and ship them back with an excuse. I was not aware of the origin of these parts when I ordered them but Israel in the UAE is taboo, boycotted, and an absolute no no. Even the country code on international calls is blocked.

Although Sultan told me Exomos was my company and I could do as I felt necessary, I knew it was not. So I always made sure every single decision was approved by Sultan, the chairman, before I did anything.

When I started I could order all the equipment I needed, but it would take months to get the bills paid. Against a general opinion, Dubai World is not rich in cash and generally pays its bills after six months—sixty cents on the dollar. It was such a lengthy process that deliveries never came on time, thus missing our deadlines for boat shows and demos during my first year of operation. To avoid annoying delays, I opted to use my own money as a loan (sometimes up to $200,000) to the company to buy equipment through Seahorse Submarines in the U.S., and then wait to get paid after a couple of months. Top management was aware of and agreed to this arrangement. But two years later, the auditors would call it embezzlement.

Once on a late evening, as I was leaving work, I saw Sultan walking on the "Exomos Beach," the beach plot next to the company. The ex Exomos beach should I say, because during the short conversation I had with him he told me that Sheikh Mohammed had allocated the entire beach and contiguous vacant plots for the construction of a palace for his daughter who was getting married.

Not only was it another project going down the drain and the end of the gigantic testing pool facility, but I was wondering if I was going to be blamed by the auditors for having started this project. Nevertheless, what a bizarre idea to build a palace inside an industrial zone.

So here I was, trying to survive Abdul Qader's and Butti's maneuvers and their blame for business I had conducted in the past—of which all had all been approved by Sultan. They were looking for a reason to turn me into a scapegoat so the government officials could lynch me. I had gone through audits before, but this one was not so much an audit as it was a witch-hunt. I was targeted personally; it wasn't business.

Abdul Qader would call me to his office without notice or explanation. I was not given any time to prepare. He would confront me with one claim after another, like pulling rabbits out of magic hats. One accusation after another—you used Seahorse Submarines to overcharge Dubai World—you were paid for orders never received.

Each time they pulled a financial statement as evidence, I would bring them my bank statements, indisputable proof that negated their accusations. Every time, I had to go through the factory myself and show the auditors that alleged missing equipment was indeed accounted for.

Most of the alleged inconsistencies they brought up were the result of the incompetence of my administrative staff or from the production staff who hadn't recognized, identified, or accounted for items that were sitting in inventory. Some were just flat out fake statements designed to paint me guilty as charged.

One auditor, who lost his temper because he could not prove anything after a five-hour-meeting, confided to me that they would never stop until they found something—that it was their job to bring me down. I heard from other sources I was a hard bone for the auditors to chew on—because I was defending myself.

Without a single shred of evidence, Abdul Qader told me I had to reimburse the company against a financial schedule prepared by his auditors, for a total of $1,500,000. He kept looking at my watch as if to determine its value to start a collection.

Itemized costs included everything from reimbursement of shipping expenses for my cars, to submarines or equipment they said they did not receive. Projects like the Stingray submarine, of which I had a picture of Sheikh Mohammed standing beside and hours of video footage in Dubai, they continued to claim was never received.

Their reason for asking me to reimburse the shipping cost of my cars was because it was not in my contract. How could it have been? I moved on Sultan's word. He signed my contract months after I moved to Dubai, after my cars were already there. Thus, there was no need to mention it in the contract. And not only did I have his word, but when the company paid for it, it was Sultan who signed the check, not me.

This is when I realized that Emiratis, as high as the executive chairman of Dubai World, could break their words and reverse their decisions just to accommodate plans to their advantage, with no remorse or fear of legal action.

Like any other managers in Dubai, I could be held personally and financially responsible for repaying monies against allegation of debts, company losses or mismanagement—even if it was when following instructions.

Mismanagement, in Dubai is a crime punishable by prison, not even a civil offense in the west. This was definitively not in my contract, but it is the law. The law provides also that the manager's passport can be confiscated, or that the manager can be jailed indefinitely without charges.

Sultan asked me to spend without counting, to build his factory without thinking the whole idea through. I was never given a budget to stay within. He had absolutely no clue about the submarine and boat business. Yet that didn't stop him from asking me to build many different designs and retrofit many of their boats at great expense—and, in the end, for nothing.

So when the cash dried up at Dubai World, they could no longer afford the company expansion as planned. The government asked Sultan to look for a way out—to protect themselves—by putting the blame on the CEO. They turned around and blamed me for the bills already paid. Sure, I had been happy to create and build the vessels that Sultan requested. I carefully informed him and the others at Dubai World every step of the way before any money was spent. But I had no clue I could be accused of wrongdoing later.

Five of my key employees told me they had been asked by the auditors to report something against me or they would be fired and deported. One of them, an engineer, had been told by the auditors I would be replaced and he had the choice to either work with the new CEO or go out with the old one—me. So, under duress, he signed a false report declaring the Nautilus submarine would sink to the bottom of the sea if it were put in the water. Abdul Qader never showed me this scandalous and coerced report because I could have proved it otherwise with my calculations and production reports. What kind of audit was that? I also had a survey from an independent naval architect who validated my calculations and certified the boat was seaworthy.

It didn't concern me executive management was looking for another CEO to replace me, because there are not that many qualified submarine engineers looking for the job. From what I gathered, Sultan planned from the beginning to bring me in to quietly shut me away for a time to build a premium factory to produce luxury toys exclusively for the Sheikhs. All the while they would beg, borrow and steal my intellectual properties to later replace me with your average, garden variety, cheap manager.

During the time they were callously spending and squandering cash, Emirati officials didn't count on the escalating popularity of their CEO. My media attention annoyed them—how could a foreigner become famous at their expense? Sultan hired me, but to spare himself the embarrassment of firing me, he selected his worst goons do the dirty work for him. Their plan was to collect enough bogus information against me to justify my voluntary resignation, but not too quickly. They wanted to keep me in the company a little while so the auditors could collect on me later. So, for the time being, they brought in another CEO—Simon.

Now the company had two CEO's, which even in Dubai was unheard of. I was the CEO for the signatures and Simon ran the company on instructions from Ahmed Butti. The company became unmanageable. I had to sign everything because Simon didn't have the legal authority. I kept a copy of everything for insurance, since I was the one taking responsibility for someone else's decisions.

Simon's job was to continue the submarine business and advance the yacht building business, with me in the background for backup and engineering. I knew him—I had seen him before when Butti had the audacity to send him to me for a job interview. The guy was a paint shop manager who had never run a company in his life. He had not a single clue about submarine technology. The guy was as dense as a sack of nails. He was good puppet material for sure— putting Simple Simon in charge was guaranteed the company was destined for doom. That is exactly what happened.

After a backbreaking two years of bringing my technology and expertise into the company, they decided to amputate my achievements at the heights of commercial recognition.

The very first thing that Simon did after moving into the office was to hire his wife under a different name for some consultant work so she could draw a steady flow of income from Exomos. Again, corrupt auditors meagerly attempted to blame me for using Seahorse Submarines (although I had done so with permission), but completely ignored this blatant irregularity.

My employees were too afraid of losing their jobs to do anything against the auditors, but at least they informed me when they knew something. Auditors came to the office at night to bug my computer and my secretary's computer. I found out about this invasion from the night guard on duty, who had been told not to tell me or he would be fired.

Dubai World IT even tampered with my private Emirati email account. They maliciously requested the state ISP to block my recipient yahoo email address so the emails I sent to myself would never be delivered. Whether my email accounts were private or company didn't make a difference. They blocked them to prevent me from copying files to myself that could exonerate me. When I found out the auditors were monitoring my emails, I launched a program to download thousands of real estate listings into my office email account to saturate it with files the auditors would have to waste time opening— and they would not be able to complain about it without exposing their intrusion into my system.

They didn't find anything in my computer, but they did catch Jennifer, my secretary. She was asked to leave because she used her desktop computer to send erotic pictures to her friends. Who cares? Half of the people in Dubai do it. The auditors threatened her with jail time for charges of Internet pornography if she didn't cooperate with them to give evidence against me. They also tried to convince her to claim she and I were having an affair so that I could get arrested for adultery. My hiring a secretary for sexual reasons would have been exactly what the auditors were looking for to hang me. Auditors also accused me of sexual harassment against a female clerk in the company. That accusation didn't go far—I barely knew her—but it showed how desperate they were to get me.

I was becoming more aware of the traitorous games the auditors were playing. They were trying hard to push me out the door, but there was nothing else I could do but stick with my job. It looked more like a battle of wills between me and them. I had done nothing wrong and, no matter what they wanted to plant on me, I was not going to resign. It was good I didn't quit. I didn't know at the time, but if I resigned while being investigated by the auditors, I would have been arrested. To run is considered an admission of guilt and a sign that you are trying to hide something.

From January 2007, executive management blocked every one of my initiatives which could have been beneficial for the company.

They blamed me for not selling anything, I thought I finally had competent employees to generate sales, and it turned out that I didn't after all.

We all knew that even one sale would have put me in a stronger position, giving them less reason to complain—or so I thought at the time. They barred all of my sales contract opportunities with technicalities from their legal counsels. I protested their biased decision-making processes. Sure, it was okay for them to sell and deliver uncertifiable, unstable boats with faulty hulls, yet it was not okay to certify a working, well-designed submarine so it could be sold. In the end, executive management would not pay the invoices for the certification, and I was left in limbo.

I was fighting an invisible enemy. I could identify Sultan, Butti and Abdul Qader as pulling the ropes to bring me down, but so many others I didn't even know were working in the same direction.

One day, one of my faithful engineers, Sebastien, a French gentleman, brought me a valve he had removed from a submarine because he noticed something strange. It showed evidence of sabotage. On a checklist, it appeared as functional, but in use it would have failed. This was a critical valve for the pressurization system. If the engineer had not discovered it, it would have caused a catastrophic failure under the water. I still have that valve with me today as a reminder of the lengths people will go to in order to ruin someone.

The auditors continued to work relentlessly, trying to find something to use against me with no success. One after another, the auditors were replaced by others to keep the pressure on. And one of them, Ferg, a South African, was fired because he got caught in his own game.

He had led Bert, one of my engineers, to believe he would replace me as CEO. Ferg even sent him abroad to negotiate a contract, but because I was the CEO of Exomos, Ferg and Bert could not set up the contract under the corporate name of Exomos without my knowledge. To try and get around that problem, they set up a dummy company, printed out phony brochures and even opened a website for it. Their plan didn't work for many reasons—not the least of which was Bert didn't have the competence to set up a business—but also, Ferg was greedy and had arranged a commission for himself. Butti found out about this scam and both Ferg and Bert were fired on the spot.

It was a bittersweet moment for me when Bert—who had been offered my position as CEO with a guarantee that he would never be fired—eventually got fired for trying to screw the company, and I was still the CEO.

Because I wasn't giving up under all of their pressure, they upped the ante and reported me to the police on completely baseless charges. I was on a weekend trip with my family in the neighboring Emirate of Fujairah when I received a call from Mark that auditors were searching my office, turning everything upside down in my absence.

This would be an illegal search in a modern democratic nation, but it was status quo in this dictatorial state. The search was related to the bullets I brought into the country with my rifle three years earlier. I left the bullets in the company store while waiting for my gun license to be issued by the Dubai government. When the auditors found my bullets in the store, they jumped on this opportunity, and Abdul Qader called the police to report that I smuggled weapons into the country.

Exomos was located inside the free zone, so technically it was the right decision for me to keep the bullets at the company and not my house—because the free zone is not the UAE. Without a license, I could not take them out of that free zone. The rifle itself was held at the airport in the custody of UAE Customs. I had the paperwork to sanction the legality of everything regarding the rifle and bullets, but the auditors ignored it.

Shortly after Mark's call, I received a call from the police. The officer asked me to come over to the police station in Jebel Ali for questioning. On the phone they refused to tell me what it was regarding, only that it was a pressing issue and I needed to come right away. I was on the other side of the UAE at the time, but this was something I wanted to clear up quickly, so my family and I packed everything up in a hurry and drove two hours back to Jebel Ali. I dropped my family at our house and grabbed my gun file. I dashed to the police station, arriving around seven o'clock that night.

I was taken to an interrogation room. Two police officers in uniform followed me in, as did two men, whom I would guess to be from the CID (Criminal Investigation Department), wearing white *khandouras*. They wore faces of contempt. They had their big case—a foreign CEO—in their grasp. Just outside the office sat an ominous jail cell. It was a filthy cage, about five by five in dimension, with five or six guys packed into it. The foul smell coming from this cage told me the cell included a clogged toilet.

They nodded at me to sit in a chair and then asked me to turn off my mobile and put it on the desk in front of them. There were four of them. The first asked me what my religion was, and then if I knew why I had been called in.

The four police officers took turns hammering me with questions for eight straight hours, during which I was not offered food or water. I was interrogated about the ammunition found at Exomos. They thought I had a contract to assassinate somebody. It seemed like they wanted to make sure I was not after a Sheikh. As a former operative, I had extensive interrogatory training, and had been on the other side of the table myself. What I saw was something out of comic book series. It was amateurish, clumsy and childish. I argued it was a set-up, that Abdul Qader had been harassing me since January, and that he wanted to frame me with anything he could find.

The interrogation took a complete different turn when I produced my file with the relevant paperwork and authorizations to prove I didn't smuggle anything. They were amazed when they saw the copy of Sultan Bin Sulayem's passport as a sponsorship label for my license. The officer with the missing button right where his belly bulged asked for the umpteenth time, in total disbelief while his saliva spewed, if Sultan was my sponsor. I kept saying, yes, yes, yes—here is the proof. That was the *aha* moment. After that, the officers seemed agitated and confused that I caught them off guard as I foiled their plan to jail me. To be fingered by the same person who had, in fact, physically authorized what I was being incriminated for was an unexpected moment for these civil servants. After they got over the documents, they moved on to playing the candid officers who wanted to know about the gun and the ammunition.

I repeatedly told them that it didn't make any sense that I would go to a Middle Eastern country on a killing mission with my wife and children in tow, then declare my gun and bullets at the border, and apply for a license to possess a weapon. It was absolutely ridiculous.

I must admit that fifty caliber cartridges look quite big and impressive for the novice, and their ignorance only escalated their accusations. They stood there and accused me of intending to shoot up oil tanks or helicopters. I disputed every single word they said, and slowly I realized it didn't make any difference.

In the end, they wanted me to sign a confession written in Arabic, so I could seek mercy from his highness. I had no idea what the document said. I had nothing to confess, and I stuck to my story, the truth. In their eyes I was a mercenary on a mission. In reality, if I were on a real mission, they would not be talking about it in a squalid police station. Finally, at four in the morning, they told me they could let me go, but only if I surrendered my passport. If I refused, they were going to put me in that cage outside with those other men.

I called Jennifer in the middle of the night so she could go to the office, open the safe, get my passport, and bring it to the police station. At this point, I felt as though I had no choice but to surrender my passport to the police officer. Something really bad was happening to me, and I couldn't help my family or myself if I was locked up in a cage.

Jennifer came to the police station, shocked to see her boss surrounded by police officers. After I surrendered my passport, they gave me some sort of receipt in Arabic and I was allowed to go. I was relieved but exhausted, and returned home to my worried wife.

I was not under arrest, but I knew the auditors would be elated to know I was trapped and under insane pressure now. They wanted me to walk with fear and feel as though they could play god with my life. Little did I know, the worst was yet to come.

The police wanted to hear a mercenary confession so they could lock me up, but what confession could I give them? I wasn't a mercenary, but I did have an imagination. Maybe I should write a fantasy about it, a story where a lethal secret agent is paid by a foreign government to send Dubai back to the Dark Ages. Perfectly doable, if that agent decided to blow up the only power plant in Dubai. There would be no power, no AC, no Internet, no phone, no gas pumps, no fresh water, no freezers, and no food. After only a week life would be unsustainable, and it would give new meaning to the word ghost town.

After the police interrogation, I protested to Abdul Qader. He denied calling the police and said he had nothing to do with it—that it was the police who found my bullets. Really? Why would the police be walking around the company to begin with? They didn't have any reason to come to the company and conduct a search unless someone had called them to report a finding.

He said he tried to call me after the police found the bullets but could not reach me. It was odd that my employees could reach me, yet he couldn't. I knew then Abdul Qader and his goons were all liars and he preferred no one know Dubai World had turned into secret police in order to justify the elimination of their prominent CEO. If it was not their intention, they could just have asked me directly about the three boxes of ammo—like they were asking me about $1.5 million of alleged missing equipment.

Later in an email exchange, I asked Yusuf Kazim, a director of the board and general manager of Nakheel Joint Ventures, to help me recover my passport so that I could go back to the U.S. on vacation. Yusuf replied that my passport was tied up with the GIA (group internal audit) and he could not help. This meant the auditors set up the whole police investigation as a pretext to try and frame me, so my passport would be confiscated or, worse, I would be arrested.

Without my passport, my plans for summer rest and relaxation in the U.S. with my family were ruined. It became increasingly difficult to do anything at Exomos, including meetings I had scheduled outside the country. Without proper a passport, I lost business opportunities.

While Abdul Qader's auditors were still harassing me, I was called into the police headquarters two more times for interrogation. The second interrogation lasted five hours, and the third one for about thirty minutes. During that second interrogation, they told me the police laboratory had tested my bullets and their findings were incriminating.

According to their report, the bullets were designed to shoot oil tanks or helicopters. I knew my bullets were not metal-piercing or incendiary, so either these cops or their lab were incompetent, or they just wanted to hang something on me whether it was true or not. I disputed the report and explained these bullets were turned, not cast, for high precision and practice shooting, with no explosive or incendiary component inside. They were dumbfounded by my quick response.

They refused to show me the report or any other supposed incriminating findings—it was all a bluff. While I was contesting the facts, they were quoting and asking the police questions about their findings. I realized their lab report was not actually based on the testing of the bullet itself or a test fire of one of the bullets. They had done some research on the Internet, comparing specifications and pictures of bullets there to my bullets. Apparently, it was good enough evidence for them if my bullets just looked like the armor-piercing bullets they saw on the net.

As I sat there, giving them more and more details about the bullets to contradict their report, I was probably looking more and more like some sort of ballistics or arms expert—so, intrigued, they asked me what my job was before I became CEO of Exomos.

I felt it would be risky to give them any details of my secret agent career or my shooting expertise, as I suspected it would give them more reasons to accuse me of being a mercenary, which would seal my fate. So instead of answering their questions, I just challenged them. I told them it was easy to sort it all out—they had my gun and my bullets. Why not have one of their lab techs or investigators take the rifle to the gun range and test fire with my bullets?

They had no response to that suggestion. I knew it was because they didn't want proof that I was innocent.

For the third interrogation, I was called to the police headquarters of Dubai, this time to be questioned by a director of the Amn Al Dawla—the secretive State Security, under the orders of Sheikh Mohammed, above the CID, above the police and above the judges. They could arrest people under the guise they represented a threat to the State, put them in solitary confinement with no just cause, and torture them if they so chose.

Just before I entered the building, I set my mobile phone to record. My recording feature could be turned on to record ambient conversations, with no indications—no blinking red lights—silently. I wanted to record the questioning, just in case. During the two previous questionings, the officers allowed me to keep my mobile phone on the table in front of me after I put it on silent. I could at least see the missed calls. So, why should this time be any different?

After I entered the police headquarters I met with Aziz, one of the police officers from the previous questioning. I thought he was from the CID. I didn't have an attorney to represent me. I was directed to an interrogation room where another officer in a white *khandoura* waited for me. Aziz told me the guy next to him was his director—he didn't give me a name.

It was a small room with just a desk and one chair, no windows. There were no documents, no files; it was an empty interrogation room. I looked for hidden cameras but I didn't see any. Like before, they asked me for my mobile phone. They placed it on the table in front of me, recording right under their noses, and they didn't see it.

One officer stood in front of me, playing the bad cop. Aziz was behind me, playing the good cop, just like in the movies. The director was questioning me while reading a document written in Arabic, as if somebody else had given him a list of questions. In his robotic tone, he told me that they had checked out my story and I was in big trouble because it didn't make any sense and no one believed me. He said I was the only one who could close the case, and by helping him solve the case, I would help myself.

They advised me to change my story and confess so they could finish the case, as if it was just some sort of formality—like I could sign some paper and leave with no problem—or so they would have me think. But I knew better. I didn't give up on my story or confess to anything. I continued to maintain my innocence. Just like before, they wanted me to sign documents written in Arabic—a confession of some sort, for something I didn't do.

For them, this interrogation was my last chance to confess my crime. They told me denying the accusations would only lead to harsher punishment—a confession carries a lighter sentence that can ultimately be pardoned by his Highness Sheikh Mohammed.

They went on to say after this last opportunity to confess, my case would be prosecuted to the fullest extent of the law. I would not see my children again, I would not drink fresh water again, and I would be locked up in an underground cave. They pushed the questioning and threatened me with torture. They gave me graphic details of the torture, which convinced me it was something they practiced routinely. They explained they would strap me into a chair and repeatedly insert needles deeply into my nose. They specifically threatened if I refused to change my story, I would be in the cave again, only this time I would be locked away in the scorching desert incommunicado indefinitely, and they would torture me there. At the end of the interrogation, they ordered me never to reveal the nature of their questioning. If I told anyone, they said I would suffer dire consequences—which I understood as death.

When I put my mobile phone on record before the interrogation, I didn't expect to hear these threats. I was stupefied. I heard of torture happening in Dubai prisons before, but I never took these stories seriously.

I sat there afraid. If they found my recording device, I would have been in serious trouble, to say the least.

The following is the exact transcript of this questioning from the recording of my mobile phone. I have included the name of one of the Amn Al Dawla police officers and his mobile number that I managed to get. No company in Dubai accepted my plea to put the conversation in writing for me. When they discovered what conversation was recorded, they feared the worst consequences. It was only much later, in the U.S., that I was able to find someone to transcribe it for me.

Transcript: Questioning in Dubai police headquarters, Murakkabat, April 22, 8:30 a.m.

Officer 1, Mr. Aziz, Mobile Phone +971 (0) 508889805
Officer 2, *Name Unknown, Director*
Officer Aziz: *Asalam Alikoum*. Good morning, Mr. Hervé. How are you?

Hervé: Good morning. I am okay.

Officer Aziz: Good . . . *Insha' Allah* . . . We will have the meeting upstairs. Please—this way. It's on the first floor. Sorry we had to cancel last week. My director had another meeting.

Officer Aziz: Mr. Hervé, this is my director. He has more questions to ask you. So we can finish this case

Officer 2: Yes. Let's go to this room. Please seat. No, no, here it is okay. So, how are you, Mr. Hervé?

Hervé: I'm fine, given the circumstances.

Officer 2: Well, Mr. Hervé. I am going to be direct with you. You have a very big problem. I have all the reports and they are all against you. Nobody believes you told us the truth. Your story does not make any sense. So you better think hard about telling me the real story. You see, we know you have been lying from the beginning. Changing your story. This is a big case—a federal case. Today you have the opportunity to tell me the truth and stop the lies. Forget about what you told us before. I can help you if you help me finish the case. So tell me the truth.

Hervé: I am sorry, sir. My story is the same from the beginning. I have nothing to hide. I told the police everything already.

Officer 2: Mr. Hervé, I want the truth. Today! This is your last chance. Do you understand that? After today we will have all the time—but you need to finish this today.

Hervé: I told you the truth already. I will tell you again today the same truth.

Officer 2: No, no, no! Tell me the real story now. I understand you have been under pressure. It is a tough time for you. You are afraid. Are you afraid, Mr. Hervé?

Hervé: Yes, I am afraid. Do you think I like being here? I have not done anything wrong. Don't you see? I have been set up by the management of my company.

Officer 2: Yes, you are right to be afraid. We can do what we want with you. We can finish this today—close the case—or we can keep you here and continue the questions later. We have all the time.

Hervé: I told the police officers before . . . I brought my bullets along with my guns with the permission of port custom authorities— and that was before I traveled to Dubai.

Officer 2: What permission? No, this is a lie. I want you to think hard. Give me another story. I am going to leave this room for five minutes. I want you to think. Then when I come back, you tell me the truth.

[At this point, both officers leave the room, and leave me alone. After five minutes they come back. One officer has a glass of water, which he puts on the table in front of me.]

Officer 2: So, Mr. Hervé, I hope you changed your mind and that you tell me the truth now. Tell me.

Hervé: I am sorry, Sir. My mind is the same. I did not try to do anything illegal.

Officer : Is that so? Tell me about it. We caught you with bullets— and there is nothing illegal? What did you want to do with those bullets?

Hervé: I am sorry, Sir, but nobody caught me with anything. It is the auditors of my company who called the police on me while I was on vacation in Fujairah with my family. The police didn't come to my facility to look and find the bullets like that. They knew exactly where to go. They have been told where to find them in my company. Mr. Hussein Ramadan called the police. He works for Mr. Abdul Kader at Dubai World Group internal audit. Why don't you ask them about it?

Officer 2: Why did you hide them?

Hervé: I didn't hide them. They were in the company store with the knowledge of my store managers. The auditors wanted to put me in trouble or—it is for revenge. I don't understand why they did that. I had the permission to bring them in the country.

Officer 2: We know who called the police. You don't have a lot of friends there. How many bullets did you have?

Hervé: 450

Officer 2: Are you sure it is not more? It looks like some bullets are missing.

Hervé: I don't think so. Well, I don't know. I didn't check for a while. They were in sealed boxes. If some are missing, I don't know. But that means they would have been stolen—by somebody in the company. I seriously doubt that. I have them since two years and a half, in the store—untouched. Don't you think that if I wanted to do anything bad with them, I would have done it already? And why would I have declared them, if I wanted to hide them?

Officer 2: How many bullets, Mr. Hervé?

Hervé: Three cases of 150. Four hundred and fifty.

Officer 2: You know, Mr. Hervé, your bullets may have been used to commit a murder. Somebody in Dubai was killed with a bullet in the head.

Hervé: Wow! Wow! I am not going to take the blame for that one. First of all, if somebody got shot in the head with one of my bullets, he would not have a head anymore—so you are not talking about the same bullets—no way.

Officer 2: Do you think it's funny, Mr. Hervé? You come to this country with bullets and guns and somebody is murdered. So you better tell me. I am getting tired of your lies.

Hervé: I have nothing to do with that. My bullets were in the store and my gun is at the airport. I don't believe that.

Officer 2: Did you give any bullets to anyone? Did you sell any of them?

Hervé: Absolutely not—never.

Officer 2: Your stories don't make any sense. I am asking you if you gave bullets to anyone. I'll find out sooner or later.

Hervé: I didn't give any bullets to anyone. I would never do that. I am responsible and a former military officer. The bullets were for my personal use—for shooting. I know how to deal with weapons and ammunitions.

Officer 2: Mr. Hervé, I am asking you again. Why did you bring these bullets if you cannot use them in the UAE?

Hervé: Well, now, I know that before I was told I could bring them.

Officer 2: Did you use your gun? Where is your gun?

Hervé: My gun is at the airport for two years and a half

Officer 2: Do you have another gun?

Hervé: Yes. A pistol. It is also at the airport with the rifle.

Officer 2: I mean, do you have another gun somewhere we don't know?

Hervé: No.

Officer 2: Mr. Hervé, I am losing patience. Do you know who we are?

Hervé: Not exactly—the CID?

Officer 2: We are state security. We are above the police. We are above the judges. We can keep you here forever. You have fresh water? Please have a drink.

Hervé: Thank you.

[At this point, I pretend to drink a sip. I don't know where this water came from, and there is no way I'm going to drink it.]

Officer 2: The water is fresh, Mr. Hervé?

Hervé: Yes it is, thank you.

Officer 2: Do you like fresh water?

Hervé: Huh? Yes, of course.

Officer 2: Enjoy it now. You won't be able to drink fresh water like that for a long time where we take you, if you don't change your story. We have other methods to make people like you talk. We are better than you to make people talk. We are state security. We are above the law and nobody will know.

Hervé: You can ask me a thousand times. And I will tell you a thousand times that I brought the bullets for my personal use with the permission of ports customs authorities.

Officer 2: Mr. Hervé, this is not France here. There is no democracy here. I will put you in a cave—300 meters underground, away from the world and your family—and I will keep you there until you tell us the truth. We have caves deep underground where we keep people like you—who are a threat to the UAE. I want you to think again—hard.

Hervé: Oofffff—this is such a waste. You think I am a criminal and you want to put me away—for nothing—just in case?

Officer 2: When I do this to you *[the officer raises his fist and puts it about three inches away from my face]* what do you think?

Hervé: I think you are going to punch my face.

Officer 2: Good, yes, this is how I feel when I see you with your guns in my country. I am asking you nicely—comfortable in this room, with a glass of fresh water. Or I can ask you—locked up and chained in a cave. Not a prison—a hole deep underground that nobody would know where you are.

Hervé: *[heavy breathing]*

Officer 2: Do you think you will continue to hide the truth when I insert needles in your nose? Do you think you will continue to lie? Do you know how painful it is to have needles put deep inside your nose—repeatedly—and then twisted around, Mr. Hervé? Do you think you can resist this kind of pain—strapped on a chair? I want to know if you are a threat to the UAE and you are going to tell me. So I can help you and close this case.

Hervé: I am not a threat. I was invited to come to this country by Sultan Ahmed Bin Sulayem. I am an engineer. You can torture me—yes—yes, but I will always tell you the same—story—I told the police from the beginning. In the end, whatever you do to me, it will be for nothing. You will destroy my life. And you will have no case. There is no case. I am a family man and a businessman.

Officer 2: Or an assassin—and we have a murder in Dubai we want to solve.

Hervé: I thought there was no crime in Dubai.

Officer 2: Funny, Mr. Hervé. No, no, no—yes, there are too many crimes—a lot. They are not reported, that's all.

Officer: I am going to leave this room again for five minutes. Think of what you are going to tell me when I come back, because you are going to tell me—nicely—or I will break you to get to the truth.

Hervé: I am going to tell you the same, Sir.

Officer 2: You can only help yourself if you tell me the truth.

Hervé: I am telling you the truth.

Officer 2: Okay, we'll see. Just put yourself together and think of your family—if you want to see them again

[Both officers leave the room and leave me alone, after five minutes. They come back to the room.]

Officer 2: Okay, well, this is your last chance, Mr. Hervé. I have time. Tonight, I go home anyways, regardless of what you tell me. The difference is with you. You can go home or you can disappear to a deep cave where we will torture you to find out the truth. Is this what you want?

Hervé: *[Deep breathing.]*. I am sorry, this is a sad situation. I have one story. If you don't believe it, I have nothing else other than trying to convince you that I am telling the truth. Believe me, you have no case. There is nobody to catch. You can torture me, but it is for nothing.

Officer 2: So, Mr. Hervé, you want to change your story and you are going to tell me the truth? Or you want me to force you to tell the truth?

Hervé: No, it is the same. I came to Dubai with my rifle and shipped my bullets with the permission of Sanil Subair from port and custom authorities. I am a former French Navy officer, licensed in the U.S. to use and carry weapons.

Officer 2: You have a family in Dubai, Mr. Hervé?

Hervé: Yes, my wife and my two sons—tomorrow is the birthday party of my son.

Officer 2: Good—and you want to be at your son's birthday or you want to call him from a prison?

Hervé: I want you to believe me so I can go home.

Officer 2: There will be an ongoing investigation. This is not over. We will find the truth.

Hervé: How long is this going to last? Because there is nothing else to find out.

Officer 2: We have all the time. We can find you and arrest you anytime.

Hervé: Why all this? Why would I try to hide my bullets when I declared them with my rifle? It does not make any sense. I came with my family and I am a businessman. I am not a terrorist.

Officer 2: We know your games, Mr. Hervé. We are going to find out.

Hervé: This is not a game. You are playing with my life—for nothing.

Officer 2: I am going to let you go—but you are going to swear not to tell anyone about this conversation—anyone—you understand? Do I make myself clear?

Hervé: Why would I tell anyone? Who is going to believe me anyways?

Officer 2: Nobody would believe you—and you will face dire consequences. We have the country completely under surveillance. We monitor everything. You talk—we catch you, for good, and nobody will ever see you again—you understand?

Hervé: If you monitor everything, then you know I didn't try to do anything bad with my bullets.

Officer 2: We are investigating. If there is something, we will find out. I'll be watching you. You can go now.

Hervé: Thank you, Sir.

[End of transcript.]

That was the end of the questioning. They opened the door, handed me my mobile and let me go. I rushed down the stairs. I left the police headquarters and jumped into my car. I turned off the recording on my phone, and drove back to my office.

After these interrogations and all the lies of Abdul Qader, I knew it was all over for me at Exomos. Sultan didn't even pick up when I called him, nor would he return my messages. He had definitely let me down. And his silence further convinced me he played a vital role for all of these incriminating and ostracizing events that were happening to me.

I knew that legally, from a Western standpoint, they would never be able to find anything to press charges against me—but in Dubai, they didn't need evidence to lock you up. It was now clear to me the Dubai authorities would use coercion or blackmail—and would even plant evidence to force the situation to their advantage. They would partake in underhandedness and treachery, going so far as arresting the wife for the husbands' deeds. They were ruthless and willing to go great lengths to wear me down.

I switched to survival mode, continuing to live and work as normal on the surface, secretly formulating Plan B to leave the country as soon as I got my passport back. I didn't know how long it would take or how I would do it, but I knew it was a foregone conclusion.

My family and I were no longer safe in Dubai.

It became worse by the week, but I was still reluctant to go to any extreme measures. My motto was: "You catch more bees with honey than with vinegar." I decided to be cooperative rather than fighting the auditors. I learned these Emiratis authorities don't tolerate contradiction. They don't like defiance, and they don't like to be proven wrong.

The questioning continued at Abdul Qader's office. Each time I had to go back to my office, gather my evidence, and return to show it to him to contradict the issues he had raised. I told him if he notified me in advance of the issues to be discussed, I could prepare my documents before the meeting and bring them directly to save everyone time, but he refused. In his view, indicating the issues beforehand would give me a chance to get away with my innocence intact.

Thinking with Western logic is a mistake. Over there, charges cannot be questioned. They are only mentioned so you could admit to them—not fight them. When I would come back with undisputable documents to prove my innocence, Abdul Qader would continue to argue.

After June, it became extremely difficult to work under these circumstances. Working had gone from the design of submarines and management of a burgeoning business to merely survival and self-defense. Not only did I have auditor meetings every week, but also the police had referred my case to the public prosecutor and I had to go to his office every two weeks for questioning. This time I had to hire an attorney, and it cost me a lot of money. Everything was in Arabic, so I also had to hire a translator. I wouldn't trust any court-appointed translator, and while dealing with the Emirati government, I needed to know exactly what my lawyer, the prosecutors and judges were saying to one another without having to rely on my attorney's words, as he might hide or distort conversations or facts to his advantage.

When I brought my grievances to the attention of Abdul Qader about the unfairness of this entire situation, his reply was always that it was the system—that it was not personal. Emiratis are really good at hiding their actions behind their organizations. They don't have the courage to face you to make a direct claim. When a problem starts with an Emirati, it never, ever, goes away. With time it just gets worse—like the wind that brings sand to your front door. You don't pay attention to a little bit of sand each day and it just piles up, but before you know it, you need a shovel. Emiratis have all the time in the world to watch the sand piling up and bury you.

The situation moved up another notch on the worst scale when executive management told me that some programs I started at Exomos had been canceled. It didn't matter Sultan had asked me to start them. They were no longer going to be funded, and the auditors asked me to reimburse the costs already incurred. Close to $3 million. Now, I was a scapegoat.

Where in the world would you see the CEO reimburse money spent by a company on legitimate business at the request of its chairman? This was absolutely ludicrous. There are no golden parachutes for CEOs in Dubai. They strip the CEO of everything he has and then throw him out the door of the plane without a parachute at all!

It was extortion. I knew then they were really after my assets—specifically, the house I bought two years earlier. They tried to convince me the confiscation of my passport by the police had nothing to do with Dubai World, but at the same time the auditors admitted that if I paid the money, I would get my passport back.

July came, and since I didn't have my passport, my family went to the United States for vacation without me, and it was tough. Just because I was being held in Dubai, I didn't think it was fair for my wife and children to skip their trip home. It's one thing to be away from your family for business reasons, but it's a whole other ball of wax when you are separated because you are being held in a country against your will and being blackmailed. I spent July alone and miserable, working for nothing.

I didn't tell anyone, but I called a friend who was a real estate agent to put my house up for sale. It was a little bit sooner than I wanted because the house was not finished, but I also thought it would take some time before I could get a buyer. Boy, was I wrong. The market was good at the time. The real estate agent called me back fifteen minutes later to tell me he had a buyer. I actually sold my house in fifteen minutes. It took two weeks to finalize the transaction. The buyer was a gentleman from Afghanistan. He paid cash. He had come through the airport with a huge sum of cash in his briefcase and nobody batted an eyebrow.

During the closing of the transaction, the real estate broker's assistant, a young lady with obviously zero experience, told the buyer that he didn't look like an Afghani because he had blond hair, blue eyes, and spoke with a Russian accent. He became upset and asked her if she had expected him to show up with a turban on. He told her to go back to school to learn some manners.

The sale still went through without a hitch. Nobody at Nakheel—not Sultan nor Abdul Qader—had tried to freeze the sale, only because they didn't know; I sold my house before it was registered with the public records, so it was merely a transfer of building contract rather than a sale. As soon as I got the cash from the sale, I wired the money to the United States. I was relieved—at least my money was safe. Abdul Qader and Sultan learned six months later that I had sold my house when the Afghani registered the house. My money was safe and they were enraged.

Having my family with me in Dubai was an impediment to me defending myself. The Emiratis knew it and took advantage of it as an effective way to assert pressure against me. It is very difficult to understand them. That is just the way they are. They see you as unbelievers on their soil and feel they have every right to build up a case against you to justify the repossession of everything you have with absolutely no compassion for family or relatives.

Although I was prepared to go to whatever extremes necessary to get my family and myself to safety, I was damned if I would roll over and admit to something I did not do. My way of life has always been about going to the extreme; living on the edge while taking calculated risks. I was absolutely determined to never give myself nor my life savings up to these thieves.

Surprisingly, top management never considered I might make plans for retaliation or escape. They knew of my past as a secret operative, but they were probably too arrogant to consider I had some tricks up my sleeve to fight back.

In August 2007, I had a meeting with Abdul Qader at Dubai World headquarters. He asked me again to reimburse monies I didn't owe. I will never forget what he said when I showed him my bank statements to prove my innocence: "Hervé, I have to discount your evidence because you are using it to try to exonerate yourself." I had to contain my rage. He was so sure of himself and arrogant. He said it was irrelevant, because he had more proof in files, but he never showed that proof to me.

I understood I could never have a fair hearing or a balanced audit, or have an opportunity to prove my innocence during an investigation, prosecution or trial. It was all set up and designed to break me down. I could not negotiate or plead innocent.

I had enough of them and their treacherous behavior. It was time for me to draw the line and get ready to fight back.

I contacted Bernard, an old friend of mine from the French Secret Service, a retired combat diver. The last time I had seen him was six months earlier while he was visiting Dubai with five other former frogmen. He was not surprised to hear from me. He had seen all of the magazines and TV shows about Exomos and me, but even with all the excitement and interest that accompanied these media events, he suspected something was not right.

I explained that Dubai was not as it appears and that Emiratis cannot be trusted. I told him I expected the worst and needed to be prepared for what was to come, so I asked him to ship me a re-breather, just in case I needed it. This diving gear is not normal diving equipment. It is a military commando re-breather—a closed circuit breathing apparatus, all in black. Unlike scuba equipment, it does not vent any bubbles into the water, so it is very quiet and discreet. It was developed for military frogmen and provided for up to five hours diving time, but there were some versions adapted for the general public.

Along with the re-breather, I asked Bernard to ship me a tactical underwater navigationboard and a full black diving suit. I expected to face some problems with Customs if I received my equipment all at once—all this black military commando stuff with no labels didn't look at all like leisure-type diving gear. So I asked him to ship it in three different boxes with the pieces split up. Just in case somebody at Customs suspected something and questioned the shipments, I had an excuse prepared. At Exomos, I was building a Swimmer Delivery Vehicle (SDV)—a commando submersible for two frogmen—so I could legitimately say that I needed the re-breather to test the submarine.

My gear cleared Customs without a problem. It is always the same with Emirati Customs—hypocrisy and incompetence. Through their ignorance and obscurantism, they cleared military equipment that could be used only by individuals for clandestine operations. But yet they never fail to seize French DVD movies if there is a girl in lingerie on the cover.

I was excited to have been able to sneak this equipment into the country. It brought many memories with it. I took it home to try it on for size and to have it ready, just in case. Helen stared at me with a look on her face that said, "Uh-oh—payback time."

Bernard, back in France, was excited, too. I told him I had no plans yet, but he was sure I was up to something and told me he would be watching the news for a big and unexplained major accident in the region.

I pressured my lawyer to get my passport back, but he told me it was a very bad and grave situation. I was not sure how much he was trying to scare me to justify his fee. According to him, the prosecutor was convinced I was some sort of deep cover sleeper or mercenary. Of course, it was all excuses, because, at the same time, he told me the prosecutor would maintain his pressure on me until I paid the money to Abdul Qader.

In September, after a year and a half of work, the Nautilus submarine was ready to be launched. I scheduled media coverage and an international press conference for the event. It was a superb high-tech vessel, looking as if it had been built in the last century, resembling a monster dinosaur fish and composed of riveted metal plates. I really couldn't wait to unveil it to the world and prove to Dubai World not only their report on the 'not' seaworthiness of the Nautilus was fake, but that a submarine could be UAE-made.

The picture of the Nautilus cruising in the Palm Islands would have circled the globe. But two days before the launch, I received the coup de grace. When executive management found out the media was at the door waiting, Ahmed Butti fired me—with two hours' notice. The next day he cancelled the launch and the media coverage.

This submarine was the pride of the company—Sultan himself congratulated me. It drew the most attention of all of our vessels whenever people visited the factory or the boat show. It had cost close to $600,000 to build, and, in the end, they threw it all away.

Money alone was not the issue. Sultan had wasted millions and millions of dollars on other projects without caring. He needed to put the blame on me. There was nothing missing from the company's inventory, and if any monies were embezzled, it was at another level. The money they were asking me to reimburse was a drop in the bucket. It was more like a vendetta than an exercise in balancing the books.

It was clear they didn't want me to get more attention from the media. Emiratis have big egos and tend to want all the attention for themselves. They begrudged an expatriate on their payroll stealing their limelight. It is not that I did it on purpose—anyone making submarines gets media attention. Everyone is fascinated not only by the underwater world, but also by the machines that can take them there. It was even more so in Dubai because the country itself was all over the news. I couldn't help it. Yet still they somehow blamed me as if I planned it all and was purposely focusing the spotlight on myself.

After they sacked me, they tried to coerce me into signing more confessions, confidentiality agreements, and other statements—all of which made me look guilty of some wrongdoing—and they put up additional conditions for me to meet in order to have my passport released. I left the company with nothing, but I paid a little. I gave the auditors $40,000—part of what they claimed I owed. I was under duress, and I had the evidence to prove later their claim was false, allowing me in turn to file for extortion against them. I also wanted to show good faith and make them believe I would give them more money later. I made no mistake here. Failure to comply and being on the defensive would have landed me directly in prison.

In the same month, I received a notice of eviction from the company villa where I was living and a statement that renovations were scheduled. Therefore, I had until December to vacate the premises. In all honesty, there was nothing cosmetically wrong with the villa—it was just another maneuver from Butti to avoid honoring my contract, since it was clearly agreed and signed on that I was to live there until my own house was completed, thus adding pressure to coerce me into paying the auditors. They knew that without a passport I would not be able to rent another house nor find other work prospects. I wasn't going to budge so I decided to stay in that villa until I was ready to leave the country for good.

All the while, I was going to the prosecutor office with my attorney and my translator to be questioned repeatedly. It was the same story—all in Arabic. The whole procedure was a farce. They never told me what charges were against me.

All public prosecutors in Dubai are Emirati nationals who pledge blind obedience to the absolute ruler in return for their judicial positions. Their jobs and incomes are subject to termination for failure to uphold their pledges. The executive branch of the government and the judiciary branch are one and the same—forget about separation of powers or the protections of checks and balances. The same branch of government that prosecutes someone was the same branch of government that defends and sentences him. In so being, the judiciary is beholding to and subject to the whim of Sheikh Mohammed. How convenient, right?

Attorneys represent the accused, but are more like assistants to the prosecutors. They were happy to take my money, but they could not do much to defend me in a case involving the government or an Emirati. They could never forget it was the government who issued their license to practice. They build a good reputation with the court and receive more referrals when they negotiate with defendants and persuade them to admit guilt for crimes, sign confessions, and pay debts. A good reputation means more defendants, more cases, and more retainers. I felt like I was up against a pack of growling dogs ready to lunge at me at the slightest wrong move. I was completely alone in front of my inquisitors. My lawyer gave me several clues that it was all about money. When I asked him what kind of judgment I was facing, he would only give me examples of what happened to other less fortunate people. He was not positive at all!

He told me about a British expatriate working in Dubai, who, after a tip to the police, was arrested with one nine millimeter bullet in his rental car. He didn't have a gun. He had nothing to do with guns or ammunition. The bullet had probably been left in the car by a previous customer or planted there by a disgruntled Emirati. It didn't matter. He lost his job, got convicted, and received a three-month jail sentence followed by deportation.

In another case, another British citizen received a six-month sentence for illegal possession of ammunition. The police caught his ten-year-old son playing in front of his house with a bullet he'd found in the street, so they accused the father of illegal possession of ammunition. He lost his job, got convicted, and received a six-month jail sentence followed by deportation—all for just one bullet.

I had 450 high-powered, large caliber bullets. By their laws, I was facing years in jail, but, if I paid the money, they would have the judge drop the weapons charges. All I had to do was to give Abdul Qader the cash and sign their typed confession, and the judge would give me just a fine with no deportation. My attorney assured me that nobody wanted to put me in jail. They were my friends—it was in my best interest to pay them money, and that it was not important; after all, it was just money. With friends like that, I needed no enemies.

They were gangsters and racketeers—and my paid attorney was just another instrument they used to strong-arm me into giving them money.

I learned my lessons then. You can't trust Emiratis, and when I say Emiratis, I don't mean Arabs in general. I have good friends who are Arabs. I mean specifically just Emiratis, who are the worst there is because they pretend to be open-minded, liberal, kind and generous. All they are really after is more power—full and absolute control over your life while you're on their turf. Bring you to your knees so you will praise and obey them.

In December, I went to trial for my case about the gun and the bullets. All trials were before judges and were usually public. There were no jury trials. All prosecutions and trials were conducted in Arabic, with a procedural right to a translator, and could last up to a year, depending on the seriousness of the charges, the number of witnesses, and the availability of judges.

I went to the courthouse with my attorney and my translator. It was a huge building with an alien atmosphere. Everybody milled about or huddled around in impromptu pre- and post-trial discussions. Only Arabic was spoken, and the room was a sea of white *khandouras*.

At my trial, the attorneys all yelled at each other in Arabic, but I had the impression it was just for show. It was over within half an hour. I didn't say a word to the judge, and the judge didn't say a word to me or even make eye contact. My attorney told me the judge would issue his judgment after two weeks.

On judgment day, I didn't have to go to court. I had to pay a $3,000 fine, and I still didn't even know what the charge was. My judicial experience cost me $80,000 in legal fees and nine months without a passport. My attorney got my passport back one month later, after the mandatory thirty-day wait to allow the prosecutor time to appeal the judge's decision.

As soon as I got my passport, I scheduled a trip alone to the U.S. to sort out urgent administrative issues that I now had there because I had been trapped for so long in the UAE.

My attorney must have gotten my passport by some sort of mistake of the court, because my name was still on the travel ban list in the police system when I went to the airport to take my flight. The airport authorities questioned me for six hours, causing me to miss my flight. I returned to Jebel Ali and took a flight the next day. Dubai World must have indicated somewhere to not release my passport, but without any filed claim, the court probably could not hold my passport any longer.

Back in the U.S., I was picked up by the U.S. immigration to explain why I stayed out of the country for so long. As a permanent

U.S. resident, I had to go back to the U.S. at least once a year, but Dubai World had affected my schedule. I had told Sultan this would happen, not realizing that I had just given them one more reason to hold onto my passport. Anyway, I sorted it out and enjoyed three weeks of freedom in the U.S., and I finally put my interrogation recording on a transcript.

Then I returned to Dubai to start packing up my house and preparing for the moving and shipping. My U.S. friends asked me why I didn't just stay in the U.S. after all these problems. It was because my family was still in Dubai. I didn't want to stay in the U.S. to save my own hide and leave my wife and children stranded alone with the wolves. I was afraid they would take my wife's passport and put her in jail, just to get to me.

Sultan probably heard from the police at the airport that I left the country and returned. I knew too well that Emiratis never forget, and never forgive, so I was expecting more troubles.

On February 27, I received a call from a police officer saying he wanted to question me about a complaint, and he wanted to see me right away—that evening. I didn't know what the complaint was, but I was fairly sure that if it got ugly, I would be spending some time in jail. It was the weekend, and anyone brought in on a weekend typically had to wait until a weekday to get any resolution. I told the officer I could not come right away because I needed a translator and an attorney to represent me. He said it was not necessary because at this point there were no charges filed against me. In Dubai, a defendant is entitled to an attorney only after the police have completed their investigation. The result of this archaic law is that police can question accused people for days, weeks, or months without benefit of legal counsel and keep them in arbitrary detention, incommunicado, indefinitely.

He didn't like my response at all and pressed me to come right away, but I politely refused. I asked him what it was all about, and he explained the complaint was from Exomos and it was about money. Here I was again. Right after I returned, Sultan filed another complaint against me with the police.

Only Sultan himself could have ordered the complaint and kept the auditors after me. Eight months earlier, his director Abdul Qader swore to me during our last meeting at the Emirates Tower a complaint would not be filed against me because they had not found any evidence of fraud. I maintained my innocence and thought they finally admitted to themselves I had not taken any money. He assured me if they decided to take any action against me in the future they would come directly to me and discuss it.

That, of course, was a lie. Nobody told me anything in person. They just went behind my back to the police and filed a fraudulent complaint. But this was not the first time I said to myself never to trust the words of backbiting Emiratis. They will lie to your face and stab you in the back the minute you turn around.

Of course, the filed complaint had not named the accuser. *The mudslinger* opted to remain conveniently anonymous. Whatever happened to someone receiving a constitutional right to openly confront one's disputer? Trust me—it wouldn't happen in this part of the world.

For me, telling the police officer I needed a lawyer was more a delay tactic than anything else.

Investigations are not about the truth. They are a tactic used to force you to confess and send the case to court. These confessions were always signed under duress either because the police have your passport and use their power to withhold it as a bargaining chip or they threaten you with prison.

The police deliberately mislead the accused into believing it would be better to confess guilt, regardless of whether it was true or not, and receive a light sentence that could be later pardoned by His Highness the Prince of Dubai. If you were to fight an accusation you would inevitably be convicted and receive a harsh sentence with no possibility of getting out. This type of exploitation brainwashed innocents into pleading guilty to crimes they didn't commit or signing false testimonies against somebody else. The promise of early release was an evil trick; it is true that a convict could be pardoned, but only after half of the prison term had been served. However, it does not erase the fine or the debt. So, the pardoned convict will remain in prison until he pays his dues at the pro rata-of $30 per day.

Now I knew how the system worked. I knew this was a witch-hunt and I was the target. I knew I could get out if I confessed to what they wanted. But I would have to give them everything I had—property, cars and money. I learned of so many people who got caught in this system who eventually extricated themselves, but in the process lost everything they had earned and worked for. They were scarred for life. They were also forced to sign confessions and or confidentiality agreements for early release that kept them from telling anyone about the terrible things that happened to them.

I was not yet in a place where I had to confess to something I didn't do. I would get out of this mess, but I knew it would not be without a fight.

There was no point trying to convince them I hadn't done anything wrong. My tactic was to play the clock. This time I would not walk into the police station alone and unprepared. I knew their games. They wouldn't arrest me at my house if I didn't show up for a questioning at the station. It takes time before the information gets there. If they want to arrest you, they don't call you and ask you to report at the police station. Instead of looking for you, they put you in the system and wait until you fall into their claws. So, I told the officer I would come in ten days.

Ten days later, my translator, my attorney, and I went to the Jebel Ali station to answer their questions—the same police station where they had interrogated me for eight hours for my bullets and guns.

Before the interrogation even started I was in hot water because the police officer in charge expressed serious agitation about having my translator or my lawyer present in the room. He said I was not entitled to legal representation. The fact that my translator was a woman didn't help either. She was certified by the court, so she was qualified to be there, but these cops didn't like to deal with women who had authority, credentials and a higher intellect then the idiots at the station. My lawyer and I insisted that both my lawyer and my interpreter be allowed to be present, and after one full hour of bargaining, these officers finally backed-off. Thanks to having these professionals on my side, the questioning was very different than the first time around. It was short and without the threats of torture and abuse.

Again, they were not charging me with anything specific—yet. They were simply telling me that if I didn't confess to the statement the auditors had prepared, I would be charged with the crime of mishandling government money. I didn't know such a crime existed. I denied these allegations and insisted that I already told the truth and had nothing to confess. The money I received from the company was my hard-earned salary, and the only money that was spent was approved by Sultan Bin Sulayem. I explained again about the coercion and threats from Abdul Qader, but all my denials and claims of innocence fell on deaf ears. The officer requested my passport as a condition of me being able to leave the station to return home to my family. He explained that if I didn't turn over my passport, they would put me in jail pending the investigation, after which they would decide whether to report the case to the public prosecution and the court or not. I knew under these circumstances they would keep me in prison indefinitely, so I surrendered my passport again.

I protested, but the officer justified it as a mere guarantee I would not flee the country and that I would show up for court appearances. Of course, that is the ploy; a travel ban alert in the immigration computers is enough to stop anyone at the airport and/or border. The real reason to strip you of your passport is to reduce you to a non-functioning human being in their society, leaving you with no alternative but to sign your life away.

It was a sick game and a widespread conspiracy that exists from the top to the bottom of Dubai government. Someone puts in a complaint to the police. The police start an investigation. The accused is either arrested or has his passport confiscated. In the meantime, he loses his identity, his job, his freedom, his money—he fades into nothing. Even if you hand over all our worldly possessions to your accuser in exchange for your freedom, you are labeled 'tainted goods' and banned from ever coming back. To add insult to injury, your signature is a must on a fixed agreement, promising your silence before you are deported.

At this point I saw myself cornered and without an honest solution. I was trapped, held in Dubai, my savings depleting, and all my plans for moving back to the U.S. delayed indefinitely. This was the goal of Dubai World. Sultan Bin Sulayem would play with me until I gave up everything I had worked hard for.

This strengthened my resolve to defend myself against this mafia state—to protect my family and what little money I had left. I was not about to pay anything or sign any confession, but I wasn't going to tell them that. I would play this thing as if I were a peasant in the medieval ages. I would act like a beaten dog, weakened from their attacks. I would play their game and tell them I needed time to get the money together. There was no point bargaining for my passport. I made the decision to escape the country without it.

I had never done that before. Not even in the service, when I secretly entered and exited countries. Sure, I used fake identities, but I always had a passport. Travelling without one would be an obstacle. But I was prepared to take all the necessary steps to go around it. I had to start the process right away, lay the groundwork and use the knowledge I gained during my secret agent career to accomplish this unexpected mission.

Emiratis prey on weaknesses. The more you show you are dependent on something, the more they are going to use it against you. I remembered Jim telling me at the beginning of my relationship with Sultan, that Sultan had asked him what my weaknesses were or if I had a dark side. At the time, I thought Sultan was being diligent in his hiring practices. Now I knew he was trying to find things he could use against me later. He didn't find anything, but I learned a lot about what Emiratis' weaknesses were and how to exploit those to my advantage.

Chapter 6

The Plan

Houdini was known worldwide for his legendary escapes. The secret to his trick he called misdirection. Well, I would show them one thing while I would be busy doing something else. The mind will believe anything it sees and hears.

My next step was to do what was called an exfiltration, in military terms (as opposed to infiltration)—or, in laymen's terms, an escape. I would put on my spy suit again and act, pretend, hide, trick, and run.

From the perspective of a secret agent, it is an operation to sneak out of a country without being detected—either through border controls with a fake passport or without going through immigration controls at all. From the perspective of the police, it is an escape and the suspect is a fugitive, illegally fleeing the country. Either way, it meant I would break Emirati laws.

What follows are techniques I used to avoid being caught and to escape. Although they may look illegal, doing them didn't make me a criminal. There cannot be a crime when you do something to defend yourself against crooked government officials, against people who condone torture and threaten to use it against you, against those who blackmail and force confessions, against Government employees who fabricate evidence, and against a corrupt system completely lacking in justice and unconcerned with basic human rights.

It is even written in the UAE law. *Article sixty-four of the Federal Penal Code stipulates that a suspect who is coerced or provoked, physically or emotionally, to commit an offence should not be held liable.*

As I felt I had no legal way to defend myself against these Government Company officials, corrupt lawyers, judges, and police officers, I was forced into taking illegal action to get out of that place.

I gave no legitimacy to the Emirati system of justice. I had zero consideration for Emiratis and their laws in the face of what I learned about them—they lie, they break their word, they are dishonest, they condone torture, and they violate human rights.

An exfiltration is no improvisation. You cannot just go and jump the border. It requires time and a lot of preparation. I needed to get the prosecutor and the auditors off my back for at least two months so I could work on my escape. The only way was to go to Abdul Qader's lair and offer what he wanted.

My plan was to act and show myself as a defeated cur, accepting to pay what they wanted and just asking for time to realize the money. I would use their weaknesses—their greed, their pride and their arrogance against them in such a way that they would not be able to anticipate my moves and would be lackadaisical in watching me.

Emiratis may not be as smart as your average Westerner, but they had the money to hire smart expatriates to hunt me down. My goal was to make them feel so confident they would not need to seek help from those who might have been more difficult for me to fool.

I called Abdul Qader direct. He didn't pick up the phone so I left a message. He called me back right away—which was unusual for him, but not really surprising given the circumstances. Although he had a very high opinion of himself and generally liked to keep people waiting on him, his greed motivated him to respond quickly. We set up a meeting to go over the payment for the return of my passport.

I went to the meeting with my attorney and it was awful. These government employees acted like Mobsters. I had six auditors sitting in front of me, hammering away at me with insults and accusations, one after the other. It was worse than my police interrogations. They used coerced testimony from former employees against me and fake financial statements to justify their demand for repayment of expenditures. These poor employees had been put in the same situation as I had been—with threats, lies, and blackmail forced upon them. I was being blamed for all the money that had been wasted due to Sultan bin Sulayem's poor decisions. The facts were distorted to such a degree they no longer sounded even realistic.

Abdul Qader was no longer asking for $1,500,000. Now, magically, the sum had gone up to $3,000,000. They said if I agreed to pay cash now, I could pay them off for *only* $800,000—but if I fought it, they would bring me to court and claim the full $3,000,000. So, for the bargain price of $800,000, they would stop the police complaint and I could have my passport back to leave the country as their good friend.

The threat was real. You have to understand that in such situation if you don't pay, you are sent to prison and you remain incarcerated until the alleged debt is paid off with no recourse and no help whatsoever. So I lied. I told him I was ready to pay. I tried to negotiate it down further, only pretending to add credibility to my promise. As Abdul Qader had frequently lied to me before, I felt absolutely no remorse about lying to him.

There can be no oath when you give a promise to a liar. An agreement or a confession cannot be valid when under threat, coercion, or blackmail. They were going to learn a valuable lesson from me—as they had sown, so would they reap.

In an incredulous voice, I asked them if they wanted me to just write a check there—sitting with them at the table my tone conveying that this was impossible. Before I could say anything else, they told me they knew I had just sold my home and that I had the money. They also said if I didn't have the whole amount, I could ask friends for personal loans.

It confirmed they were after my earned personal money. The purchase and the sale of my house was a legitimate, personal real-estate deal. I bought the house on my own and it had nothing to do with the company. They had no evidence of me taking any money from the company, so it was my personal assets that bought the house.

I protested, insisting that in a Democracy, only a court order could require me to pay corporate debts with my personal funds and only if fraud was proven. I knew the word Democracy and its concepts did not count for anything with these men. They even said it didn't mean anything to them. They laughed at me and mocked my naiveté. They even added that they could send me to prison for just saying the word.

Their careless disregard for the greatest governing premise in our world angered me and further strengthened my resolve.

I acted as though I was defeated. I said I needed time to gather all the money together and they *graciously* gave me two months to pay. Bingo. I had just bought the exact amount of time I needed to prepare my escape, and it was they who came up with this number, not me. So far so good, I got what I wanted out of them.

My lawyer made it perfectly clear through the whole ordeal that he was on the auditors' side, working with them to get me to pay. After the meeting, he had the audacity to tell me I was lucky to get such a good deal—that they could have asked me to pay $5,000,000 and sent me to prison. He emphasized the quicker I paid the money the better it would be for everybody. How could I trust a guy who was so willing to roll over on my case—so willing to give me up to these auditors for the money he would earn brokering a deal? I felt no loyalty to someone like this. I knew if the money wasn't easy for him, he'd drop me like a hot potato. I couldn't trust him any more than I could trust Sultan.

I noticed during the meeting how close my lawyer was to the auditors. They were all Emiratis of course, all on the same side of the gate. I decided my best strategy would be to avoid the auditors from this day on and use my lawyer to talk to them. This was the best way I could see to keep their animosity at bay and keep them from knowing too much about what I was doing. I had been fighting with them for a year now, and I felt my lawyer was in a better position to appear credible to them than I was.

I would play French pool *Billard à 3 Bandes* or *Three Banks*. It is a pool table game with only three balls—two whites and one red—with one of the white balls carrying a black dot to differentiate it from the other. The players must play in three banks which means that they have to strike the banks at least three times when they hit the two other balls. It's very difficult and requires a high level of skill in anticipation and calculation. It is a French expression that does not translate into English very well—all it meant was that I would hit the lawyer with my bluffs, who in reaction would hit the auditors with my endorsed bluffs, who in turn would authenticate my bluffs to the prosecutor. I would make sure to always be three steps ahead of them. Sultan, at the end of the food chain, would swallow the whole soup.

Under this scheme, the prosecutor would never be able to predict my moves and would trust the information coming from the auditors, since they were the ones who initiated the whole mess. All I had to do for my part was to manipulate the lawyer for the next two months, and he would do the rest of the work for me. This plan was very much like the ones I had put together and operated while in the secret service many years before. It is a sophisticated game of manipulation and the Emiratis were no match for me.

After a full year of harassment, fear, lies, coercion, restraints on my freedom, illegal searches of my office, loss of income, loss of business opportunities, threats of torture, threats of imprisonment, loss of my eligibility for U.S. citizenship, loss of compensation for not showing up in U.S. courts in a separate case where I was a plaintiff, defamation of my character, insults, and last but not least, loss of family time and vacation—I decided that I would show Sultan my response to his sending this posse after me to do his dirty work. He overlooked my resume. He would read it again with pain this time.

I went home and told my wife that I had no choice but to go for an escape. She didn't seem surprised, but she was angry at the whole situation and the extremes we had to go through. She, too, was involved and would have to play a role. The plan was for her to leave Dubai with our young boys as soon as possible on a commercial flight. We would send our household goods and vehicles back to the U.S. Then I, alone, would make my way out of Dubai by clandestine means. It would be a multi-task type of operation—physical, technical, administrative, and financial. The risk factors had to be reduced to a minimum because my family was my first concern. I knew if I got caught it meant life in prison.

This was a very serious situation, and more than once I almost backed out and considered borrowing the money to pay the auditors. But I kept coming back to myself with two arguments against bowing to their demands. First, it was not just about money, but about my name. If I paid them, everybody would think I was guilty of something because nobody would ever believe I paid $800,000 just to get my passport back. Secondly, I could not reduce myself to pay for something I didn't owe. It went against my nature. And even if I could have paid them $800,000, they would have come after me with more demands later. I could see their thought process—if I could pay that why not three million? No matter which way I looked at it, I had no choice but to go ahead with the escape.

An escape requires good health, strong mental condition and excellent physical condition, in case there is a need for self-defense, to outrun a pursuit, or for emergency survival. After I returned from the meeting, I began to prepare myself physically. I started a program of running two miles every day and additional exercises to build my strength and endurance. I purchased a treadmill some months earlier and I used it in my home. I didn't want the Emiratis to see my routine change, so I didn't run outside. It was impossible to run outside more than five minutes anyway because of the heat.

I knew that down the line I would have to go into hiding so I decided to change my appearance—ten pounds less and a trimmed beard-mustache the same way Emiratis do. All together with a suntan and a pair of sunglasses nobody would recognize me.

After I sold my house I had some money to use for my escape plans and it wouldn't be cheap. I withdrew cash even filled out the slip at the bank with the notation *auditor pay off* just in case they went so far as to monitor my account.

I contacted Bernard, my friend who had shipped me my frogman gear, and asked him to come to Dubai to help me. Long ago, I had done him a favor and pulled him out of a messy situation, so it was time for him to return the favor. Even so, it went without saying that whenever I asked for help, my friends would give it, like I would help them if they needed it. We were members of a special kind of fraternity, bound by strong ties between fellow comrades. My plan was to start the evaluation and recon alone until I could send my family home. Then, I would go into hiding and he would join me in Dubai.

I knew he'd do anything to help me—but I didn't want to take advantage of our friendship and put him at risk for helping me. I found though, it was not difficult to motivate him. He heard about other similar situations of people getting forced to pay off some Emiratis, and he saw my escape as well-deserved revenge. I wanted to make sure that Bernard wasn't taking unnecessary risks. This was no movie of the week. It was the real deal, not just talk. You might hear a lot of people in a bar over peanuts and vodka puffing about how they would accomplish this feat, escaping from Dubai. They say they know someone who knows someone who could get them out—but they're full of it. Talking about it and doing it are two completely different animals.

Bernard had the capabilities to help me escape and he knew how to do things secretly. He had been an operative and we had worked together before. I knew from experience he had the skills and stamina to perform under pressure. Most importantly, he was a Dubai outsider. Most expatriates in Dubai are afraid to do anything that might give them even the slightest problem. They live with the constant fear of losing their jobs and getting deported. I knew I wouldn't get much help from them.

This operation was different from those I had done in the past. The context was completely changed from the one I had used before as a spy. When I was working undercover, it was like being a ghost— I didn't exist. Nobody knew me—I was invisible, almost insignificant. I always made sure nobody would be interested in me so no one would pay attention whether I was there or gone, nor would they know what I was doing. Here in Dubai, it was different. The enemy knew very well who I was, and my name and picture were in all the immigration computers and in the police system. I could turn into a ghost, but this time I would be a ghost with an $800,000 bounty on my head and plenty of bounty hunters out there looking for me, ready to collect their reward.

They didn't care that I had been a secret agent for years with espionage skills at my disposal, because they were too arrogant to believe it would make any difference. Ahmed Butti said once that without a gun in my hand I was not dangerous. I remember smiling to myself when he made that statement. If he only knew… But it was good. It would only help me escape that much easier with them having a false sense of security.

Emiratis are so confident in themselves they lose an important quality—the ability to anticipate or, even think for a moment that a situation may be something other than what it appears. They are so used to proudly receiving false honors and forced, disingenuous compliments they have handicapped themselves. They would never have imagined somebody like me could or would try to escape right out from under their noses. I would use this handicap to my advantage while always being vigilant to their possible awakening to the realities of what I was planning.

Besides Bernard, I needed help from a few other Cooperative Individuals, what we called CIs. I had only one CI who was aware of what I was doing and the extent of the help he was giving me, but all the others were involuntary or unconscious CIs, helping me without knowing the real reasons or sometimes without even knowing they were helping me at all. I told my CI's only what they needed to know to do the job. It was also a precaution. Under questioning, no one could reveal what he or she didn't know. For example, if I needed to ask a CI to rent a hotel room for me, I would tell him I had a girlfriend and I didn't want my wife to find out about it with the credit card receipt. I would not tell him I was hiding from the government. When I needed to be dropped off at a specific building, I would ask the CI driving me around to drop me off two blocks before the building and walk the rest of the way, so he would not know where I was really going.

One of these unconscious CI's was the person who provided me with the means to escape from Dubai—he even expedited the process for me. He was no ordinary man. I will laugh about it for the rest of my life—Sheikh Khaled, one of the brothers of the President of the UAE himself and friend of Sultan Bin Sulayem.

My lawyer was another CI. First we met in person, and then we agreed to have meetings on the phone because I didn't want him to notice my change of appearance. He would keep me updated about the auditors and the prosecutor and I told him how I was getting the money together to meet their demands. I never put anything in writing or signed anything—it was all just talking and acting. I kept him believing

I feared the auditors and that I was in agreement about paying them $800,000.

As the deadline grew near, the lawyer began preparing the final agreement for the auditors. They were pressing me for payment. I told my lawyer I would bring two checks to the final meeting—one for $300,000 and another for $500,000—as if the money for the auditors was coming out of two different accounts—all this to make it sound authentic. But the lawyer was desperate to get his hands on the money, so he asked me to send the checks early. He said he would keep the checks in his possession until our final meeting with the auditors.

I told him it was not really legal for me to write checks from accounts that didn't have sufficient funds and doing so could make my situation worse. I believe it was another of their traps. The truth was I didn't want to write and sign any checks because I never intended to pay them a penny, and I didn't want accusations of bad checks floating around out there after I was gone. I had enough trouble with them as it was without other accusations being aired.

The lawyer himself came up with a weird solution—he asked me to give him the check numbers instead. I could not believe they were being so naïve and desperate. What would the check numbers do for him? I went ahead and gave them two check numbers that I pulled out of my hat and which meant absolutely nothing. It seemed to satisfy him and assured the auditors as well.

The lawyer prepared the agreement with the check numbers only and told me I could continue on with my progress in securing the funds until our next meeting. I never saw that agreement.

On our next call he informed me of a change in the process. The meeting to finalize the deal would be with Sultan Bin Sulayem on the forty-seventh floor of his Emirates Towers office. I would hand the money over to him directly, sign the agreements and I would get my passport back from the prosecutor office. After avoiding me for almost a year, now he wanted to see me…because I would have the cash in hand? Well, he had a surprise coming. So I continued with my progress, but it wasn't securing funds I was working on—it was my preparation for escape.

The first thing I had to do was to secure my means of communication. The UAE have the best technology in the world for Internet, land line, and wireless phone services. The UAE government uses this technology extensively for censorship and monitoring phone conversations, emails, and Internet usage.

The police use these same channels for surveillance without warrants.

I know from experience that reading phone transcripts and spying via email intercepts, requires tremendous amounts of manpower to manage the high volume of data, text, messages, translations, and pictures. Finding one valuable piece of information in that mess can be like finding a needle in a haystack. The more advanced computer resources used for intercepts and analysis exist, but having the best technology in the world does not mean the capability to use it.

I doubted very much the police would have the intelligence and skill it would take to anticipate, intercept, interpret, and understand my activities through interceptions of communications in general. Rules, machines, and computers can never replace the human intellect. Although the UAE has the financial capability to acquire artificial intelligence technology, I didn't believe they had it or they would even be allowed to have it. I was also counting on them being too arrogant to consider an expatriate could outsmart a machine.

Even being pretty confident their intercept skills were not the best, I was not ready to take the risk of getting on the phone or Internet without precautions. In the UAE, getting a phone number or wireless service requires a passport. You can buy a mobile phone anywhere, but to activate it you need a SIM card and a passport to buy the SIM card. The SIM card is the small computer chip that you insert inside the mobile phone to activate the wireless service. Anytime somebody buys a SIM card in Dubai, it is directly linked to his name and passport and recorded in the police computer system. If the name is flagged, it becomes easy for the police to track and locate the person through his mobile phone and monitor the calls and phone conversations.

The phone conversations are not the only valuable information that could be intercepted. There are also the numbers that are dialed and call in. How many and for how long, and their location? The police can track who you know and who knows you, how often and for how long you talk to these people, and from where you call them or from where they call you. For the purpose of my escape I needed several untraceable SIM cards and mobile phones so the police could not track me or monitor my calls, and I would still use my known phone as bait, to make them believe I was where I said I was, and whom I was calling. I had plans not only to use my own phone, but also to use the phones of others to help me.

The Emiratis could have never suspected I could use mobile phones to track their whereabouts. For my plan to work best, I needed to know precisely when Sultan was out of Dubai. It was ironic that the one who had an interest in tracking my moves would not be able to, when in return I would be able to track him. The key to getting this information lay in the fact I knew he was traveling most of the time with Jim. I could not track Sultan's phone, but I was able to use the information from Sultan's entourage to track his travels.

This was one of the basics in intelligence work. If you can't directly reach the objective or target, you enlarge the circle around him to find a weakness—and boy, did I find a good one! When I discovered that Jim and my former employee, Amin, were lovers—the day I stumbled upon their 'pink room' in my factory, I made an important discovery. I was not able to track Jim's phone at all. But I did manage to get access to Amin's mobile phone account via the Internet. Amin had been my employee at Exomos, and, because he was in a managerial position, the company paid his phone bills. This gave me access to his mobile account and he never knew it. When I fired him he asked me if he could keep his mobile number, and I said yes—not realizing how convenient this could turn out for me in the future. If he had bought a new phone and new number, I would have lost this access.

Every time Sultan traveled out of the country, whether by yacht or by private jet, Jim was with him. He was Sultan's errand boy, and the guy who handled what Sultan called his *special projects*. Sometimes Sultan traveled twenty days a month outside the country. He always maintained secrecy about his trips; very few knew where he was traveling. Now, whenever I needed to know where Sultan was, I only had to access Amin's phone records. I found a way to hack in and check his records live. All I had to do was look for Jim's calls—and it wasn't hard because Jim and Amin called each other about eight times a day, every single day. I love my wife but I don't call her eight times a day. These calls weren't even work related since they no longer worked together. I wondered how Jim was hiding this obvious personal relationship from Sultan, who I knew would disapprove.

Amin's phone records showed the location of Jim's calls via the roaming system, therefore I knew where Sultan was every day, whether he was in China, Tanzania, Colombia, or Coronado California in his vacation house. All the efforts of this supposed sophisticated businessman to keep his travels secret were destroyed by a thoughtless member of his entourage, who needed to talk to his secret boyfriend.

I also could track Sultan's private jets and flight plans by its tail numbers, A6-DPW and A6-NKL but it was not as good as my Jim link, because I didn't know which plane he was flying and other people could be very well be traveling in his planes.

I looked over personal ads in shopping centers in the Filipino cluster—tiny pieces of paper pined on a board of items for sale with a phone number to contact. I found many phones for sale by people cashing in on their phones before returning to their country. I bought a few used prepaid phones with their SIM cards. Nobody would ever check or care about a Filipino housemaid's mobile phone. I put some cash into buying units, so there wouldn't be any traceable bills. At this point I had secured untraceable phones or black phones. Even though my calls on these phones would be completely anonymous, I still had to take precautions when I used them. I made sure that if I was going to talk on the phone about anything related to my escape, it would be with someone who was also on a black phone. I gave a black phone to my friends, CI and Bernard. I didn't have to tell them to only use them for my clandestine communications. Outside my covert calls I never used my black phone to call my friends or people I knew, because I didn't want to link the black number to anyone I knew or leave a trail of my calls if they were monitored.

All of the planning and preparation for my escape took discipline. I had to pick only friends who already had the restraint and control needed for the operation. It couldn't be taught in two months. I couldn't take the risk of trusting someone who would ruin everything by using the black phone to call a girlfriend and blow my cover indirectly. I have seen it, it happens.

Even on an untraceable phone I had to be cautious. There are certain words in the police computer surveillance systems that are flagged and are known as keywords. Your phone individually may not be monitored, but these keywords are, and they can be intercepted in the flow of thousands other conversations and red flag a phone. Words such as, nuclear, bomb, terrorist, drug, or escape could raise a red flag and uncover the caller indirectly.

Deception was always part of my strategy. If I needed to talk about a boat with my friends, I would call it a house. I always renamed things to confuse the issues I was discussing in the event anyone was listening in. When I arranged a meeting for an undercover action, surveillance, or with a source, it would always mean six hours later than the scheduled time. If there was a trap to be set, no one would be caught.

Because I wanted to check emails and use the Internet to access websites, check phones records, track Sultan, and access certain police files, I needed to secure my online access entirely. I had to ensure the Emiratis could not track my log on communications, identify the data I was downloading, or see what sites I was visiting. The last thing I wanted was to have the police monitoring my screen and know everything live that I was looking up on the Internet. Especially I didn't want to have concerns if I viewed a map of a specific location for an escape route, that somebody would be there watching and waiting to catch me jumping the fence.

Using Etisalat, the UAE proxy, was not an option—I had to bypass Etisalat and use another proxy outside the country for my Internet research. I set up a VPN or a Virtual Private Network with an Internet provider in the U.S. on my laptop. A VPN works like a tunnel through the local Internet provider (IP). In Dubai it uses the Etisalat infrastructure while maintaining privacy through security procedures and tunneling protocols such as the Layer Two Tunneling Protocol (L2TP).

It was totally anonymous and not even illegal to have my data encrypted and travel to and from my Internet connection without Etisalat being able to decrypt the data. The VPN also concealed my real IP address and replaced it with another.

Once my VPN was set up I could type a website address into my search box and it would be encrypted. It would then go through Etisalat without being detected. The final server in the U.S. I accessed through Etisalat would decrypt the data and connect me to the websites I wanted to log on to. Anything that got sent back to me would be encrypted and then decrypted once it reached my computer. The only thing Etisalat could know is that I was connecting to a server via VPN. They could not see what was going through and of course, they couldn't block what they couldn't see.

Not only could I access any website I wanted with total privacy, even the ones that were blocked in the UAE, but the police could not see what sites I was on or track my log on activity. Using my VPN, I was able to access websites for the Dubai Police, Customs, and other government entities for crucial and useful information which I needed to plan my escape.

For many other reasons, anyone living in Dubai should consider using a VPN if they are concerned about censorship and government intrusion into their private life. I should have done it long before my problems started.

I discovered too late that all the emails I was sending from my local private email account to myself at my Yahoo email address didn't go through, or, if they did, all of the attachments were gone. I was aware that my company email account could be legitimately monitored by Dubai World IT, but I did not know the auditors, through the government ISP had put a block in the system on my known private Yahoo email address to prevent me from sending copies of my files, work emails and any evidences of their wrongdoing, to myself outside the country. As a result I lost a lot of files, and had to use a few tricks of my own to be able to save some files and emails, and it's lucky I did it because they are now proof to support my accounts. It shows how the government of Dubai interacts between its agencies and companies to make sure people have no rights or the liberty to secure private communications. It is a common procedure done in Dubai when key employees are about to be terminated. If I had used a VPN from the beginning, they would never have been able to block me from sending emails to my Yahoo address.

To prepare my escape I needed to reproduce all sorts of documents, make fake passes, identification cards, licenses, and various permits—so I designed and built a portable document creation laboratory—which, thanks to modern technology, fit into a small suitcase. It included a portable laser printer, my laptop, stationery, a laminating machine, tools, chemicals and my digital camera with a stand to take pictures of documents. Twenty years ago a laboratory to do all these things required three large suitcases.

The digital camera allowed me to take pictures of everything, even something showing on the screen of a computer that I couldn't print or download because of website content protection. For instance when I accessed the Dubai police system, it would not let me print the pages, so I took a picture of it. With the latest technology and today's graphics software, like Photoshop, it was actually not very difficult to make fake documents—and it was considerably quicker and easier than it was twenty years ago. I remembered when I used to make fake documents, manually with classic photography and photo development in a bathroom; it would take me three days. With my small mobile laboratory, it took me two hours to make a fake access pass for Port Rashid. But don't get me wrong here—easier did not mean I could get sloppy with my work. The making of a fake document requires a lot of artistic skill and precision. It must be as close as possible to the real document so you don't get nervous and start sweating from fear when you face the security guards.

Two important factors are in play when you use a fake pass to enter a secure area—one is against you, and the other helps you. A security guard checks IDs all day long—that is essentially all he does. He checks hundreds of IDs, all authentic and all looking the same—

some new, some worn out. Without knowing it, the guard develops a sixth sense that allows him to spot a fake right away. It's like that Sesame Street game my children used to watch on television—which one of these IDs is not like the other? Which one of these IDs doesn't belong? This explains how he gets suspicious when something is not right with an ID—something that nobody else would even notice. Because of this phenomenon, it is important to make sure that nothing is missing, out of place, or done in haste, during the making of a fake document.

What is in your favor when you face a guard is that if he has been there a long while, he is likely to be lazy and bored by the nature of his work. So when the fake document is convincing enough, he does not bother to go to the second level of scrutiny and look for details like holographic imprints. There is an interesting paradox here—as the technology gets more advanced, it should make it more difficult to prevent forgeries. But that can only be true if you eliminate the human factor, because humans do not change—they are still lazy and naïve, impatient and pressured. The guards cannot closely scrutinize every ID or they will have people lining up outside the door and protesting because of the wait. Even when security does decide to begin a program of heightened awareness and oversight, it does not last long. The guards soon get bored because nothing happens to make their extra efforts worthwhile. The same authentic IDs come in day after day, week after week, so why bother?

Back in the day, when I was undercover, my team and I used all sorts of tricks to get weapons and electronic surveillance equipment across borders. One time I had to smuggle a silencer and a gun, driving across a border for a job on the other side. To accomplish this, I disassembled all the parts and mixed them up in a tool box and, throughout two different cars, I concealed the unmistakable shape of the frame of the gun into a toy gun, but there was no trigger or moving parts to indicate it was a real gun. It looked like a toy in its box. Then I chewed on fresh garlic just before I was entering the control area. It made me relax just to think about how the guard would be repulsed at my weapons-grade bad breath. Besides, I looked decent, dressed in a suit, and was clean-shaven—so the only thing that guard wanted to do was get far away from me as soon as possible.

To make sure the guard would let the good-looking guy with bad breath go; I put some bait right behind me to eliminate the chances of any remaining overzealous inquiries being directed towards me. The bait was one of my teammates—a guy with a face you wouldn't want to see in a dark alley, and a bad looking car with boxes on the roof. He made sure to act nervous on purpose to catch the guard's attention and make him suspicious. Of course my teammate didn't have anything illegal on him—he was squeaky clean underneath that scary face. Racial profiling helped when you knew how to use it to your advantage. Guards were not trained for these tactics. They were puppets in front of trained operatives.

In Dubai, I didn't try the bad breath trick because there are already so many people going around with such a stench that my bad breath would have seemed normal. The racial profiling bait trick would not be necessary either, with so many people from so many different countries there was no need to put bait behind me—it was already there.

The special tactic I used in Dubai I hadn't used in other places before was made possible by the pride and arrogance of Emiratis. They gave me the perfect cover to use with fake documents. When I acted like one of the VVIPs, with a pass attached to my *khandoura* and a smug face, the peasant security guards didn't even dare look closer at my tag. Society programs these foreign workers who are hired to be security guards to act subservient to these pompous fools—the Emirati pride had created a security risk for all of the UAE. Security guards were just like everybody else in Dubai. They were imported workers who didn't care about what or who they are guarding. They feared their employers, but that fear did not equal respect. I made a dozen IDs and VVIP passes that looked genuine at first glance. They allowed me access to buildings and other restricted access properties disguised as an Emirati.

With my communication covered, my IDs handy, and disguises on hand, I was now ready to investigate ways to get out of this place.

The UAE is located in the Persian Gulf surrounded by neighboring Arab countries that I had to consider unfriendly. Looking at the map, I saw I was trapped not just inside a small country but inside an 800-mile radius around the UAE. Surrounding me was Saudi Arabia, Iraq, Qatar, Bahrain, Iran, Pakistan, Kuwait, Oman and Yemen. There was nothing appealing or friendly about these countries if you were wanted in any one of them—they are all ruled by theocratic governments at war, or on the verge of hostilities, and often hosts to terrorists or religious extremists.

I had three avenues by which to escape the country—by air, land, or sea. Based on my professional experience, I already had a basic idea of how to get out of the country—but my experience was twenty years old—a bit rusty. I wanted to study all available options to make sure I was making the best decision. The biggest difference from what I faced twenty years ago when I was an operative was that, this time, instead of crossing just one border with one set of variables, I had to cross three borders in one—an electronic border (by far the most difficult to evade), an ethnic or politic border consisting of a belt of hostile countries, and a physical border consisting of fences, mountains, deserts, or oceans.

Of all the options available to me, the safest one was an escape route over a distance of a minimum of 800 miles. It was not the shortest route, but it was the only one to avoid the sphere of influence of the UAE and other Muslim countries. I had to evaluate all the ways I could travel these 800 miles, analyze them, and eliminate one after the other to keep the one that would work.

The only possible way to leave the country by air would have been on a commercial flight, which meant going through the airport and immigration control. Taking off from unregistered airfields in the UAE with a small airplane, a helicopter, a balloon, or any other flying machine would not get me very far and would not be realistic. I believed air traffic control and air defense in the UAE were not as tight as one would think, so it was more an issue of the flight range than how to get airborne that concerned me. I heard stories of people going in and out of the UAE in private planes undetected, but they did that staying within the Gulf countries. Who knows what or who they were carrying and under whose orders? I couldn't use those rumors to guide me into a sense of security for that would surely be a very risky avenue of escape.

Obviously, traveling on a commercial flight requires an authentic passport. Fake passports don't work in the UAE even if they look perfect, because they cannot pass through the electronic controls. The computer records entry and exit of everyone coming into and out of Dubai plus passenger manifests—if there are no records in the system the passport is easily tagged as a fake even if it is authentic. Many people in cocktail conversations in Dubai mention that consulates can help their citizens get a new passport with a new name to get out, but that does not work either. If there is no record of entry into the UAE for a given name, the police see it when the person shows the passport to exit the country and will hold this person indefinitely until they have an explanation. I have seen people miss their planes for simple wear and tear on their genuine passports. There is no way a ghost passport would make the grade. It would be a passport to prison.

A new passport under my name would not have worked either because my name was on the travel ban list at the airport, so I did not even bother to apply for a new passport at the French Consulate.

The only way I could get through border control at the airport would be if I were to borrow the passport of someone traveling to Dubai—a friend, a tourist or a business traveler—and change my facial appearance to look like the picture. It would not work to tamper with the picture on someone else's passport. This type of fraud is detectable due to the latest technologies and holograms imprinted within.

The 'borrowed passport' is a technique I used while I was in the service. It actually works quite well. It requires a little bit of preparation, using makeup artistry and subtle manipulation of the hair and other features, but I have done it successfully. The traveler who gave up or lost his passport could always later claim that it was stolen. In the UAE, that person would probably be trapped in Dubai for at least a couple of months when the police discovered somebody else traveled out of the country using his name and passport. I didn't have a friend whose passport I would want to borrow, since I knew how much trouble he would be facing once I was gone. And, I could not see myself banking on the uncertainty of hunting in hotel lobbies, searching for look-alike candidates whose passports I would liberate from their possession. I wouldn't want to put someone I liked in that position and it wouldn't be fair to do it to a hapless stranger, either. I didn't feel right about putting someone else in the situation I was working so hard to escape. I decided it was best I put the air option aside and look at my other options.

Leaving the UAE by land would inevitably take me to a neighboring and unfriendly country. From there I would have to continue by land or air, only to find myself in the same situation I already realized wasn't going to work. Controls at the border checkpoints between countries were the same as those at the airport, although somewhat more laid back. It was fairly typical for border officers to rely solely on their computer systems to make decisions about travelers. They took no initiative to address issues. Even when there is an obvious mistake by immigration, they will keep the traveler stuck there at the border for hours until the central immigration office resolves the problem.

I learned this firsthand when I was held once going to Oman with my children, before the auditors had the police take my passport away for the second time. We were preparing to return to the U.S. My children's visas were going to expire soon, so to renew them for another sixty days, I had to leave the country with them and come back the next day. When we reached the UAE border station, my children's visas were not in the database—as if they had never entered the country. The border officials decided that since my children had never officially come in, there was no way for them to let my children out. It was an obvious mistake by the immigration office, but it didn't matter to them. We were held at the border for four hours, and they had no compassion for my two young boys suffering in the heat. Finally, some government employee in the central immigration office sent a waiver to the border patrol office that gave us clearance to go through for our exit.

This unfortunate event almost ruined my weekend, but it was very informative. I watched for those four hours, all the things going on around me and how the guards worked. Besides the bureaucracy and red tape, there was no control at the gates—they didn't inspect cars, they didn't visually check the identity of veiled women, and they didn't search luggage. I could tell they were lazy. I guessed they only checked cars and luggage when they got a tip that something or someone would be smuggled into or out of the country.

Going through a border station to exit the country hidden inside a vehicle was a possibility, although it carried some risk. Or a man disguised as a woman could easily exit the border station with a female Arab passport. 200 yards after the exit gate you have to pass the same immigration controls at the entry gate of the neighboring country border station. I would have to get through an exit from the UAE, an entry into another Gulf Country, and then another exit from that country. It was too many passes with too much risk.

Between the two border stations laterally there are fences or mountains. Fences are pretty much all around the country—they are high and in very good condition. They must have cost a fortune to build. It could be passively monitored by local citizens eager to make some extra money reporting anything unusual they see to the police. Where there is no fence, it is a maze of mountains and boulders. Trekking through those mountains in the heat would require serious training and at least one donkey to carry drinking water and food. People there say the fences are to keep the camels off the roads and to keep cattle from going south. I am sure some of that is true, especially when you consider the Emiratis place more value on their camels than they do human foreigners. They would be sadder to learn of one of their camels being hit by a car than one of the south Asian workers being killed by one. But on the other hand, there is really no need for fences because the livestock have nowhere to go. They live in a vast desert, dependent on humans to survive, so they don't stray too far from their shelter, water, and food. The fences came with the expatriates—to keep the expatriates from escaping, not the camels or the cattle.

To leave Dubai by land without having to deal with border officials, a person really needs to go deep into the desert areas to be sure no one would be watching. I spent hours exploring all the UAE borders on Google Earth. This is a fantastic tool. There is not ten meters of the UAE borders I didn't inspect looking for weaknesses. Google Earth shows all the details of the borders, the fences, the barracks, the parking lots, the deserts, the roads, and the police stations. It shows the terrain and how some border stations like Hatta or Kalba at the border with Oman, can be bypassed with a four-by-four vehicle on a 1,000 yard detour. I noticed another passage in Dibba, close to the Musandam peninsula, on the northeastern side of the UAE.

Every time I logged onto Google I used my Internet bypass software, my VPN, to avoid being tracked or monitored by Etisalat.

Later I drove around with all the information I had gathered in hand. With maps and the Google Earth pictures I downloaded, I drove to various sites to rehearse jumping the fences several times and crossed the borders in different areas. I entered in Oman and Saudi Arabia without being detected and practiced going around border stations. I drove all around the country to check escape routes. They would have been really nice rides with the spectacular scenery and landscapes that were there—unfortunately, I was not in a proper frame of mind to appreciate the beauty around me. I was going through a detached, professional process to design a plan of escape. I was too busy working to enjoy driving off-road.

During these recons, I took the precaution to leave my mobile phone in Dubai as bait. If it was monitored it would appear locked in on a phone tower in Dubai, and not roaming around the borders in the desert revealing my intentions.

After my various tests, I realized the problem was not exiting the UAE itself or entering another GCC country. The problem was more about the whole region in general. Yes, I could jump the fence or fool the border police, but once I surmounted one barrier, there would be another one waiting for me. All GCC countries are connected to the same police system and they share the same database. So if you are wanted in one of them, your name is in all of them. I might have been able to apply for a new passport at a French consulate in Oman or Qatar, but if I went to the airport to take an international flight, I would be checked in the computer the same way as I would be in the UAE and from the same database. They would block me and send me right back to the country from which I had escaped, this time in police custody. Not only that, but with no records of entry in the computer, I would be stopped by the Qatari airport police and extradited back to Dubai under UAE police escort. They keep their borders open to the neighboring police who can pick up people caught this way.

Even if you are not on the travel ban list, you are still on the database. I managed to verify this through a friend, a fellow resident in Dubai. He traveled to Qatar once and when he was questioned by the Qatari officer for some glitch in the system, he discovered his personal address was in the Qatari police database. The only way it could have gotten there was because it was a shared database.

This system of shared databases is similar to the one in place in Europe, where all country members share a common database under the Schengen Treaty. If someone is wanted in France, he can be stopped in Italy as he flies in from outside Europe because they all share the same information. The differences between the UAE system and the Schengen Treaty system are that in Europe, only people with an outstanding warrant are in the shared data base and the police don't cross each other's borders at will. They must abide by laws regarding extraditions and procedures to be followed. If you are arrested in one of the Gulf Countries on only suspicion from any of the others, you have no right to an attorney, nor do you have any type of extradition hearing before being shipped to the other country.

In Europe, people may cross the borders of the state members without being checked, which is definitely not the case in the GCC countries. The UAE has a border with Oman and Saudi Arabia. Qatar does not have a border with the UAE—you have to go through Saudi Arabia first to get to Qatar. The risk of going through Saudi Arabia without documentation is extremely dangerous. The same is true for Yemen. People, in these places they can just disappear or get shot by locals. It has happened before. I remembered the four French nationals who were killed in Saudi Arabia and the French who were killed in Yemen for no reason. I could not risk that kind of danger.

With today's technology, immigration and travel control through border checkpoints are absolute and effective nearly 100 percent of the time. This allows governments to set up networks, centralize the information coming from different sources and locations, and to document, monitor and verify the identities of travelers with iris scans and fingerprinting as they pass through. It is no longer just an entry and exit stamp in your passport. These newer technologies are almost impossible to deceive.

In Dubai, all the personal information you give to your employer or sponsor, can and will be leaked to the police to be used against you in case of conflict. Right after I recovered my passport in the gun case, I was held at the airport for six hours, missing my flight—all because they wanted to further validate my ability to travel. Before letting me go they asked me to confirm the names of my parents and their address. How did they know that in the first place? I had never disclosed that information to anyone but Dubai World. Sultan Bin Sulayem or his lieutenants must have disclosed personal information to the police to better control me.

The UAE is able to afford the best immigration control system in the world. All border control checkpoints are connected to police headquarters. No one could enter the country without a visa. But, most importantly, you cannot exit the country without permission either—there is a hidden exit visa.

Nationals of many countries must apply for a visa prior to leaving their home countries for the UAE. If a person has traveled to the UAE before, the police will check the person's records. If he is flagged 'not wanted' like a reporter or a writer who criticized Dubai before, his entry will be denied. But if the person has an outstanding police record or a debt, they will let him in, and arrest him at the gate.

As a person enters the UAE, his passport is stamped for entry with a date and a time limit for his stay. The police log this into their computer database: name, date, point of entry, the ID of the immigration officer and the reason for the trip to the UAE. The visa grants a certain number of days to stay in the UAE and indicates who the sponsor is.

In exiting the country, the police check the computer to see if there are any reports against the visitor, any unpaid balances for anything like fines or tickets, rental cars, unpaid hotel bills, claims made by people alleging monies owed to them, etc. If there are no records in the system, the person is allowed to exit the country without knowing his name has been checked in the database. If there are outstanding items showing, he may have to pay a fine or reimburse a debt or a bill before he can leave or be detained in case of a complaint. The system is extremely rigid—if there is the slightest difference or even a mistake, he is not allowed to leave the country under any circumstances. It's a good idea when leaving the UAE, for a person to have a chunk of cash on hand to buy his way out.

I have seen terrible things at the borders—women who could not exit the country with their children because the father of the children was not present, sick people who could not leave for medical treatment in their home country, arrests at the border for being behind on car payments, and arrests for mistaken identity. Believe me, it is harder to leave the UAE than to enter it. It's not an isolated incident to be delayed or detained at the border when trying to leave the country—it's a common practice.

A friend of mine who visited Dubai had a valid passport but it was old and the picture was coming loose. It wasn't a problem when he entered the UAE, even though it was loose then, but it caused a six hour delay and a missed flight when he tried to leave. The airport security police had a big issue with the loose picture and didn't want to let him go.

Although I knew how to make a fake passport and how to duplicate exit stamps, it would have been totally useless because there would be no electronic records to substantiate the validity of these documents.

I think it is possible to bribe certain border employees or officers who have access to the system—but it would have taken a long time, six months or so to make it foolproof—so I eliminated this option as well.

Because Dubai is surrounded by other GCC countries and they all shared border-crossing information, I decided it was too risky to jump the fence and escape from Dubai by land. I had to find another way. I needed to narrow down my options and go for the safest means of escape that could be achieved in no more than two months. The last option, by sea, was the one I most preferred anyway. I am a sailor and an accomplished seaman. There are no fences and no police stations on the water—no flight plans, no routes. I have come in and out countries before by the ocean, as a secret serviceman.

Due to the tensions brought on by war in the region (Iraq is not far), security checks and patrols in the Persian Gulf are common. The Strait of Hormuz, where half of the world's oil is transported, is one of the most patrolled areas in the world. I was used to this type of security level on the sea because I used to sail between Cyprus and Lebanon during the civil war. The level of risk I would undertake would vary, depending on the manner by which I would traverse the ocean.

I had three possible means by which to escape from Dubai by sea—boarding a commercial ship departing Dubai, boarding a cruise ship departing Dubai, or boarding a ship in international waters. Each had their own, individual pros and cons.

Before I left Exomos, I scanned my permanent port access pass and put the image on my computer so I was able to use this image to make a new passes with a different name. I was able to enter the two commercial ports of Dubai to test my possible escapes—the port of Jebel Ali, a commercial port only, and Port Rashid, a commercial port and a cruise ship terminal. I was very familiar with these ports because I worked in one and my line of work often necessitated that I be at the other.

Boarding a commercial ship meant traveling as a clandestine passenger, hidden somewhere inside the ship. At some point I would have to sneak off the ship to avoid immigration controls.

Despite the fact that there was a lot of information available on the Internet about commercial lines, ships, destinations, and schedules, it was a very uncertain scenario with lots of risks and little control. I would also need to find a way to survive while I was onboard or find a way to bring food and water with me, because I would not have access to these things as a stowaway. I had neither a plan nor the time to formulate one to bribe someone onboard to assist me with my escape. I heard rumors about commercial ship offering safe passages for $200,000, but it could have been traps set up by the police.

Boarding a cruise ship with a reservation seemed to be a more promising idea. On a cruise ship I could choose my destination, make a reservation, and leave in luxury. These cruise ships were headed to Egypt, India or farther East. I observed that it was easy to go onboard a cruise ship disguised as an Arab woman with a borrowed passport. There was no visual identification because of the heavily protective *abayah*, so I would only have to concern myself with passport controls. This scenario required the help of an Arab man who would accompany me as my chaperone and a passport borrowed from a Muslim woman.

I had made successful preliminary arrangements with a man from Oman who agreed to accompany and travel with me, so I would not have to talk. It was normal for a man in the UAE to do all the talking for his women. The women usually walk about six feet behind the man and wait quietly for him to handle everything. Going through the immigration controls accompanied by an Arab male to show a passport on my behalf would make it much easier, and it would actually work. I would have to pay my accomplice for his business of course, but it was affordable. I had a few Emiratis and Omanis contacts willing to help me for money. They themselves had been in trouble with the police before, and were therefore happy to help me trick the government as payback for their past misery. Making money doing it was just icing on the cake. I learned in doing my research this method of smuggling people in and out of the UAE from neighboring countries is quite common and very successful.

In the event it would not be possible to board the ship in disguise with a borrowed passport and the help of my Omani friend, I could plan for Bernard to be on the ship with a reservation, and I could then go through the water at night on the unexposed side of the ship with Bernard waiting for me with a rope ladder to help me get inside the boat. Bernard would need to have a reservation for a cabin for the trip, so I could travel with him under his cover and with his assistance. I felt that this method would also be pretty safe and reliable. I would need to avoid immigration or swim away from the ship on arrival because I would not have a passport and would not be on the passenger manifest either. Generally speaking, it wouldn't be difficult to sneak off a ship by water because cruise ships were not a primary target for the police— they are usually full of law-abiding tourists just there to have a good time. I had done this a couple of times to infiltrate islands in the Caribbean on cruise ships.

There was another cruise ship, a little bit farther down the pier, outside the cruise terminal premises and fences. She seemed much more accessible because she was outside the immigration perimeter controls and there were no security cameras or checkpoints. I investigated this cruise line's details further, including its routes and reservations, and I found out the ship had only one destination: Iraq. I decided it was definitely not a good idea to go into a war zone without a passport. It would be like leaving a prison for hell.

In all, getting on and off the ships would be straightforward, the security around the ships easy to bypass, and I had access to a borrowed passport and a local who was willing to help me. Unfortunately all the cruise ships were fully booked until December. There was no way I could wait that long to leave when I was in a country where life in hiding was costly, unfriendly, and too far away from my family. I reluctantly put aside these options, at least for the time being. My local friend who would be my date on the cruise ship would continue to help me with other things.

I explored other extraction options with other ships, like stowing away on Sultan's own boat. I also looked into cargo ships which were viable options but required months of preparation—months I didn't have.

In the northern Emirates and further north in Oman and the Musandam Peninsula, there were fleets of smuggling boats. They had fast boats going back and forth between Iran and Oman with loads of contraband, both human and otherwise. I could not see myself in a situation where I would be arriving in a country worse than the UAE without a passport. I remembered that two years prior, two French students on a sailboat drifted into Iranian waters due to a navigation error were arrested. They spent eighteen months in jail for nothing but a lapse in concentration. I needed to find a method of escape with less risk.

The last scenario I considered consisted of escaping the country on a dinghy—a very small craft, a mere beach toy that didn't need to meet registration or numbering requirements. In a dinghy, a person could cruise around without a permit or passport and without being questioned. If I could get far enough away from Dubai undetected, I could no longer be questioned anyway—once I reached the international waters. Technically speaking the jurisdiction of a country on the ocean stops at the limit of international waters twelve nautical miles off the coastline. Once in international waters in my dinghy, I could meet up with another and bigger boat, at a pre-planned rendezvous point to continue on a journey across the ocean.

In this type of scenario I would have full control. It required experience, navigational skills, seamanship, which I had—and a boat of course, which I didn't have. I didn't have any friends with a boat who could pick me up in high seas either, so I decided the best was to get my own boat in Dubai, ask Bernard to take it to the international waters and I would meet with him in high seas. It had to be a sailboat in the thirty-foot range—an ocean capable boat or what we call a passage maker. This moniker was a very apt description of what I needed. It would help that sailboats have a friendly non-threatening appearance like a tourist or recreational craft that no one would suspect would be used as an undercover escape vehicle.

A power boat the same size has a very limited range between refueling because of the gas consumption. These boats get about one mile per gallon of fuel and I was looking at a range of about 1,300 miles. A power boat would also get more attention—and I needed to stay under the radar, not screaming across it. I immediately looked for a sailboat for sale while I also decided what my destination should be.

My destination had to be outside the Muslim sphere. Not only the Gulf countries surrounding Dubai, but also Pakistan a little further away, because of the security problems and terrorist threats, I didn't think it was a good idea to show up there at all, let alone without a passport. This region was very unfriendly and risky nowadays. It used to be nice. I worked in Karachi in the 1980's and liked the place.

On the other side of the UAE, going South West towards Africa you have to sail off Yemen; but there we are no longer just talking about unfriendly waters, but total chaos, lawlessness and waters with sea pirates. There may be a procedure for boats in the region to pass through in convoys accompanied by armed navy ships—the skipper of the boat simply calls his embassy to check if there are any convoys to join. The problem with me doing that was I would find it very difficult to explain why I didn't have a passport. If I traveled outside of a convoy I would probably end up taken hostage or dead. I had to find another destination.

There was only one more direction open to me—east. The first friendly country where the view of a sailboat would not seem out of the ordinary was India. I had never been to India. There were many advantages in going to India. India and the UAE do not have a good relationship, partially because of the way the Emiratis treat workers from India.

India had refused to enter an extradition treaty with the UAE, thus their police did not share data. India was a very friendly country and the laws are not as restrictive as they are in the UAE. More good news was that the French Consulate in India had no relations with the UAE. As long as they didn't know about my problems in Dubai, they would not look in that direction when I showed up at their door, asking for a new passport. The downside was that administration is a nightmare of bureaucracy with lengthy and complicated procedures for whatever documents or authorizations you need. Without a passport and a visa for entry, it would be difficult.

The French consulate in Dubai could not help me leave the UAE. They knew me very well and I had a very good relationship with Robert the General Consul—but they also knew the Dubai police had confiscated my passport. I could not blame them. Giving me a new passport would have put the consulate in the middle of a diplomatic dispute—and, even with a new passport; I would not have been able to exit the country because of the travel ban that had been put on my name.

The French consulate in India was outside this sphere of influence and this jurisdiction, and would be free to give me a new passport. Because the French consulate was located in Bombay (now called

Mumbai), a large city on the Arabian Sea with a commercial port and marinas, it was perfect as my escape destination.

After eliminating all other scenarios, I had come up with my final plan. I would escape on a dinghy with a full load of fuel, water and food, reach high seas and wait there for Bernard to rendezvous with me in a sail boat. We would meet in international waters and together we would sail to Mumbai in India. Before entering Indian waters I would simulate an incident at sea to justify an entry without visa for emergency reasons. Once there, I would ask for a new passport at the French consulate, and we would fly back to our respective countries.

My next steps were to acquire a Zodiac dinghy and a sailboat, and to get my family to safety.

Chapter 7

Resource Acquisition

I started to look for a boat before sending my wife back to the U.S. Buying and registering a boat is a long process and is even more complicated for a clandestine operation.

Stealing a boat was not an option; there were already too many administrative hurdles in Dubai that needed to be cleared before taking a registered boat out at sea. If it was not registered—or even worse, stolen, it would become a really high-risk operation. I was innocent of any crime and I was not going to put one on my tab now.

I discreetly continued pulling the strings on my lawyer to stall Abdul Qader with the same story, to make him confident I just needed time to get the money, and as planned, I would go to the meeting with Sultan to finalize the deal. He was doing a much better job of convincing them of my intention to pay than I could myself. Postponing meetings and giving justifications for delay is just how business is done in Dubai anyway. It gave me a little more time to complete the acquisition and preparation of the boat. It was important that all the paperwork and the preparation for my escape be in the most advanced stages before the deadline was set to meet with Sultan. After that deadline it would a whole different scenario because I would have to work while in hiding. I had a strong suspicion my lawyer would get a cut of the blackmail money I was being forced to pay because of the way he was dealing with both them and me. I didn't trust him, but I still found him to be a good resource of information—sometimes when I expected it the least.

One time he told me I needed to relax and suggested I go fishing for the weekend. He didn't know if I even had a boat, but I used this opportunity to get some information from him. I told him that without a passport it would be unlikely that I would go fishing on a boat because I would not want to be caught by the police and accused of running away from Dubai. He confirmed what I already knew—that while cruising in a small craft in coastal waters, you are not required to carry a passport or any other permits because a small craft does not have a registration and obviously cannot go very far. I spoke with my attorney about these things not only to get information from him but also to keep him from getting suspicious about me having a boat or worse, planning an escape.

To minimize risks during my escape, I had to limit illegal actions to only those absolutely necessary to accomplish my escape. Attempting illegal activities that weren't critical to success and involving police action could be fatal to my plan. There was nothing illegal about me going out to sea in a dinghy. If the police were patrolling the waters they would think I was just fishing. There wouldn't be any reason for them to interfere with me. It was different for boaters on a registered boat. Larger vessels, I would say above fifteen feet in length, are not allowed to go to sea without a sailing permit, and if they plan to go beyond the territorial waters they need to have their passport stamped by immigration. But there is no fence or border station out there in the water. There is no physical border. Passport control, exit and entry procedures are not processed at the limit of the territorial waters, but at the immigration station in the port. And immigration officers, the Coast Guards or the police have a right to search the boat for contraband or undeclared passengers. Once you pass the territorial waters limit, you are outside the police jurisdiction and they cannot do anything to stop you.

Because the police cannot put patrol boats all along the territorial waters to stop people from going into international waters, it is fairly easy to just sneak away with the right boat and reach the twelve mile limit. My plan to rendezvous with a sailboat on the high seas wouldn't be a problem since Bernard would be leaving the country alone, onboard the sailboat going through normal port immigration procedures. His passport would be stamped and checked exiting the country.

The plan was pretty much foolproof, and could probably be repeated by anyone else trying to get out of the UAE. Of course, once my story gets out, my guess is the Dubai government will start registering all watercrafts, stopping boats without cause and will possibly institute more control and administrative procedures making it even worse to go sailing in the UAE.

I had some money put aside so I could buy a used sailboat. I could not purchase a new one because the time it would take for delivery would have far exceeded my deadlines and there were no sailboat manufacturers in the UAE. It was a not just a money issue but a time issue. I needed a boat right away. I didn't want to buy a single use boat either. After my escape, I wanted to be able to sell the boat and recoup at least some if not all of my money.

I searched the local pre-owned sailboat market which is very sparse in the Gulf. You don't see a lot of sailboats on the Persian Gulf and the Emiratis are not sailors. Their egos are more satisfied with power boats and they rarely go far from their marinas. I will admit though, that Sultan impressed me with his new boat, the *Dubai Magic*. She is an exceptional, forty-five-meter motor sailboat. All the other Emiratis I knew went for three-deck power yachts, but Sultan bought this sailboat as junk and had it completely refurbished in three years by Dry Docks, another one of Sultan's companies. It seemed an awkward choice for an Emirati, a three-mast ketch—it was the only one in Dubai. They are slow, less maneuverable than power boats but they are the best solution to circumnavigate the globe and live comfortably at sea. I am still wondering where Sultan got his idea to acquire this type of boat because he was not an experienced sailor. I liked his boat but I couldn't afford to splurge on a boat like this, I needed to find something seaworthy and cheap.

Through ads and boat listings I found six sailboats for sale in the UAE. Six listings was not a lot of boats—especially for a place with as much disposable income as there was in Dubai. I contacted the boat brokers to make arrangements to inspect the boats. I introduced myself with a different name, and already my appearance was different, so it was unlikely I would be recognized. Two weeks earlier, just after my last meeting with the attorney, I had started to change my appearance. It takes a couple of weeks to grow a beard and mustache, so I had to do it early enough so if anybody was looking for me after not showing up to the auditors meeting, I would look different. I trimmed my beard the same way Emiratis do. I also had a suntan and wore large sunglasses; all together I looked very much like a Middle Eastern man.

I needed a boat that was in good condition and seaworthy, a boat I could just jump in and sail the following day. I didn't have the time to fix a boat, nor did I want to risk the exposure of sitting out on a marina working on one. Most of these boats were not immediately available for various reasons, but two of them got my attention. The first boat was a small sailboat, a direct sale from a private owner. The seller was a gentleman from Australia. He and his wife were living onboard on weekends and working in Dubai during the week. He wanted to sell his boat, but only after summer because they were going with the boat on vacation to Indonesia first.

I could not wait until September. I was already pushing my luck and getting stir crazy in Dubai. I needed to leave no later than June. The couple was leaving at the end of May for Indonesia, and the boat was already loaded with supplies and fuel. When I went to see it, I made up a story about why I wanted it. I told the owner that I needed the boat as soon as possible to join my friends and wife for a vacation in the Maldives. I could not risk giving him any hint of my escape plans. He suggested that I go with him on the boat for his trip to Indonesia, take possession of the boat from him in Indonesia, and he would come back to Dubai by plane. In his mind it was a good option, because I could sail from Indonesia to the Maldives easily, since it is not too far.

Actually this was a good option that I considered accepting. I thought it through and considered that I could actually find an excuse to make a stop in Mumbai, he could just drop me off there, and I would pay good money to compensate him for not buying the boat on the condition that he kept my passage quiet.

Dubai is like a village and the expatriate community is small. As we became more acquainted, I learned more about him and I had to be careful to not reveal anything to him about myself for fear of jeopardizing my operation. I was surprised to learn he was working on Sheikh Mohammed's yacht as the chief engineer. This in and of itself was a problem because I knew a lot of people working on that yacht. An even bigger problem was his wife. I knew if went on the boat with them, she would expect me to give her a full story of who I was and why I wanted to travel with them. Wives are always the hardest to convince if something sounds out of the ordinary.

I kept the option of traveling with this couple open in the back of my mind, in case I couldn't find something better. I maintained a relationship with the Australian gentleman and continued to indicate interest in buying the boat, explaining that I needed time to figure out how to sort out the travels back and forth to Indonesia.

Another reason I maintained the relationship was because when people are eager to sell, they are very talkative. I encouraged him talk to me about his job and his employer, Sheikh Mohammed. I learned of Sheikh Mohammed's habits among other things. Not only did this gentleman tell me all about the boat, he also told me all about the security they had in place and how paranoid all the members of the ruling family were. He told me about the drinking, the women and shooting guns at sea. I learned Sheikh Mohammed kept a submachine gun, an Uzi, on the floor next to his bed. Was he afraid of a coup? The Australian invited me to come onboard Sheikh Mohammed's boat I would just have had to leave my ID at the entrance. I was not concerned about the ID, since I had a fake one I knew would fool any of the security guards. Rather, I was concerned about being recognized and identified by someone else on the boat. I had been onboard this boat before, and I knew a lot of people and officials who might be on the boat. Although I had a beard now, once inside without my sunglasses on, my eyes would surely give me away to anyone who had seen me before.

The Australian's contract with Sheikh Mohammed was ending in December. After his stint was done, he planned to return to Australia. I know he is now safe and sound in his home country, so there is no reason to worry that the Emiratis, who may want to punish him for speaking to me, would want to grab him for questioning or anything else.

Once I determined the Australian's boat was an alternate solution, I took a closer look at the second boat I had found. It was more interesting, but also more expensive. I contacted the broker under a fake name who represented the owner, and he proudly told me the boat belonged to his boss, Sheikh Khaled Bin Zayed Al Nehayan, brother of the President of the UAE (Sheikh Khalifa bin Zayed Al Nehayan) and member of the royal family. I saw an advantage to buying this boat immediately. The transaction would be finalized quickly with less scrutiny, because that's just the way things are done in Dubai when a Sheikh is involved. I did three sea trials on the Sheikh's boat to check that everything was all right, and given the few other options available to me, I decided to buy his boat.

I could not believe my luck and the irony. If I could manage to acquire the boat of Sheikh Khaled and keep it for a couple of weeks under the registration of His Highness, I would be able to go anywhere around the UAE waters without being stopped by the police. Having his registration on the boat would be like having a free pass to go anywhere I wanted, untouched. It was the same with cars in Dubai— some license plate numbers were just not to be questioned. A bill of sale for a sailboat with the signature of a member of the royal family was quite a powerful document.

I had to move fast and get this transaction wrapped up as quickly as possible, yet without raising any suspicion. I told the same story to the broker, my pretext, what I called the Maldives Story. We were a group of friends visiting the UAE and looking for a boat to go to the Maldives Islands to pick up our spouses and continue our vacation at sea. According to my story, our wives were already in the Maldives waiting for us on the beach, so we needed the boat as soon as possible. If we were delayed in getting the boat, it would be too late for us to reach the Maldives by sea, so we would not buy the boat at all.

The broker wanted his commission so he didn't want to lose this sale. The Sheikh wanted to sell his boat pretty badly as well. The boat had been listed for more than a year, sitting at the marina, and the cost of its berthing was accumulating. The broker did his best to expedite the transaction. I dared to ask the broker to have Sheikh Zayed sign the paperwork in one week. The boat could not be under my name indeed because I was in the police system so I gave a power of attorney to a friend of mine, French also, to sign the paperwork, buy the boat on my behalf under his name, and he would attend closing with the Sheikh for me, so I would not need to be present. I made sure my friend who signed as my power of attorney was not doing anything illegal. It was a normal business transaction and he didn't need to know what I would use the boat for. He was leaving the UAE anyway a few months later. I pressed the broker to close quickly, telling him time was of the essence. I told him if I could not get the boat in two weeks, then I would not buy it. With my deadline, the broker and the seller sped up the process.

Normally, it would have taken about two months to finalize a boat purchase with all the legalities that must be accomplished, but I was able to get the boat within my time frame. At no point did the Sheikh or the broker know my true identity. The deal was closed in one week. It was practically a miracle too, as it was not easy to catch the Sheikh because he was always traveling. In a weird twist of events he signed the bill of sale the day before he was going on a trip to China with Sultan and Sheikh Mohammed. I discovered this once the acquisition was in process and it worried me a bit. If the Sheikh were to mention to Sultan he was selling his boat to a French guy, Sultan might connect the dots and ring the alarm. On this trip to China they would have lots of free time in the plane. They both love boats and the Sheikh owns the Marina where they both keep a yacht. My worries were for naught though, because if they did share information, the alarm was not raised. Either they didn't discuss it at all or Sultan didn't put two and two together.

I found it ironic that some government executives had trapped me in the country, and yet a member of the royal family was helping me to get out. I was incredibly lucky they were either too arrogant or too idiotic to not pay attention to details, like "Navy Officer and secret operative," all over my resume. They didn't realize I could pull something like this. They never realized if I were convincing enough to make them believe I would pay them nearly a million dollars to get my passport back, I could very well invest $200,000 in an escape.

In addition to purchasing the sailboat, I also bought a small inflatable with a soft bottom—a twelve foot dinghy with a fifteen-horsepower outboard motor. It was green, which would make it less visible on the water.

Once the boat purchases were complete, I worked on them to get them ready. The sailboat was berthed in a marina south of Dubai, in Ganthoot—a remote place with nothing around it but a hotel frequented by Emiratis and their Russian prostitutes. The sailboat had not been maintained for a long time. The broker told me that Sheikh Khaled had kept her in the marina without visiting her for over a year. My first order of business was to conduct an inventory of what was there, what was missing, what was working and what wasn't.

I bought two identical portable GPS systems for Bernard and me to use. The boat came with a life raft that was still certified. I would never go across an ocean without one. There was no radar system onboard, and this was disappointing because it meant I would not be able to sleep well, always having to scrutinize the sea. The radar was an important feature necessary to monitor surface activity and to avoid collisions, especially at night or in poor visibility. It was a good thing Bernard would be onboard with me for the trip, so we could take turns on watch and sleep longer.

I removed the radar reflectors to reduce my radar signature. Radar reflectors are metal shapes tied up to the mast; they work as mirrors for radar signals, reflecting the radar waves back to radar receivers so that the sailboat is highly visible on the screens. I didn't want to be visible to the UAE Coast Guard station to avoid more hassle. I would put them back on once on the high seas.

I had a satellite phone with an Internet connection. The phone was a necessity for safety reasons. If I had an emergency in the middle of the ocean I would need to call for assistance—and I knew I would have one. I planned to stage one to justify an emergency entry to India. I would not be calling the UAE Navy of course. I doubted they could actually rescue anybody. The UAE Navy ships never took to sea and when they did they were either driven aground or broke apart. No wonder the UAE agreed to let the French Navy open a base in Abu

Dhabi. They out sourced the task to a foreign naval force that could do the job the UAE Navy was not capable of—defending their own country. Unlike other countries, Dubai has almost none of its citizens engaged in the police or the Armed forces to ensure the security of their Nation. It is not a risk; it is an invitation for invasion or coup.

I needed the phone and a satellite Internet connection for other reasons; I had to download documents on my way to India and maintain the illusion I was still in the UAE with emails and messages to people and friends.

Because I wanted to leave Dubai as soon as possible, I was not going to wait for all the required documents for the new boat registration. When I purchased the boat it was registered to Sheikh Khaled. I then had her registered in the Mauritius. I planned to take my mobile lab, printer, and plastic laminator on the boat so I could print a new registration cards and other certificates. I would retrieve these documents online and print them onboard, change the registration to a new one with a UK London registry, and everything would be authentic. I bought a set of flags and decals so I could match any registration numbering and change the numbers on the hull—lower one flag and raise the French flag. Boats flying the French flag are very welcome worldwide, except in the UAE of course where no boats are welcome whatsoever. With this plan, it would be difficult to track my boat, because the boat that left Dubai would not have the same registration as the boat reaching India. This would create delays if there was an investigation and it would give me more time to fool whatever administrations were involved and get farther away.

Although I had sails, I took 600 liters of fuel for the diesel engine. The weather forecast was showing winds of fifteen miles per hour, which wasn't much. Under those weather conditions I would have to run the engine to help maintain a ten mile an hour cruising speed. My destination was 1,300 miles away, so at ten miles per hour, that would be an eight days crossing.

My real destination was Mumbai in India, but because I was pretending to go to the Maldives, I took documents with me to support my pretext. I had a set of everything I needed—charts, maps and books, all for the Maldives. Of course I also brought navigation charts and books on India and Mumbai, which I planned to dump in the Ocean just before arriving in Mumbai so that nobody there could accuse me of planning to go to India from the beginning.

India requires an entry visa prior to arriving, for any type of stay, but because my official destination was the Maldives I didn't have a reason to have a visa for India, without a passport I could not get one anyway. The accident, (the details of which were as yet unclear) I was planning to stage at sea when approaching India, would justify an emergency entry into the country. With an emergency onboard, they could not deny me entry and they would issue me a crew visa, a common practice for seamen. It's like a permission to come on shore. Thanks to my Internet satellite link, I would be able to explain how after my accident, I logged on to inquire about Mumbai and downloaded useful information, such as the contact information for the French consulate and the port authorities, so I could call in and report the accident.

This is the beauty of the sailboat; you can go anywhere, and you always have a good reason to stop anywhere you want. If you arrive in India by plane, car, train or on foot without a visa, you are kicked back immediately. When you arrive on a boat after an accident, they don't know where you came from, they cannot deny you entry, and they cannot throw you back to sea. Instead, they help you.

I would have at least six days to decide what kind of emergency I would stage. I had other things to figure out and finish first. Back at the marina where the boat was berthed, my preparation and activity around the boat triggered some curiosity among the neighbors. A German couple was living on a big sailboat in the marina, stranded in Dubai. They had been lured by an Emirati national to come to Dubai to start a boat charter business and they bought the sailboat from him. Unfortunately for them, they discovered too late the fifty-one percent Emirati business ownership law. They could not operate the company successfully with this inequitable control and loss of incomes. As they were working and chartering their boat, the Emirati kept taking cash, as often as he could. The German couple had to stop offering charters because they could no longer afford to operate the boat. They were stuck with a boat they could not sell, or charter, and they could not go anywhere. At that point they were living on the boat like bums, with no resources and entangled in legal issues that I was sure would only worsen in time.

They held no jealousy or bitterness towards me. They told me their story because, to them, I was just a tourist visiting who needed to be warned. Had I met them before they entered into this business deal, I would have told them to walk away from the idea of starting a boat chartering business in the UAE! I had explored this possibility myself and quickly came to the conclusion that it was just asking to be scammed by an Emirati. As they were explaining to me how they got ripped off, lured into doing business in Dubai and became trapped, I could not resist asking them why they didn't just sail away on their boat. They had no idea I was in the same situation and I certainly wasn't going to tell them, but I felt compelled to plant the seed of this idea in their heads.

Unfortunately they could not leave the country because their Emirati partner and sponsor took away their passports, and because the boat was under his name. Without the approval from the Emirati, they would never get the required sailing permit and their boat would never be able to exit the marina. The coast guard station was right at the exit of the marina, and they would spot them right away.

While working on my escape plan, I was shipping my entire household out by sea freight. It was a potential problem because my house was located on Nakheel's grounds and under the surveillance of Nakheel's guards and administration. I was concerned my container could be blocked or seized by Ahmed Butti, also head of Customs. Both Chairman of Nakheel and Customs were after me. Fortunately, I was once again able to use their lack of foresight to get out of the guarded community. I shipped my household goods under a different name so it would not pop up on Ahmed Butti's desk. The guard showed up at the door to inquire about the container in the street being loaded with my stuff. He asked if I had a non objection letter from Nakheel and I just showed him the eviction notice Butti had given me earlier. I pretended I was just vacating the villa as requested. I was using his words against him. The guard had a valid document and a viable story, so there was nothing to report. Butti and the others would only find out too late that I had left the house.

It is crucial when doing something undercover, to always have a good story and the documents to support it, so when asked to present them upon request, people don't dig into the details any further than necessary. That way you don't look suspicious trying to invent something on the fly.

In our professional jargon we called that pretext. A successful operation was all about pretexts. When a situation doesn't look suspicious or important, the reporting takes more time to move up through the administrative pyramid—and, when it finally makes it to the top, it is too late.

After the shipping company picked everything up, we left the house and checked into a hotel. Timing was everything. I wanted my family to leave before the red flags reached Dubai World. Every step had to be done quickly to prevent Abdul Qader from stopping my family at the airport. My wife had resigned from her job only a week before; her visa was canceled a few days after. We were on Easter holiday so the school would not start asking where my son was for at least two weeks. I booked a last minute flight for my wife and kids and, two days later, she was picked up by her employer's driver so he could take them to the airport. As it would be with most expatriates, her employer had held her passport, only to release it at the airport to be stamped at the departure gate.

It was an emotional time for all of us. My wife and children were going back home and I was staying behind. I didn't know how long we were going to be separated, but I knew it would be at least a six weeks before I could join them. If things went bad for me, they would probably never see me again—but I didn't tell her that. We tried not to think about that possibility

There were always problems at the airport when anyone left, so it didn't surprise me when my wife called to tell me she had a situation with immigration. For a moment I feared the worst, but this time it was again a problem with the visas for my children. They took her to the police for questioning for forty-five minutes. Because she was aware of what I was going through with the auditors, she told me later, it was the worst fear she'd ever felt in her life—not just for herself, but for our children. She knew if she was detained, the police would not have the slightest consideration for the two little boys left alone. She paid a $300 fine, cleared immigration and boarded the plane.

At that point I knew they were gone and safe. I was relieved of the worry over my actions harming my family. Now I could focus 100 percent on my plan.

As my family's plane left Dubai airspace, I was on the phone with Bernard asking him to come back to Dubai.

The time to go into hiding was coming, bringing me closer and closer to escape day. I didn't want to end up like this German couple, trapped in Dubai indefinitely and bankrupt, or in prison with no charges, like other Dubai World executives who had turned into scapegoats. My family was waiting for me in the U.S. and my means of escape were in place. The pressure was building from the auditors and Sultan to get their ransom. I had to disappear soon.

Chapter 8

The Escape

My family was gone, and I was waiting for Sultan to schedule his meeting with me, my lawyer, and Abdul Qader. I would not go to the meeting, of course. I would go into hiding the same day instead. Timing was tight, and the scheduling would be stretched to the limit before suspicion could rise.

I got a call on Tuesday night from my lawyer informing me that the meeting was set for Thursday—in two days. He wanted to make sure I knew I had to go to Sultan's office and bring both checks. He said that, as per the agreement, I needed to sign a confession and a settlement agreement, as well as another agreement stating I would not work in the submarine industry anywhere in the UAE unless I paid another $1,500,000 to them in compensation. In addition, I had to sign a gag order in which I was forbidden from contacting the press and discussing the terms and conditions of these agreements, the functioning of Exomos and its relations with Dubai World, its executives, and its subsidiaries. In return, I would get back my passport, the travel ban would be lifted, and they would let me go back to the U.S. These additional agreements confirmed the blackmail would never end until I was completely ruined.

For over a year I had been coerced into signing all these documents and agreements. The whole scenario constituted extortion, blackmail and the illegal confiscation of my passport, but I was about to put an end to it.

In the end, His Excellency Sultan Ahmed Bin Sulayem, a man who considered me as a friend, the man who invited me to come to Dubai to come and work for him, was the one to actually deliver the coup de grace to a family man, an engineer, and a businessman—a man who had committed no crime, a man who had invested so much of himself to build their company. Now I knew for certain he was behind all of the harassment, mental torture, threats, lies, and coercion—that he was not some unwilling participant, ignorant to what the auditors or Butti were doing. The small piece of me that hoped he was not involved was gone.

Here I was at the end of the road, the point of no return. There was no reason in postponing the meeting or meetings with Sultan without the money and with only excuses—or worse, refusals. I would face dire consequences—an arrest for certain. This was the day I had to go under the radar—to become a ghost.

I had two days left to look for another place to stay until Bernard arrived in Dubai to help me by renting a room with his passport.

My best option was to share an apartment with somebody I hadn't yet met. I didn't want to be a liability to my local friends, and the risk of a leak was too great with them. When I was an undercover operative, I would look for places to stay other than hotels or rentals because of the surveillance and ID trail. The most successful and quickest way was to look for a woman with whom to share an apartment.

So I was back in business. There were many single working women in Dubai who have difficulty paying rent and who are lonely. So it didn't take me long to find Ms. Leila in a bar. She was willing to offer me her couch for a week or two. The world had not changed, but what I had done in the former Soviet republics was far more difficult than it was in Dubai. I posed as a nice French gentleman, telling Leila my wife kicked me out of the house—that we were going through a divorce, and that being a roommate would cost me less than a hotel until I could find another place. Leila felt sorry for me, and she appreciated the extra money I offered her for the inconvenience, so she took me in—and I had a place to stay.

On Thursday night, I checked out of the hotel and switched my phone to silent. I didn't go to the meeting: I vanished into the city.

After I didn't show up at Sultan's meeting, I received twenty messages and missed calls. It looked like they were getting nervous. Good. I checked out of the hotel, because they could be looking for me. If I was in a hotel, anywhere, under my name, they could find me with a single phone call to the police.

I called Leila and told her I was on my way to her place. I moved in with a couple of duffle bags. I was able to sleep, eat, and watch TV for a week without checking into a hotel. I knew she would never tell anyone of our arrangement because it was illegal to sublet an apartment in Dubai, and it was also illegal for an unmarried man and woman to share a home.

I know what you are thinking, but you can stop right there. This was no James Bond movie. I didn't get the room, the food on the table, and the bed with a beautiful girl waiting for me. That was not the case by a long shot. In real life when you want to live clandestinely, you go with the casual lady, not the supermodel. They are not only easier to hook up with, but they also don't call too much attention to themselves, and you are not seen as another guy trying to get into their pants. They are totally unsuspecting.

After one week in her apartment, Bernard arrived in Dubai. I told my makeshift roommate I found a place. In all, it worked out well. Leila had been very nice. I put on the charm, but never lost my focus to keep myself out of harm's way—to get out of town. I gave her one last kiss good-bye and never saw her again. I paid one month's rent in exchange for one week's stay, hoping she wouldn't look at me as a moocher.

I took a taxi to the airport to pick up Bernard. He didn't recognize me. My change of appearance worked. I looked like a Middle Eastern tourist, wearing sunglasses and a cap.

I had a list of select hotels that met my requirement, which was to be able to reach my room without being seen by the front desk clerks. Side pool entrances, restaurants on mezzanines, or gallerias, all with direct room access through elevators, were the ideal setting.

Before going to the hotel, we made a brief stop at a coffee shop just across the way to discuss check-in arrangements. Then Bernard walked to the hotel to make a reservation under his name for a double bedroom. When Bernard came back, he gave me the key to the room. I went to the room alone, using a different access point. Bernard joined me about half an hour later to talk in more detail about our plan.

All hotels in the UAE are under passive surveillance. Undercover police and employees report anything out of the ordinary. They don't actively search or investigate unless they have reason, but they are the eyes and the ears of the police. In big hotels there is always a CID officer in a *kandourah* in the lobby—watching. When you check into a hotel, the clerk at the reception desk takes your passport to make a copy and scan it. But, the scanner is the property of the Dubai Police. This inconspicuous wallet-sized device is the Dubai Police's direct link, allowing for immediate transmission. So, they know who is checking in and who is checking out—live.

When the UAE government recommends that everyone hold an E-passport (with a barcode), don't be conned into thinking it's for the traveler's convenience. It's to make things easier and quicker for the government officials to know where everyone is at *all* times. For this reason, I asked Bernard to come to Dubai with his old passport, so when his passport was scanned it would be processed manually, thus taking more time to track.

As a general rule when living covertly, you segregate your activities into three different locations. You set a place to meet, a place to work and a place to live. Never, ever mix the three. What I had to do was considered illegal in the UAE. It involved producing fake documents and elaborate disguises. These were elements that I didn't want found at my resting place. A hotel was not the best option for my workplace because of the surveillance and the risk for the housekeeping staff stumbling across my covert tools and documents. Bernard could not rent rooms in three different hotels at the same time, because that could have raised a red flag in the Dubai Police Department, so instead Bernard and I shared the same hotel room and we changed hotels every two nights.

Whenever we left the room to go out, I left a webcam connected to my laptop and logged on to monitor the room, and, before returning to the room, for added measure, I checked online to watch for any traps waiting for me set up by the police. Blending with my surroundings and subtlety were keys to avoid raising suspicion during my stay and to prevent a team from bursting through my door at 6:00 a.m.

Right: Hervé Jaubert standing between Sheikh Mohammed and Sultan Bin Sulayem

Middle: The Goby Submarine landing on the sea bed

Bottom: The 40,000 sq. ft. Exomos facility, in front are the mockups of Nautilus and Adventurer Submarines

Top: The Nautilus Submarine in the production bay

Right: The Stingray Submarine ready to be deployed

Bottom: The Adventurer cruising at periscope depth

Hervé Jaubert in conversation with Sultan Bin Sulayem at the Dubai Boat Show 2006

Hervé Jaubert with Sultan Bin Sulayem on vacation in Africa

Bill of Sale

**DUBAI
UNITED ARAB
EMIRATES**
10th of April 2008

C201

(revised 1999)

Official number	Name of Ship `KAREB AL AMAL" (BENETEAU OCEANIS Clipper 473 # 127) To Become : LADY LUCIE	Number, year and port of registry

	Feet	Tenths	Sailing, steam or motor ship	Horse power of engines (if any)
Overall length	47	7	SAIL AND MOTOR, SINGLE SCREW	75 BHP
Main breadth	14	2	Gross tonnage	Register tonnage
Depth	6	9	(for dual tonnages)	state the higher)

and as described in more detail in the Register Book

Body Corp:	Company name	Principal place of Business	
Individuals	Full Names	Address	Occupation
I the transferor	H.H.SHEIKH KHALED BIN ZAYED AL NEHAYAN	BIN ZAYED GROUP PO BOX 53793 DUBAI U.A.E.	GROUP CHAIRMAN

in consideration of the sum of ▄▄▄▄▄▄▄ DHIRAM paid to me by
Dhiram **ONLY**

Individuals	Full Name	Address	Occupation
the transferee(s) (Add "as joint owners" if this is the case)	Mr ▄▄▄	▄▄▄ CANOVANAS PR 00729 USA	TECHNICIAN

the receipt of which is acknowledged, transfer **64/64** shares in the above ship and in her boats and appartenances to the transferee

Further, I the said transferor for myself and my heirs or successors covenant with the said transferee and his assigns, that I have the power to transfer in manner aforesaid the premises hereinbefore expressed to be transferred,

and that the same are free from encumbrances

(Leave blank unless there are any outstanding encumbrances when 'save as appears by the registry of the said ship' should

For completion when sale is by Individual or Joint Owners
Executed as a Deed by the above named transferor on   date 10 Mo of April 2008

Signature of transferor   in the presence of

Full name of witness	Signature of witness	as witness
AHMAD IBRAHIM REFAI		
Occupation of Witness	Address of witness	
EXECUTIVE SECRETARY	P.O.BOX: 11092, DUBAI -UAE	
Full Name of witness	Signature of witness	as witness
MARIAM KHODR MIRI		
Occupation of Witness	Address of witness	
PERSONAL ASSISTANT	P.O.Box: 11092 DUBAI -UAE	

Bill of sale of the escape boat purchased from HH Sheikh Khaled Bin Zayed Al Nahayan, brother of the President of the UAE

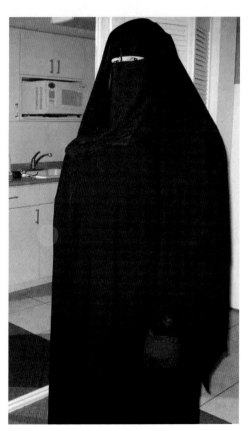

Transformation, Frogman under Arabic woman disguise

A: *Bernard leaves Ganthoot with sail boat. Hervé takes the land route to Fujeirah*
B: *Hervé & Bernard meet in Fujeirah, Hervé escapes on rubber dinghy, Bernard leaves on sail boat*
C: *Hervé & Bernard rendezvous in high seas, and sail to India*

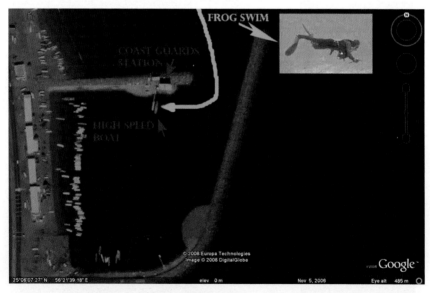

Frogman night swim in Coast Guard station to disable the high speed boat

Top: *Mumbai Police receipt for Hervé's passport loss report*

Right: *Mumbai Immigration clearance with Hervé's New Passport*

*Top Left: Hervé sailing
the Arabian Sea
Top Right: Moored in
front of Gateway of India
Right: First arrival on
shore to Mumbai on boat
ramp side of Gateway
of India
Bottom: Hervé in
Mumbai streets*

I figured it would take two weeks from the meeting with Sultan for them to realize I had gone AWOL. Then there would be another two weeks before the prosecutor reported me to the police. So, that would give me at least a month before they started looking for me—by then I would have already escaped the country.

In their eyes I was already guilty, so now that I had become invisible I'm sure they wanted to put me on the barbecue more than ever.

I had to throw whoever might be following me off my trail. The CID can easily locate a cell phone and narrow it down to a 300 yard area using triangulation and by tracking the phone tower the cell phone is connected to. You can spot these masts with a bunch of antennas sticking out all over the landscape and all along Sheikh Zayed Road and the main roads. There are hundreds of them in Dubai, and along each are diesel generators for backup in case of a power outage. Their areas of coverage overlap one another. There are so many of them it is possible to be very precise in locating a given cell phone. It shows the strategic importance Emiratis put on their phone network. The loss of the cellular phone network due to a power outage is not an option in Dubai.

I remember in 2004 when Florida was hit by three hurricanes. The state didn't have cell phones transmitters and repeaters backed up with generators. So when the power went out, the cell phones didn't work for days. However, Dubai wanted to make sure that in the case of a power shut down, cell phones would still be usable. In addition, the cell phone network allowed the police to locate people through their mobiles.

Once again, I found more of their own tools to set them up as a fool. So, if they were tracking my phone, this time I would provide the location. I silenced my phone as I stopped in a gas station in town, and entered the attached store. I wandered the aisles looking for a good place to conceal my phone. I picked a box that contained some sort of useless camping device. I figured they wouldn't sell this article for months, since no one goes camping in the desert where the temperature is over 120 degrees. I dropped my phone, fully charged, inside the box and put the box at the bottom of the pile without anybody noticing. My phone would stay there active, taking messages and missed calls for three weeks before the battery went dead, all the while indicating to the police that I was still in the area. Of course, I would never know who called me because I would never go back to my phone. If the police were looking for me by my cell phone, they would be searching around a gas station surrounded by apartment complexes in vain. Even if they found it, they would know I had planted it to toy with them.

Two weeks after my no-show, my attorney sent me an email asking my whereabouts. It read it was not too late and I still had a chance to come up with a solution. He also wrote they understood if I just had a delay getting the money together. They were either naïve or desperate at this point to believe that I "just had a delay." Because I was not responding, he sent somebody to my house, only to find it empty. The timing had been perfect for getting my family and me out of there. He mentioned the huge embarrassment I had created for him, not showing up at the meeting—and that everyone was pointing fingers at one another for buying my horseshit.

I not only changed my appearance, but I also used disguises to stay under the radar. Regardless if I was in my *kandourah*, disguised like as tourist, or dressed like an Emirati woman, absolutely no one would have ever recognized me. Even if I sat next to Sultan himself, he wouldn't have noticed. The only risk I was actually taking was while wearing the *kandourah,* someone could have spoken to me in Arabic. Since I am not fluent, it could have raised suspicions. It did happen on several occasions and I had a hard time dodging the conversations. The adrenaline rush reminded me of an experience I had twenty years before, in Karachi, where I disguised myself as a Pakistani for two weeks during a covert operation to track down a terrorist cell planning to hijack an Air France jumbo jet. Passengers on this flight never even knew how close they came to being the victims of a terrorist attack.

In Dubai I dressed sometimes like a tourist, wearing a cap, with padding under my clothes to change my silhouette. I was able to go around Dubai, buy my equipment, check my routes, check the borders, try out my escape scenarios, go to restaurants, and meet with my contacts, all without ever being recognized.

But when I disguised myself as a fully-covered woman; I completely blended into the streets. This was a perfect camouflage. I dressed in black from head to toe with an *abayah*—veil, ponytail, perfume and all. This is the best way to go around Dubai without being questioned or even addressed by another person. It is like being invisible. No one, not even a police officer, could address an Arab woman in the *abayah*. I was able to use their culture against them.

I had dressed as an Arab woman before, in another Arab country. Back then I carried guns and explosives in pouches under a robe that made me look like an older, fat woman. I did it again, only this time it was minus the guns and explosives.

In Dubai, the *khandoura* and the *abayah* are deeply anchored in the Emirati traditions. This cloth is probably the most important object in their culture and makes them feel as if they belong to an elite class. But if criminals were to use these outfits to hide, they would be reduced to a criminal accessory. It would be a huge insult to Emiratis and a direct threat to their culture. This reminded me of the armed robbery in a jewelry store where the perpetrators disguised themselves as Arab women and used plastic guns. The news agencies were not authorized to report these facts because the government feared that another gang would use the idea. And it started already—my disguise with an *abaya* revealed in the media triggered a group of women to file a petition with the municipality, requesting that women who present themselves in *abaya* at "women only" private beaches, should be checked by female officers, to make sure that none are men in disguise attempting to peep at women.

I was still in contact with some of my friends but only by phone or text message because I didn't want to show myself as a bearded Arab. They would be on a strictly need-to-know basis to avoid any leaks that could be caught by the Amn Al Dawla.

I had to make sure I could never be identified by my new appearance at all time. For instance, whenever I went to the ATM machine to get cash, I would stand in front of it holding my cap with my teeth in such a way that it covered the whole lower part of my face, including the beard and the mustache. There is a time-lapse camera on every ATM machine, and they record every face of every person who comes to withdraw cash. A man in my position would remain free only by taking every precaution. I expected those Mafioso to make some effort to catch me so they could collect.

The beauty of being in disguise was that I took on another persona—just as I had in my clandestine life before. But this time, without the fear, I felt relieved and powerful in my element, like a fish in water. The moment was mine to take over the reins of control, and there was nothing they could do to stop me. I knew their habits, their schedules, the location of their vehicles, their addresses, where they docked their yachts—I knew too much about them. What I didn't know, I could find out. I could take action as needed. If they wanted to play dirty, I would gladly return the favor a hundred fold.

Beside the disguises, I decided I needed some self-defense devices—non-lethal, of course, in case I was detected or followed. Something strong to incapacitate my pursuer, so I could get away. In my previous career, I got the best results from pepper dust bombs.

These are much stronger than the self-defense pepper sprays that you can buy in security stores in the West for personal protection, but they are illegal in the UAE. Pepper dust bombs are easy to make and the components are available everywhere. In comparison, pepper sprays would feel like a sore throat medicine. Sultan was not the only connoisseur of hot sauces. This natural chemical in its pure form is a thin powder of capsaicin crystals, fifteen times more powerful than police-grade pepper spray. It incapacitates instantly, and the effects last for half an hour, anyone who has been exposed to it will have extreme burning sensations on the skin, the respiratory tract, and in the eyes. It is really nasty stuff, but essentially harmless long term. Its effects wear off with no permanent damage.

I ordered some on the Internet, enough to make three pepper grenades the size of my fist. The shipping paperwork read hot sauce component and the packaging also indicated hot sauce, so if customs opened the box it would look like innocuous hot sauce stuff and it would be delivered to Bernard. Customs confiscates mail order vitamins but pure capsaicin is let through without question. There were no import restrictions because everybody puts hot sauce on every dish. I also bought some mortar fireworks in Dubai. I never questioned why it was that fireworks are such big business there. There is also a lot of smuggling of fireworks. I don't know where they all go or who uses them, but in any case, this big market for fireworks made them available to me for my purposes.

Once I had all the components, Bernard rented me a room in the cheapest hotel possible. It was dirty with no Western tourists who would raise hell if they felt any burning sensations or a severe rash for no apparent cause. I knew the kind of occupants of this hotel wouldn't say a word to anyone. I used that room only to make my pepper grenades. I set the room up with a plastic hood in the shower, and I used gloves and a mask so I could manipulate the powder without contaminating myself.

I separated the lift charge from the firework shell so I could use it as a propulsive charge to vaporize the powder in the air. I discarded the mortar shell—I didn't need the shell that creates showers of colored sparks. I put the charge and the powder inside a small polyurethane bottle with a friction igniter, the same type used in some firecrackers. There were no hard parts in these grenades that could hurt anybody, even with high velocity. In the event I was pursued or followed, or if I were going to be stopped or arrested, I would trigger one pepper grenade and throw it behind me while running away. Nobody would get through the pepper cloud for sure, and they would further contaminate anyone asking them what happened, touching them or trying to help.

I did my best to clean up the room; I didn't want the cleaning people or the next guest to experience severe itching. They would probably blame it on the filthiness of the hotel.

I carried one pepper grenade with me at all times. I felt more comfortable with its silent protection in my pocket. Once I went underground, I met local people I had no idea existed—they were not exactly the law-abiding-citizen types. I spent time in the Musandam

Peninsula and sympathized with local smugglers and fishermen who where engaging in illegal trafficking with Iran on speedboats. They would speed through the Gulf Channel fifty boats at a time, overpowering any patrol boats that got in their way—like a flock of birds. Some were armed with AK47s. I didn't think I needed one, but I had a feeling that if I changed my mind, I easily could have bought one from them. These people travel back and forth regularly between the Emirates, Oman, and Iran—fooling controls and smuggling people, tobacco, guns, and drugs.

While I was working on my plan, I heard that Sultan was planning to sail to the Maldives Islands on his new sailing yacht, *Dubai Magic*. He had her berthed for a short time in the local marina. I thought the option to travel hidden on his boat could be quite the ironic escape—getting out of the country with the very same person who had brought me in and who had brought on the trouble. So I decided to go on the boat to check out the possibility while he was on a trip.

Once I knew he was away on his jet, I made my move. I disguised myself as an Arab woman. I wore flat shoes to keep my height as low as possible, and I added some padding to make me look older and fatter, and to break the height and weight ratio of my male stature.

There was very little chance anybody would discover what I was doing. I knew from my previous visits on Sultan's boat as his guest there were always prostitutes and women onboard, for entertainment. No one would ask these ladies where they came from or what they were doing there, and I sure didn't look like someone who would be dragged off to some man's cabin.

There were guards in the marina, but they only controlled people in the parking lot ten minutes before Sultan was due to arrive. He would call them to tell them he was coming to his boat. Since he was away on a trip, nobody would call to check and clear the parking area.

Bernard drove me in his car, and I sat in the back as if he were my driver. He dropped me off at the dark end of the parking lot. I boarded the boat, and within seconds I passed two crew mates who didn't even look at me. The boat looked pretty far along in its rehabilitation compared to the last time I had seen it, a year before. I looked inside the cabins that were open, and I inspected some of the living quarters as well. No one asked me anything or stopped me. I felt like a ninja, boosted with adrenaline and power. Anyone who would have bothered to stop me or ask me something would have had the surprise of his life. However, the boat didn't look ready to go anywhere anytime soon. There were still a lot of unfinished construction and mechanical jobs onboard which made it impossible to predict when the boat would be ready to go out, so I decided it was best to abandon that idea.

The female *abayah* and veil worked out to be an unbelievably good disguise. In the beginning, I had concerns that a man buying a woman's dress would raise suspicion and someone would call the police, but then I saw they were available in Carrefour, the French retail store chain, and nobody paid attention.

In public, a police officer cannot ask for the driver's license or identification of a woman wearing a veil—he has to call for a female police officer, and there were not that many of them. If a female police officer did decide to engage me, she would not have the strength to stop me, and the surprise would surely have thrown her off her game long enough for me to get the advantage.

When I was a covert operative, Arab countries were the easiest ones to work in because of the traditional clothing habits that could be used to conceal weapons and identity.

Without exception, guns are not allowed in the UAE. I knew that now. But there are guns—on untrained and soft police officers, holstered un-cocked, with no rounds in the chambers. Sometimes the police officers are not even allowed to put a clip in their guns. When they finish their shifts they have to leave their pistols at the police station. There are no armed off-duty police officers in Dubai. It shows the lack of trust the government has in foreign labor employed as cops. They are underpaid, lazy, and unwilling to take any risks to stop a determined and skilled fugitive. They are definitely not trained in close combat techniques, either. I found it so ridiculous when they accused me of smuggling weapons for a hit. Idiots! If I had needed a gun, I could have just served myself right out of their holsters.

And you may not even need a gun, in the UAE the men's clothing is a weapon that can be used against them. Spies or police officers call it a weapon of circumstance or a dual use item. It's an everyday object that can be turned into a deadly weapon. Emiratis hold their head cloth on with a black rope wrapped around their heads, called an *igal*. This rope is long and strong enough to be turned into a strangulation device in the blink of an eye. CID officers are so sure of themselves, displaying arrogant attitudes and disdain for peaceful foreigners, they don't see how vulnerable they could be in front of a determined individual. They are careless. They can approach a suspect with a ready-made noose or garrote sitting right on their heads. They should consider themselves lucky they never face hardened criminals or secret agents ready to fight.

The security checks that used to be second nature to me before became normal again—while moving, entering and exiting buildings, or going in and out of hotels, I continually checked to make sure I wasn't being followed or under surveillance. Some will say everything I did was like firing a canon to kill a mosquito, but I respond it was the difference between getting free and getting caught. There is no such thing as too many precautions when you go clandestine. It was not a comfortable life for sure, but it was the price I had to pay to assure my freedom. I was not perfect, I still made mistakes—but I did my best to limit them to the bare minimum so they would not be noticed.

Dubai has an extensive network of informants, and counter surveillance was very difficult. You wouldn't see it because it is not just a person reporting information. It is paper trails, tips, phone calls and other bits of information gained through technology and informants.

Anything you leave behind with a link to your passport or your name can be picked up by the police. It was imperative that I never show anyone or give anyone documents with my name on them. I made sure never to carry my real identification with me. If anybody were to recognize me or notice something unusual about me, I would be reported to the police, and the informant would receive remuneration. The Dubai police pay between $100 and $1,000 or more to informants for any useful leads. In the Service, we were told about the 'old lady behind the curtain.' You don't notice her. She has nothing else to do but to stay there for hours, looking at the street, but she will notice if she sees anything out of the ordinary, and might call the police on you.

A friend of mine in the service got caught in just such a way. He was on a training mission, but in real conditions. His mission was to place a real bomb (without the detonator) in a locker outside the train station. A lady behind some curtains spotted him and he was arrested. He spent two days in jail before the Service had him released, but his career ended there because the media had published his mug shot and he could no longer go undercover. In the UAE, there may not be any old ladies behind curtains, but there are hundreds of people wandering and sitting around doing nothing. Most of the time they have nothing to report, but the network is there.

A person can actually be followed without ever having someone physically behind them. All they do is use people in the network as checkpoints—there to report your position as they spot you. If police can track you, it is because the information is traveling with you, not the informants. A police officer can track his target without leaving his office. This type of surveillance is undetectable. I had to make sure not to do anything suspicious in open view that would alert this network of informants.

Even though Dubai is big and filled with over a million and a half people, somehow it is still like a village. You always bump into people you know. One day I was in a hotel going to lunch disguised as a tourist when I saw a group of Dubai World auditors—the very same group that was after me. They had rented a meeting room for one of their sessions, and I saw Abdul Qader himself. I followed him a bit to see what he was doing and where he was going. He didn't recognize me even when I was in the same elevator, standing right next to him. He was going to the restroom.

It was a weird feeling to be alone in that small elevator with somebody who had been instrumental in creating the problems I was going through. The urge to strangle him with the black rope he wore around his head was strong, but I restrained myself. It was not part of my plan to hurt anyone (even if he deserved it), and I am not a violent man. My plan was survival, not revenge. It served as a strong reminder to me though, that I could always bump into somebody I knew and I had to be careful and limit my outings to only those absolutely necessary. I was getting close to my time to leave, and I could not afford to make mistakes.

Finally I got the boat ready. I had my paperwork, and the time came to move the sailboat to Fujairah, on the other side of the UAE, the open ocean side on the Arabian Sea. The sailboat was located on the wrong side of the UAE, so to speak—on the Persian Gulf. Escaping from that side was too risky for me without a passport, even if the boat was still under the Sheikh's registration. It is an enclosed sea, with Iraq on one end and Iran across with a bottleneck through the Strait of Hormuz. Security is enhanced there and fully enforced with frequent checks by Navy patrol boats. I could not afford to be checked by a naval vessel from any country.

Sailing in the Persian Gulf is not like sailing in the Mediterranean or the Caribbean, where you are free to go pretty much everywhere without much hassle. In the Persian Gulf, you need permits and visas to travel from one city to another. There are territorial disputes that cause problems, private islands where the owners shoot on sight if you get too close, armed smugglers and God knows what else. On top of all this, when you arrive somewhere, you are likely to be sent away because there are no available berths to accommodate visitors. As non-Arabs, we would stand out too much. There were only a few boats cruising around the area, mostly containing Arabs, so when there is one that does not contain Arabs, everyone notices. Suffice to say, it is really not a recommended area for yachting, especially for fugitives.

Because the route was located in such a politically strategic area with lots of patrols, I had to escape to an open ocean, and for this, I needed Bernard. I needed him to take the boat alone all the way around through the Strait of Hormuz to reach the Arabian Sea, and head south to Fujeirah. This would be a day and a half trip. He had all the maps, routes and instructions to meet with me in the marina on the other side of the UAE, and we would be in contact with the satellite phone.

Once the boat was ready to sail, with all the reserves and supplies onboard, Bernard and I had to drive to Fujairah to prepare for my escape on the dinghy.

He rented a hotel room for a week. From there we went back and forth along the forty-five miles of coast, scrutinizing the sea to observe marine activity and traffic—watching the beaches and every fishing port from north to south. I was looking for any and all coast guard or police boats. I needed to know how many boats there would be, where they were being docked, and the power of their engines so I could to estimate their top speed. Speed converts into time and distance. At the end of the day, I would need to keep as much distance as possible between myself and these boats.

We played tourists scouting the area, being friendly with the locals, fishermen and even police officers. I spotted several police and coast guard high-speed boats; they were mostly located north around the port terminal.

Going south, ten miles from the border with Oman, I spotted a high speed police boat. It was docked in a little fishing port with a small building serving as the coast guard station. The forty-foot speedboat was powered by three large outboard engines. I estimated it had a top speed of at least forty-two miles per hour—way more than the fifteen miles per hour of my dinghy.

Between the border of Oman in the south with its single police boat and the north with its flotilla of police boats, the best I could do was to distance my point of exit five miles away from the nearest police boat in the south. All the other police boats were stationed north twenty miles away. Five miles from the closest and only police boat was a little too close for me to be comfortable. If I was detected they could catch me before I reached the international waters.

I needed to even the odds a little. So I looked at Bernard, and with a smile on my face, I thanked him for sending me my frogman's gear. He knew immediately that I was not going sight seeing under the water.

All he said was, "Arma?"

I replied, "Yes."

An arma is an operation in which we engage, destroy or sabotage an infrastructure, a building, or a—boat.

To keep my exit point twenty miles from the police boats and eliminate the threat five miles away, I would have to swim underwater, infiltrate the small port in the south, and sabotage their only police boat to make sure she wouldn't go anywhere if I was detected going offshore with my inflatable. Now it was getting exciting.

With these observations and my searches on Google Earth, I chose my point of exit and set my escape route.

It was another irony, in a boatload of ironies, that one of the partners who was blackmailing me, Ahmed Butti, the man who called me an idiot and fired me for no legitimate reason, was also the director of Dubai Customs. Dubai Customs was the same outfit that allowed me to receive my military-grade diving equipment I would use to disable a military boat. Any problem with Customs could have stopped my escape. Under his watch, and right under his nose, I brought into the country a Navy Seal—closed circuit diving apparatus that helped me escape Dubai.

I memorized the make and model of the police boat, so I would know the exact arrangement of its interior and engines. I knew the best and quickest way to sabotage the boat was to go for the fuel lines and clog them, leaving no clues. The motors wouldn't run, and it would take them a long time to discover the reason for the malfunction.

I showed Bernard the marina where he had to arrive after his trip around the Straight of Ormuz. He took note of the berth arrangement, the fuel station, and the entry of the marina, and he informed the marina staff he would be coming with his boat to refuel so there would not be any surprises, such as no available berths.

After that, we returned to Dubai and I prepared Bernard to take the boat to Fujairah. I briefed him again on how to get there. He was a sailor and former Navy Seal, so I trusted him with my boat—my ticket out of the country. But I had concerns about the overzealous cops on the sea to stop him for nothing.

In order to go from Dubai to Fujairah, Bernard had to leave the UAE, enter Omani waters, pass through the Strait of Hormuz (without entering Iranian waters), go around the Oman peninsula (also called Musandam Peninsula), and then reenter the UAE waters on the opposite side of the country. Prior to leaving, he had to get a sailing permit from the Omani Embassy to pass through Omani waters, get a sailing permit from the UAE Coast Guard, and stop at Immigration in the port to get an exit visa.

While we made final arrangements for the trip, I was at the marina every day preparing the boat for the crossing. I brought supplies and fuel so we would be able to stay at sea for at least twenty days. We had 150 gallons of fuel, spare parts, tools, safety equipment, and plenty of food. This was a lot of activity for this small and quiet marina, so it didn't surprise me when it caught the attention of some other people who were there, living on their boats.

It is always the same, people ask you questions when you bring water bottles and food on your boat, but they don't ask anything to the other boater who brings women onboard. They didn't give us any problems; they were just curious, maybe a little jealous to see someone leaving this place for good.

Everyone living at the marina was a foreigner, and I wasn't worried about anyone recognizing me with my disguises in place. With my story of my vacation trip to the Maldives, everything they saw me doing made sense.

Bernard practiced the exit out of and entry into the marina with the boat several times to get the coast guard officials used to seeing it and get the boat handy. It was Sheikh Khaled's boat, after all, but I wanted to make sure that there wouldn't be a problem leaving the marina on the day of our escape.

The next day, in the morning, we went to the marina and, as Bernard was about to leave with the boat, at the very last minute, a problem surfaced—and a big one. In Dubai, just when you think everything is good to go, a spanner usually appears to wreck your plan. The marina management didn't want to let the boat go because the payment for the rent of the berth was six months behind, to the tune of about $6,000. It had nothing to do with me; I bought the boat, not its liabilities. Most likely Sheikh Khaled had overlooked his payment schedule and forgotten to pay the bill. Sheikh or not, owner or not, they would not let the boat go without the bill being paid.

Adrenaline flowed through my arteries, and my mind was one hundred percent focused and sharp. I called the boat broker who sold us the Sheikh's sailboat and explained to him how embarrassing the situation was. I found out that it was actually the broker who had not paid the bill. I suspected he wanted me to pick up the tab so he could pocket the cash. I was angry and extremely frustrated; the boat was paid in full and I could not leave? Yet another Dubai scam. The broker asked me if I could pay and he would reimburse me later. I asked him, later as in never?

I was obviously not in a position to take the issue to the police, but the broker didn't know that. I couldn't go against the Sheikh, either. It is always like that, people in Dubai trying to rip you off with anything. Six thousand dollars was not small change. He was an expatriate on a visa sponsored by the same Sheikh who sold me the boat; he thought I was just a tourist passing through Dubai wanting to buy a boat, so when I revealed to him my knowledge of Emirati laws, he knew he could be in big trouble if the police called his sponsor to tell him his employee was screwing him with the marina fee.

After we finished our conversation, somebody quickly arranged for the payment, and two hours after the incident, the marina authorized Bernard's departure. At last.

I untied the boat and watched Bernard sail out of the marina. He had over a day to get to Fujairah. I urged him to stick to the plan, watch the route, and call me on the satellite phone should anything happen.

I was on a very tight schedule. My plan was to escape on the dinghy on Friday before noon. Weekends fall on Fridays in Dubai—it's like a Sunday in the Western world. At that time of day, everybody would be at a mosque praying. It would be unlikely to see anybody on the ocean to chase me.

As I was waiting for Bernard to make his trip to Fujairah, I stayed at the hotel, rehearsing my escape in my mind over and over. I also prepared a special tool kit to sabotage the coast guard boat. I needed a cutter, some clamps, super glue, and a tube of special resin for gas tank repair. The technique I would use consisted of placing two clamps, twelve inches apart, on the fuel line. They had to be strong enough to squeeze the fuel line to avoid a gasoline spill when I would cut it open.

I would then cut a three-inch slit, lengthwise between the clamps, using a cloth to absorb the gas caught in that section. Through the opening created by my knife, I would insert the end of the resin tube and squeeze in a cork of resin deep enough to make sure it sealed off the fuel line. Last, I would dry the gasoline off the edges of the cut on the line and glue the edges back together with super glue, remove the clamps, and collect all tools and debris inside a watertight bag to take with me when I left. The tampering of the fuel lines would be invisible. No one would figure out for a while the fuel lines were clogged, especially since they are hard to check—they are securely tightened on each end to the engine and fuel tank.

At one point inside the Strait of Hormuz, Bernard was boarded by Omani Coast Guard officers. He lost two hours answering questions. Two hours was not too bad, but it proved I was right to not be on the boat when it went around the peninsula. In these countries, it is easy to get in trouble for nothing. First they arrest you, then they ask you questions.

The next day, as Bernard arrived in Fujairah early in the morning, I checked out of the hotel in Dubai. I paid cash, pretending I was Bernard. I would go to Fujairah by car. It was too risky for me to rent or drive a rental car, so I wandered around for a while in the lobby of a hotel until I found a German tourist who was looking for a passenger to split the cost of his rental car to cross the Emirate. While I rode as his passenger, I was lectured for two hours about the Munich Oktoberfest—however, it was an acceptable price to pay for the discreet trip.

In Fujairah, the atmosphere was different than in Dubai—more relaxed. There were a lot of tourists around, and I did my best to avoid any eye contact or conversation. I didn't want to exist to anyone. After my German friend dropped me off at his hotel, I took a taxi to the Fujairah marina. There I saw the sailboat berthed at the fuel station. There had been no wind on the trip, so Bernard had to run the engine all the way and burned half of the fuel. I greeted him and took some of my things and my diving gear from the sailboat to bring with me to the hotel. I was anxious to move to the next step. After refueling, we went to the hotel, Bernard rented a room, and we moved in. I then prepared for my underwater mission. I needed to make a covert entry into the water, 800 yards from the coast guard station. I had noted my bearings and distances earlier and waited for nightfall.

At one in the morning, I put on my black skin suit with the hood and my frogman gear—the re-breather on my stomach, my fins, navigationboard mask and knife strapped to the inside of my legs, and my tool kit under the re-breather. Then I strapped two small towels rolled in balls that I placed just on top of my re-breather to bulk the *abayah* so it would cover all my stuff and give me the shape of a woman with big breasts. Then I put on a bathrobe to soften the sharp edges of everything that was strapped to me, which I would also need it to dry myself off after I came out of the water. With everything in place I put on the *abayah*, the black veil, the fake pony tail, and the mask. I had black diving gloves to cover my hands and black diving booties. To the rest of the world I looked like an Arab woman; the *abayah* hid everything. All the stuffing under it made me look like a chubby woman, but I felt like a ninja ready to strike. It took me forty-five minutes to get geared up. Bernard joined me and disguised himself as well.

We left the hotel looking like a couple of women. It was not easy to keep a natural walk with all that stuff strapped to my body. It was a weird feeling, because once again, I felt invisible with people treating us like ghosts. Bernard was all excited to be part of an undercover operation again. We both had been away from this kind of work for a long time.

It was almost surreal. Four years earlier, when I first arrived in Dubai, I would never have thought that I would be walking through the lobby of a hotel in full combat diving gear, under a black robe looking like an Arab woman. It was like a scene from an action movie—or a comedy.

We took Bernard's rental car from the hotel to a breakwater near the coast guard station. The hotel was only five miles away. We got out of the car and walked together to the end of the breakwater. The moon was nearly full and nobody but us was around. I removed my *abayah*, gently entered the water, put on my mask and fitted my mouthpiece. Bernard stayed on the jetty, standing and watching, waiting with my black robe and the bathrobe.

I was breathing pure oxygen; my tank was two-thirds full. I hadn't been able to find a shop with a compressor rated high enough to fill my military grade oxygen tank completely, but I had a good two and a half hours of oxygen, which was more than I needed. I had my watertight tool kit, supplies, and tactical board in hand. A tactical board is a combat diver board with a compass, a timer, and a depth gauge, all used as navigational aids. There is also a bubble level to indicate the horizontal attitude of the diver; when you're in total darkness in the water with no bubbles coming out of the breathing apparatus to trail up to the surface, it is difficult to figure out which way is up.

Because of the darkness of the water, I kept my eyes locked on my glow-in-the-dark instrument board. I had a timer to track my progress, and I used the old and proven technique of counting fin kicks to measure the distance. It is good and accurate for distances less than a mile, but you have to keep focused on the counting so as not to lose track.

The water felt great—cool and soothing. My underwater training from so many years ago kicked in, and I remembered the rhythm I had to maintain to keep a speed of one knot under the water. It was very shallow there, so I maintained a depth of only six feet.

I had to make two changes of direction before entering the fishing port. I made only one dead reckoning to check that I was on track. I came slowly to the surface and stuck the top of my head out of the water to look around and be sure I was where I thought I was. Counting fins kicks is like having a grid in your head—it is necessary when there are no points of reference swimming blind and it keeps you from going crazy thinking you are lost—and it is easy to get lost in pitch black water.

After my count of kicks, I assumed I had just passed the rocks of the jetty at the entrance of the fishing port, so I made a ninety-degree right turn. I swam another twenty-five yards, came back up to the surface and hit the hull of the patrol boat with my hand. Touchdown! I could not see the hull, so I raised my head out of the water and peeked around. It was the police boat. I looked around—all was clear, and after almost a half hour of swimming, I removed my fins and started to climb onto the boat. This was not very practical, because I had a bunch of equipment hanging on my harness and my breathing apparatus on my chest was in the way—and I weighed twenty more pounds now than the last time I had done this. But, high on pure oxygen, I flipped over inside the boat like it was nothing. I didn't want to make any noise either.

Once on the boat, I looked at the coast guard building and gazed around for a good two minutes to make sure nobody had noticed me. I was out of sight of Bernard. It took me five minutes to pull out the three fuel lines I would work on. It was dark and out of the question for me to use any sort of flashlight to do my work. To keep a tactical advantage and be able to work inside the boat, I used a skill I had learned in the secret service to enhance my natural night vision. This is a technique I always use to see in the dark. It is called scotopic vision, and anyone can do it to dramatically improve night vision without the use of any devices.

Our eyes are wonderful organs. The human eye can provide high resolution, focused, and binocular color vision in daylight with the central area of the retina. For the most part, the human eye is primarily a daylight color system and does not work as well at very low illumination levels—unless you know how to use the peripheral area of the retina. The human eye provides us with natural night vision using this peripheral area.

The first technique I used to increase my natural night vision acuity was to focus fifteen degrees off-center. Instead of looking straight at the object, I looked at it a little bit off-center at an angle, so that the image was formed on the peripheral area of my retina, and it became more visible. Then, while still looking at the object off-center, I moved my eyes in a slow, circular scanning motion around the object. Instead of fixed focusing, I slowly and constantly moved my eyes fifteen degrees off center, up and down, right and left.

The second technique I used to prepare my eyes for night vision was to wear dark sunglasses during the day in sunny and bright Dubai, because it helped to preserve the levels of chemicals that enhance night vision inside my retinas. Incidentally, a diet using bilberries helped increase the level of these chemicals, and my thirty minutes' swim under pure oxygen definitively boosted my night vision.

Now inside the coast guard boat, I was able to work on those fuel lines without a flashlight. It took me twenty minutes to operate on the fuel lines and put them back in place. When I was finished, I gathered up all the evidence of my presence, slipped back into the water, and swam back to the breakwater where Bernard was waiting for me. He gave me an all clear sign, and I got out of the water, put my bathrobe right back on over my wet gear, and then put on my *abayah*.

The whole operation took me an hour and a half. We got into the car and returned to the hotel. We had the rest of the night to get as much rest as we could, as we would need it for the next day—Escape Day.

With their fuel lines clogged, the coast guard boat was dead in the water. If I raised an alert while I was leaving, they would not be able to chase me. The other patrol boats were twenty miles away from my exit position. Even if I was detected, it would take the police at least forty minutes just to reach my initial position, and that would give me the time I needed to get to international waters.

On the day of my escape, we had a solid breakfast before we left the hotel. I checked the marine weather forecast and wind patterns on the Internet for the last time, and we went to the marina. Just as I suspected, nobody was around. It was a quiet and peaceful Friday morning—prayer day, so everybody was at the mosques.

The weather was calm, a little foggy with about three miles of visibility, which was perfect to cover my escape. There was a little wind and the surface of the water was flat, which certainly made travel in the inflatable dinghy more appealing and faster. The wind was blowing in a favorable direction, one that would push me all the way to India. We took the dinghy off the sailboat, put it in the water, and prepared it for my escape.

It was a pretty small craft but safe and nearly unsinkable. It was not very comfortable, but it was very maneuverable, lightweight, and it could carry a significant load. In essence—it was a perfect boat for the job.

I inspected the sailboat for the last time to make sure that everything was in order. Bernard and I reviewed our procedures again and checked our portable GPS units to verify our point of rendezvous. I had programmed our units with the same rendezvous point, like clones so there could not be any mistakes. With this modern technology I would say it was easier to find our way on the sea than to find our way on the roads of Dubai.

I may sound like I was confident, like this was an easy trip I was about to take. However, I warn you not to try going out on the high seas in a small craft like this to escape. It is dangerous and can be lethal without long and proper preparation and skills. I'm sure my desperation fueled some of my bravado—but I also had years of experience on the sea and a lot of special training from the military made it less of a gamble for me.

Bernard and I each had a portable satellite phone for our communication once we were out at sea. They are now very small and cheap, but because the batteries were so small, we arranged to keep them off and only connect five minutes every hour to check-in with one another. Our mobile phones would be out of range after two miles, and talking on a VHF radio was out of the question because the coast guard could monitor the radio frequencies.

I had two cans with thirty-five liters of gasoline in each, enough to go 150 miles, if necessary. I wanted plenty of gas in reserve to face any unexpected events. I had water and dry food to last two days at sea and a small tarp for shade. I left my re-breather on the sailboat, but I brought a fishing rod with me to pretend I was fishing in case somebody approached me. I was ready, and it was now or never.

I looked around and checked the marina to see if anybody was watching. It was all clear.

With huge excitement burning inside me, I jumped into the dinghy and started the engine. I had been waiting for this moment for the last two months, and now, here I was—leaving Dubai at last.

I felt the call of the sea again. I just loved the ocean. I waved and said good-bye to Bernard, and I moved away from the sailboat. I passed the marina entry and took a route south with a slight angle off the shoreline to reach my exit point, slowly, in case there was anyone watching who might be suspicious of me going in a straight line out to sea. I changed direction, turned around, circling, pretending to do something other than what I was really doing, but surely going away and away.

As I was increasing the distance between me and the shoreline, I opened up the gas throttle to go full speed ahead. I was now moving at a seventy-degree angle to the shoreline at fifteen miles per hour.

The area I was aiming for was empty of vessels and traffic. Further north was a different story, with lots of cargo ships, tankers waiting for entry into the Fujairah port, ferries taking people to and from the cargo ships, and other marine activities that I didn't want to be around.

There was about three miles of visibility, so I became quickly invisible from the shoreline. I had my binoculars stuck on my eyes, watching every detail on the horizon to see if there were any boats coming towards me. Even a fishing boat would represent a threat to me. It took me two hours to reach international waters.

I was in my element, a part of the ocean, in total solitude, the sky above and moving water all around me. It may seem scary to be alone like that on a small raft on the water, but I knew where I was and what I was doing. With this beautiful weather, I felt so comfortable and totally free. Finally free of those corrupt government officials who had been harassing me for so long.

I didn't want to be in the gray area just outside of territorial waters where police could pursue someone committing a crime. This is why I put the rendezvous point for Bernard and me beyond the twenty-four-mile distance from shore. It was quite far and in the middle of the ocean, but for certain outside the UAE's jurisdiction.

I actually enjoyed this temporary aloneness. There wasn't a soul or a boat in sight. A huge weight lifted from my shoulders. I wasn't all the way home yet, but I was well on my way.

My reverie was interrupted when I checked in with Bernard. He was experiencing some administrative problems at the immigration office on shore because it was Friday. I told him it wasn't just because it was Friday. There were always administrative problems to exit the country. Most of the employees had gone to prayer, so when we talked on the phone, he let me know that it would take three hours for him to have his passport stamped and clear the marina with the sailing permits. I didn't expect it would take that long, but it was still going to fit into our plans. So long as I knew what was going on, I could prepare myself for the wait. I got comfortable and enjoyed the view.

After a while, the beauty of the day started to fade. The sun was terribly hot. I had to drink water every fifteen minutes. Current caused me to drift two miles per hour back towards the territorial waters. I had to start the engine every hour to go back to the rendezvous position. At least it gave me something to do while I was waiting.

While I was stopped, I felt big fish bumping the soft bottom of the dinghy. I played with them a while. The water was so clear I could see them circling around.

Eventually Bernard left the marina and followed his route to the rendezvous point. Going ten miles per hour, it would take him two hours to reach me. I had been waiting five hours, eating peanuts, and playing with fishes when a plane came out of nowhere without warning, flying right over me at a very low altitude, maybe 500 feet.

It was a military patrol plane. I recognized it immediately as a P3 Orion submarine hunter plane. They have that long boom tail which houses a sensor for the detection of the earth magnetic distortion caused by the hull of a submarine. It flew over so quickly that I didn't have the time to identify the markings on the wings. I didn't think the plane was from the UAE, because to my knowledge, the UAE didn't run submarine hunting patrols. It was probably an American or British plane. They had a crew of ten or twelve and were equipped with powerful radar and high-resolution cameras. I was worried my escape was now in jeopardy. I didn't know where it had come from, but I could tell it was going in the direction of Fujairah.

The plane must have spotted me from far away and must have changed direction to make a fly by for identification. My concern was not that the crew would think I was a threat or a fugitive; rather, because I was way too far from shore for a dinghy, even for just fishing, I was worried they might think I was lost and needed to be rescued. That would be a normal reaction when you see a small dinghy in the middle of nowhere. Now I was afraid the pilot would call Fujairah to send a rescue boat to pick me up, and Bernard was still one hour away from rendezvous. I cursed. I could not believe this—out here in the middle of the ocean, to be spotted by a military plane. What were the odds? Just after it flew over me, I jumped on the motor, started the engine, and went full speed in the direction of Fujairah. The plane didn't circle around. It just continued its flight, heading straight to Fujairah. I knew I was still on their radar or camera monitors after they passed me. I wanted to try and show the crew that I was going back to shore and that I was not in need of any rescue. I had one hour before the rendezvous with Bernard and plenty fuel to speed toward the shoreline and convince them I didn't need help. I didn't need to go far—I just wanted them to see that I was able to do it.

Because the closest patrol boat to my area was sabotaged, I estimated it would take at least two hours for a rescue or police boat stationed in Fujairah to come to me—if they had been given the order. I would transfer onto the sailboat before then, so there was no real threat, but it was still a concern.

Damn, I had made the right decision in having disabled the coast guard boat the night before.

The following hour was the longest hour of my life. I kept searching the horizon for boats, making sure no rescue was on its way. But nothing happened, and nobody came. Then I spotted the sailboat with my binoculars, so I went back to the rendezvous point.

The sailboat was still so far away that the mast looked like a toothpick on the horizon. I estimated the distance to be about five miles, which meant about thirty minutes or so waiting time.

Bernard could not see me from that distance, as I was too small and too low on the water, but when we got closer to the rendezvous point we aimed our boats at each other and met up as planned. I threw a line to Bernard, who secured the dinghy, and then I climbed aboard the sailboat. I let out a big sigh of relief and grasped the hand of my friend.. I had been baking in the sun for six hours, and I was glad to have that leg of my journey behind me.

Once on the sailboat together, we continued on our route, away from the area. I was still concerned about the patrol plane. After an hour, we were far away enough to no longer be worried about anything.

The night was falling, and what a beautiful night, the best I have ever experienced. Was I ever glad this day was over. I had done it—I had gotten out of the UAE, and I was on my way to India. I felt immense relief knowing the police and government people were still looking for me, but in all the wrong places. After a year of harassment and threats, I was at last out of that caged country. I kept the upper hand all the way, and they didn't see it coming. I played it by the book and left them no chance to catch me.

Being in a dinghy provided a low profile that did not get the attention of the police. It appeared to others as a mere beach toy when it is so much more. I used to operate the same way twenty years ago, taking hostages out of Lebanon or infiltrating countries. It worked then, and it still works now. It's not likely regulations would change much, even after my secrets are revealed to the government of the UAE. It would be an administrative nightmare to try and regulate every little dinghy that's over there, and it would only make the life of every other normal weekend sailor miserable.

While Bernard and I were sailing away, I was overwhelmed by a double feeling of freedom, being in open sea and being released from the claws of the Dubai government.

I looked back to watch my nightmares recede behind me. After the dreams of the beginning, after I gained popularity with my submarines, I had stepped onto a higher platform. And it was Sultan who had decided to pull it from under my feet. In the end, he didn't want me to leave Dubai a better man. He wanted to take me apart, making sure that I would leave the country broken.

Sultan had let me down. He'd ordered his auditors to go after me for personal reasons, and they had kept me hostage for a full year. But they could not break me, and they could not bring me down. I never gave up, never gave them the money they wanted from me, never signed their confessions.

By now, it had already been three weeks since my no-show at the meeting with Sultan. I could only imagine everyone's embarrassment, not knowing my whereabouts, and their frustration when I would not pick up the phone. With close to a million dollar bounty, for sure they were looking for me. The prosecutor was left with an open case and no defendant. I was laughing because they had no idea I was on my way to India, free and sailing away with the ocean breeze blowing through my hair. I managed to send my family back home, I successfully shipped my household and my cars, and the only things I left behind were my passport, a lot of money and my 400 gallon salt water aquarium.

It was beautiful and I regret having to leave it behind—but it was too big and too complicated to take apart. I had tried to sell it before, but expatriates would not buy a huge aquarium for a temporary stay. Forget the Emiratis; if they were interested in fish, it was the cooked kind. I ended up donating it to a school, under the condition that they would remove it from my house. I left the key to my house in my door, so they just had to go there, take it apart, and move it away. I did get some value out of donating the aquarium, though. By checking in with the school, I would know if the police or the auditors had stormed my house. That would give me some idea what stage they were in looking for me. Nothing happened, and I hope the children will enjoy that small piece of the undersea world I left behind.

I lost a lot of money as a result of this ordeal, but I was free. My determination and my accomplishments had paid off. I may have been a retired spy—a little bit older, rustier, and carry a few more pounds—but I had written my own destiny. I was still able to do what needed to be done to survive, on my terms. I would never go back to Dubai.

I'd turned the page already; Dubai was history, my mind was already in India. I would find a better life back home. In the middle of the immensity of the ocean on my small boat, I reached plenitude.

After we passed the fifty miles mark, I took a heading east-north-east to catch some winds in the main sail.

Hervé Jaubert

Chapter 9

The Crossing

I was sailing the boat with Bernard, relaxing and thinking, and preparing the procedure for my arrival in India. There wasn't enough wind to give me a ten-knot cruising speed, so, like I had expected, I had to run the engine.

Sailboats are the best option for traveling on the sea. Combining wind and motor reduces fuel consumption significantly. You can circle the world and go anywhere. Sure, it takes longer because it goes slowly—slowly but surely, just like the tortoise in the old adage. Sailboats are also safer and more stable in rough seas. Even if the boat capsized in a storm, it would return to its normal upright position due to the ballast in the keel. A capsized power boat does not return to an upright position and is doomed thereafter. Best you can do on a sailboat caught up in a storm is to reduce the sails, close all the hatches, throw a drift anchor, duck, and just wait for the end of the storm. It is scary and very uncomfortable. But if there are no obstacles, it is relatively safe.

After the first day we had our routine—gourmet cooking on a small stove, Internet connections, boat maintenance, and watch. We didn't have much entertainment, no TV, no radio. As we didn't have radar onboard, we had to keep an eye out on the horizon, especially at night, looking for navigation lights from other ships to avoid accidents.

It happens all the time—you sail for days without seeing anybody, but the first boat you see on the horizon is heading straight at you. The sooner you see it, the better you can change course to avoid collision.

Radar gives audible warnings of oncoming boats so you can sleep. But, without it, if I didn't have Bernard, I would not have been able to sleep more than two hours at a time. Bernard and I worked out a routine where we would take shifts watching for oncoming boats. We each got to sleep six hours at a time. I got the evening shifts, 8:00 p.m. until 2:00 a.m.

One danger on any boat is the risk of fire, and we experienced one during our journey when the gas hose came off its fitting on the stove. When I turned on the gas to cook lunch, released gas ignited all over the stove. I grabbed the extinguisher and screamed at Bernard, who was on the deck to open the hatch and close the propane tank valve. He took five long seconds to do it. I was holding onto the trigger of the extinguisher, looking at the flames, ready to shoot. I didn't want to create more of a mess with the extinguisher dust, but at the same time, I was making sure the fire didn't get out of control. Fortunately, it didn't burn long enough to cause damage to the cabin, which fortunately was built out of fire retardant material. The cooking stove and area around it was blackened, but the black marks came off with a swipe. It was a serious reminder to us that any accident on the boat would be a serious problem as long as we were closer to Gulf Cooperation Council countries than India. Because, in case of an emergency, we would be rescued by and sent to the closest country. We had to observe extra precautions to prevent any accidents, and in case of a catastrophic emergency, I had two backups—the dinghy, of course, and a life raft. The winds were pushing us to India, so in the event we had to ditch the boat, we could just wait to drift close enough to India before we would make the emergency call.

On the third day, we had another emergency. Early in the morning, during an inspection, I found a lot of water in the bilge (the space between the hull and the floor)—at least 200 gallons. I didn't know where it had come from, but Murphy's Law sure seemed to be working well on my boat. When a problem occurs, it is always at the worst time. And just when you think everything is going to be okay, another one crops up.

Normally, water in the bilge is automatically evacuated from the boat by a bilge pump. The pump drains any water in the bottom of the boat and dumps it outboard. So not only did I have a leak somewhere, but the bilge pump was not working. I had two manual pumps onboard, so we pumped water into buckets for two hours and dumped it overboard to remove all of the water.

Then I looked for the leak. It didn't take me a long time to find it. It was a faulty gasket on the propeller shaft. There was no way I could have predicted this. I checked the propeller shaft and sea trialed the boat before, and there had been no leaks. And trust me—I am good in finding leaks. I build submarines.

It probably happened because Sheikh Khaled hadn't used his boat for such a long time, causing the seal to dry up, get weak, and become loose as soon as it was put to work. It was not a big leak in the scheme of things, but it was big enough to be a concern. I fixed the gasket and stopped the leak, but I could not repair the bilge pump; it had to be replaced.

This wasn't all bad news though, because this problem gave me the idea and the perfect pretext for our arrival in India. I hatched a plan for how I would get away with arriving without a passport. When we got closer to India, I would loosen the gasket again and let the boat fill up with water. With a faulty bilge pump and water coming in, I would have full justification for entering Indian waters without a visa or a passport. I turned a problem into an advantage, and I actually didn't have much more to do to stage an accident. I sent another silent thank you to Sheikh Khaled for selling me his boat with a built-in excuse to get into India without a visa.

After the leak incident, I checked the bilge twice a day. Although I was very excited about my escape, it was not time to celebrate yet. There was no party, and there was no swimming in the ocean. I didn't want to take any risks or delay our arrival, even by a little bit. I only allowed myself a glass of Grand Marnier at sunset every day, with a cheer to Sultan—"Here's mud in your eye—you back stabbing liar."

We passed Iran, and were now off Pakistan. We still had a long way to go to get to India.

Nights were strange. They would start pitch black after sunset with no moon and a fog that hung in the air around us half a mile away. We were sailing in a hole of clear weather in the middle of a fog, and it looked like a curtain of fog in circle around the boat. I could not see the stars or the horizon. Later, after two hours, the moon would rise and lighten the night.

Nights would always bring curious sightings, like phosphorescent plankton stirred to glow with the hull cutting through the water or lights in the sky, too low to be of an airplane, and too high to be of a structure on the water—impossible to identify through the fog. With little wind, the humming of the engine was the only sound I could hear.

We didn't have air conditioning on the boat, so it was not very comfortable and we could not sleep well in the heat. We left the hatches open to cool the cabin off a little with the night breeze. I spent most of the day on the deck, enjoying the air and the wide open sea, looking forward to my arrival in India. The cabin was a little claustrophobic and too hot during the day.

Sometimes we had visitors, dolphins swimming around and jumping next to the boat and dozens of flying fish, jumping out of the water and planing. Bernard tried fishing, pulling three lines behind us. It was good we had plenty of food so we didn't have to count on his fishing to feed us—because the only thing he caught during those eight days was a single baby tuna fish.

I called my wife Helen everyday on the satellite phone—giving her my status and position so she could log it and track my journey with Goggle Earth. Three days into the sea, I changed the registration of the boat, and I downloaded the new paperwork and certificates. We were on a different boat now, with a different number and different flag, which would make us much more difficult to track—though I thought it very unlikely he could have followed me this far. I was three lifetimes ahead of Abdul Qader, Sultan and Butti, who would never figure out how I pulled this stunt.

We passed Pakistan and were getting closer to Mumbai. At this point, things started looking different. There was a shift in the direction of the few ships we encountered. More were going in the direction of India—as opposed to the beginning of our trip when ships were headed towards the Persian Gulf.

Finally, the time had come to begin the process of securing my entry into India. Two days before our arrival in India, I initiated the arrival plan. I called the French consulate in Mumbai with my satellite phone to report an emergency at sea. I reported that while in route to the Maldives we were taking water through the propeller shaft and the bilge pump was not working. I reported that during a partial flood of the cabin and as we were moving our bags outside to keep them from getting wet, we lost two bags that fell off the deck into the water and sunk. Unfortunately, my passport was in one of them. I told the consulate that I didn't need to be rescued but that I needed to enter India to repair the boat and request a replacement for my passport, after which I would leave India.

I knew this would cause some confusion at the consulate. This situation may have never occurred before because are so few people traveling by sailboat, and even less having an accident at sea. I was counting on this confusion to help me. India has a heavy and complex bureaucracy, but my boat emergency would help me through it. It was perfectly understandable that one could lose his passport at sea. This does not happen in a commercial plane. First, you can't board a plane without a passport, and second, if you lose it, it can't be far.

Airport authorities are also very familiar with and prepared for crazy stories from travelers who try to invent anything to justify illegal entry. So when the police face an unusual situation, there is no confusion. Routines and professionalism take over, and most often, they uncover the truth behind made up scenarios.

But when it comes to an accident at sea on a private boat, nobody is prepared. It just does not happen. They would have no choice but to accept my accounts.

Once in Mumbai, with a new passport and an exit visa, the authorities would be more than happy to see me leave the country either by boat or by plane to wherever I wanted—so they could close this administrative issue. After the repairs, I planned to contract a broker to sell the boat, as it was not in my intention to continue on sea.

The French consulate told me they would call the port authorities upon our arrival to help us with the entry procedures. I knew their call would never find its way to the proper authorities, but it didn't matter. For the records, I officially reported the accident and the loss of my passport and requested a new one to replace the confiscated one by Dubai Police, at Sultan's request. But of course I wasn't going to tell them this part of the story.

We were approaching India when we encountered some heavy weather. At about 300 miles offshore, there was a strong wind and a well-formed sea. I shut down the engine and the boat was going a good ten knots under sail. It was magnificent, going up and down six foot waves. I didn't have a rain coat and I was soaked by splashes of water breaking on the deck. At night it was beautiful and warm. The moon was up and shining, reflecting on the waves.

I changed my heading; the boat was taking the swell from the side so she was rolling like crazy with Bernard down in the cabin trying to get some sleep. Ahead, the lights of small vessels indicated some traffic. Later in the night, as I got closer, I identified fishing boats— rather small ones, about twenty-five feet in length. I was surprised to see so many fishermen there in such small boats this far from India. Then, for the next twelve hours we didn't see anyone.

Around seventy miles from the coast of India, I approached a restricted area, an oil field owned by the government of India. As indicated on the map, no vessels were allowed to enter this area because of the oil extraction and the presence of a lot of structures and oil rigs sticking out of the water presenting a hazard.

I wanted to go through this restricted area for many reasons: first, it was a shortcut to avoid a 150 mile detour, which equated to about fifteen hours of sailing; and second, there would be very little chance that I would encounter any police or military vessels for the next fifty miles. Restricted areas were commonly patrolled by private security companies, not national law enforcements such as the coast guard, police, or navy; also there is a separation in the chain of information, and direct reporting was unlikely. I believed no one would make it difficult for me. I was hoping to get stopped by a security patrol of some sort, so that they would keep a report of my entry into the restricted area for emergency reasons, but without investigating it because they aren't qualified to. This report could later endorse my story, when I would find myself in the immigration office telling it to them. I would know their report would be somewhere to back me up—to show good faith and total innocence.

My maps clearly showed the restricted area and its boundaries, but since Mumbai was not my official destination, I was not supposed to know because I would not have any maps. However, during my career as a secret agent, I always used maps against the people who depended on them, so they would never find me. The secret is to use the map and the terrain to go where nobody is looking. People are lazy—when they have a map, they follow the routes that are indicated on it. But a map is never perfect and sometimes paths or updated roads are not put on the map. I always made sure to take those paths, knowing no one would search a route that was not on the map. This is thinking outside the box. If I had one piece of advice to give to anyone, that would be the one. Two times in my career, in the former Soviet Republics and in the Middle East, I escaped a lethal situation using paths that were not on the map. No one ever thought to put a roadblock there.

Restricted areas are even a better distraction. Because they are labeled as such, everybody is making the assumption that nobody goes there. The public assumes it's covered by law enforcement officers waiting to catch people straying inside the limits. Bad guys think it is patrolled by the police. And the police think it is a waste of time to patrol an empty area. So, restricted areas are left to some private security guards who are unprepared, unmotivated, bored to death, and outside the chain of command. It was a perfect choice for me to approach India without being detected by law enforcement.

We reached the restricted area in the early morning. It was strange—the wind had dropped but was steady and the sea was calm with a long swell. I ran the engine again to keep up my speed; I had enough fuel to reach India even without wind. There were abandoned oil rigs all over. They looked like gigantic arachnids—junk, metallic, skeleton monsters and rusty. No wonder it was off limits to sail there. It was dangerous, creepy; an amazing sight.

Already the scenery looked different. After two hours of sailing in the restricted zone, I saw a huge platform on the horizon, dead ahead. Smoke was coming from it, indicating some human activity. Boats surrounded it. I kept my course, hoping to get near the platform and gain the attention of the security guards. I got closer and closer, but nobody seemed to be paying attention to us. Eventually, I passed the oil rig about 300 yards to port. Some people were working; a helicopter dropped off others and headed to another platform two miles away.

I continued, as nobody seemed to be paying attention to my boat, but after half a mile on our course, a boat that looked like a fishing boat came toward us. She was quite slow and started using her horn to signal us to stop. Because the boat was going so slow, I knew they would never catch up. I didn't know what they were after, so I slowed down and waited for them to reach us.

As they got closer, I identified some men in uniform on the boat. It looked strange to see people in uniform on an old, wooden fishing boat. When they reached us, they identified themselves as oil rig security, although there were no signs, markings or anything indicating it was a security vessel.

There were two officers in blue uniforms and six crew members in red jumpsuits. They were trying to impress us; one of them held a machine gun on a bipod pretending to be ready to shoot at any moment, but there were no belt rounds loaded to it. It was an old MG42, the infamous WW2 German Burp Machine Gun. It was an old design, but a good gun—which explained why it was still in use. I trusted they were who they said they were, and began my act. This was the opportunity I had been looking for. I told them about the leak on the propeller shaft, the water inside the boat, the loss of my documents, and my decision to go through the area to get to Mumbai quickly for repairs.

I invited them to come onboard so they could see the damage and the water on the floor. After about ten minutes, they let down their guard and became friendly. One of them told us they had become nervous when they saw us, because it was quite unusual to see tourists in this area. In the last five years he had worked there, they had not seen a single foreign boat around, let alone a sailboat. We found out that the whole site is strategic because it provides natural gas to India. I had been right—nobody was sailing there.

I let them use my satellite phone so they could surprise their families with an unexpected phone call. I gave them some cookies and tea. They were not suspicious at all. The fact that Bernard and I were French and being on a sailboat helped a lot. I bought 200 liters of fuel from them for $100—a good deal for everybody. It's not that I really needed it, but I wanted to look like we had problems.

The guy who seemed to be the officer in charge of the group prepared a report, and after one more hour of talking, we left the area in the same direction we had been headed before. They told me they would report the accident and radio Immigration to make them aware of our arrival, which I was sure they would never do. VHF radios cannot transmit that far. It was not a completely innocent gesture when I offered them the use of my satellite phone. I wanted to verify they had limited phone or radio contact with the continent. So it confirmed my suspicions when they jumped at the chance to use my phone. They didn't have contact—or if they did, it was limited.

I crossed what was left of the oil rig restricted area, and I put the boat on a course to Mumbai. We were getting closer. We could tell by the changes in the water around us. When we were still fifty miles away, I saw yellow and black striped sea snakes swimming across my path. Later, a couple of dolphins followed us for about fifteen minutes. I felt like they were my welcoming committee.

I reached Mumbai territorial waters at one o'clock in the morning under the cover of a moonless night, in total darkness. Nobody would be able to identify my boat, see the registration on the hull or my French flag, so nobody would stop me to check our documents. Nevertheless, I was surprised by the insane traffic. Cargo ships and all kind of vessels were arriving from all directions. The radio was screaming in different languages, and everybody was talking to one another. I wondered how much crazier it could be during the daytime. It was difficult to find safe passage through these congested, pitch-black waters. With no visibility and no radar, I had to pay extra attention to the navigation lights of the other vessels to make sure I was not on a collision course with anyone.

We crossed an Indian Navy war ship 100 yards portside that had no lights on. I easily recognized her black shadow silhouette and big guns. They ignored me. As a former navy officer, I was happy to see some busy seamen. At last I was seeing some real navy ships at sea, not like the ones in Dubai that were just for show. In the four years I was in Dubai, I never saw, not even once, a UAE Navy ship going out to sea. The Exomos building was next to the Navy base. Every morning when I went to work, the war ships were berthed, always at the same place. From what I heard from the French military contractors I knew, the UAE Navy grounded three frigates during delivery trials two years earlier.

Given the heavy boat traffic, I followed the channels and buoys indicated on the map so I could get to the port without incident. It was like a virtual highway—there were no markings on the water, only buoys and lights. But this time, I was not going to follow a route that wasn't on the map. We arrived at the port two hours later in the middle of the traffic. Like I had suspected, no one from the oil rig had called on the radio. So no one was there to stop me or call me on the radio to ask me for documentation. I didn't radio the port either; I just slipped into port without being noticed.

I was not going to stop and report to the port authorities, so I decided to anchor the boat in the bay close to the Mumbai gateway like a tourist. I had several pictures of the marina and the gateway, with the beautiful and majestic Taj Mahal Hotel on the waterfront, but in the middle of the night the pictures were not very helpful—especially with so many boats and floating obstacles around. It would have been difficult to find a mooring or dock in the dark. I preferred to wait for the next morning to see exactly where I was.

I dropped the anchor about 1,000 yards from shore, secured the anchor line, took down the sails, and took a good look around. Nobody seemed to have noticed my arrival. I could see the city, hotels, cars, and people in my binoculars. I stayed there for about an hour on the deck, excited by this sighting and the thought of finally being in India. I observed the port, and then I went to my bunk for a few hours' sleep.

Bernard and I woke up the next morning with the boat rolling from one side to the other like a giant was shaking the boat. I thought initially that we had drifted and got grounded, but it was only a sensation caused by the strong wind and choppy waters.

Up on the deck, I took in my first sight of Mumbai. It was an amazing feeling. I left Dubai eight days ago and now I felt like I was in a different world. I left a place which meant to harm me, to find myself in another country—a much friendlier country. It was Sunday morning, and the consulate was closed. I had to wait until Monday to call and notify them of my arrival.

The area where we dropped anchor was too far and unstable to stay another night, so I raised the anchor and moved the boat to the gateway of India Marina. I was prepared to respond to immigration officers or the police, being new inside the area, but as we got closer it seemed unlikely that anyone would show up. Nobody seemed to bother with formalities like immigration at this busy port. There were at least 200 yachts and recreational boats moored in front of the gateway. It was busy with a lot of boaters going out, quite normal for a weekend. I had no problem finding a buoy to tie the boat to.

Bernard cursed at the line he pulled out of the water—it was filthy and covered with some sort of disgusting muck. I couldn't keep from laughing. He managed to secure the boat with a repulsed look on his face.

"Next time, I am the skipper," he said with a funny look on his face.

I double-checked the line to see that we were not drifting. The last thing I wanted was to damage another boat without having a passport, papers, or insurance. Once I knew we were secure, I shut down the engine. I expected to stay in India two weeks. This was enough time to get a new passport, clear Indian immigration, and take a flight back to the U.S.

I called my wife. She was happy to know I had arrived safe and sound, although she didn't seem to be surprised. I may be a sailor and former operative, but this was not a picnic, I told her.

I was thinking of what would have happened if my trip had been the other way, with an emergency arrival in a Dubai Marina rather than an Indian Marina. I know it would have been a most unwelcome experience in comparison.

In Dubai, thirty minutes after a foreign boater arrives, a marina official comes onboard to notify the captain he has to leave within the hour because there are no available berths and he cannot stay there. Then, the captain would have to report to the Dubai police station in town where immigration officers would fine the passengers and the captain for bypassing the immigration office, and take their passport for investigation. The marina official would not be lying.

It is true there are no available berths in Dubai. All they have available for visitors are a couple of buoys for which they charge $300 per day, without access to fresh water or power. Fujairah is the same; Bernard had to stay docked at the petrol station because there were no available berths.

Here I was, in India, anchored 200 yards from the waterfront. From the boat, the view was fantastic. I could see the Gateway of India, the Taj Mahal Hotel, thousands of people in colorful attire, and wooden ferry boats taking people to Elephant Island across the bay. The Gateway of India is an unmistakable landmark, a large monument on the waterfront, with a huge esplanade where thousands of people gather. This was the departure point for the British troops when they left India in 1948. I didn't get to India through their back door, but through a main point of interest.

After we checked everything on the boat, we put the dinghy in the water, started the outboard, and headed for the Gateway of India. The water was really disgusting, with garbage floating everywhere. There was a lot of activity—people swimming in the filthy water, and small boats and passenger vessels going in and out.

I took the dinghy to a boat ramp next to the gateway, like everybody else seemed to be doing. I threw a line to a guy standing there who secured the dinghy alongside, and I jumped up onto the ramp. I gave him a one-dollar bill tip—for this much money he would keep an eye on my dinghy for the entire day. Then I passed a gate up the ramp and walked to the street.

At last, I was walking the streets of Mumbai, among Indian people and visitors; some looked at me as if I were just another tourist. Little did they know that in this post-Mumbai bombing era of enhanced scrutiny and security, I had made it to this country without a passport and walked the streets without even being checked for ID. I walked out from a beach in the United Arab Emirates to walk in the streets in Mumbai, all the way in a transparent bubble, without a single uniform to check me. Mumbai had been bombed two weeks prior to my arrival and was on high alert. That didn't prevent me from getting into the country unchecked. Scary to think about, really. It wasn't that I came through because of a glitch, either. I came through because I dared to, and I knew how to get around obstacles. It was like living in a parallel world where rules and values didn't apply the same way.

I crossed the street and walked to the Taj Mahal Hotel—and saw that it was a marvel of history, architecture, and craftsmanship. It was impressive, to say the least. I changed some dollars for the local currency, and I invited Bernard for a real solid breakfast.

We spent the rest of the day visiting the city and shopping. Later we returned to the boat. Everything was normal. Nobody came to the boat or checked anything.

The next morning, after a sweaty night, we both went onshore. I called the French Consulate to report that I had arrived in Mumbai and to schedule an appointment to file an application for a replacement passport.

Later that same day, I squeezed myself into a taxi to go to my appointment at the French consulate. The taxis were very small there, with no air conditioning. They're old and have been all fixed up, and they run on natural gas. Now, thanks to my trip through the restricted area, I knew where the gas came from. The huge restricted area was an oil field and a gas reserve for the country. Thousands of taxis were available everywhere in town. There were so many there was no waiting. The traffic was insane—drivers passing each other with only a few millimeters to spare, and without causing accidents.

I could tell the city was on alert because there were armed soldiers at the entrances of buildings. I met with the consulate officer, and I told him my story. He told me he was sorry for my troubles and confessed that it was unusual. In the ten years he had been working at the French consulate, it was the first time he had to deal with a lost passport at sea on a private boat.

Before my passport was confiscated by the police in Dubai, I had taken the precaution of making several color copies. I scanned them and emailed them to myself through my VPN so I could download them and print them from anywhere in the world by just accessing my email account. I did this in front of the consulate officer, going online at his desk and printing a copy of my lost passport. He was able to use this copy to check my identity and process the request that usually takes forty-eight hours. Then I would get a replacement passport valid for one year.

Although a demand for a replacement passport is filed and processed in the local consulate, it has to be approved by the consulate with which you are registered or by the office that issued the lost passport. Before going to Dubai, I was registered at the consulate of Miami. I had never registered at Dubai's French consulate as required. It wasn't that I had planned anything, it was just that I was reluctant to go through the administrative procedures.

My reluctance was my luck. Thanks to my not registering with the Dubai French Consulate, my request had to be approved by Miami and not Dubai. If I had needed to depend on the Dubai consulate, I might have been in trouble. The French consulate in Mumbai would have contacted Dubai and might have learned that my passport was not lost, but had been confiscated by the police. I wondered if the French Consulate would have authorized the issue of a replacement passport in this case. They would have been in a difficult position and could have later been blamed by the Dubai government for having given the authorization to renew a confiscated passport.

The Miami office didn't give a damn about the UAE, nor did it know anything about my situation in Dubai. So, not surprisingly, Miami approved my replacement passport. The Miami consulate only required that I renew my registration card once I got back to Miami. I forgot it was due, but I was more than happy to proceed as soon as I was back in the U.S.

I now had two days to wait before I could get my new passport. The consulate gave me a credential letter so I could report the loss of my passport to the police. This was necessary in order to regularize my entry in India and to get an exit visa for my departure from India. It was an emergency exit visa—not a visa to stay in the country. Once the exit visa was issued, I was required to leave the country on the next available flight. It was not my intention to overstay anyway. I went to the police station to report the loss of my passport. All I had to do was file a form and answer a couple of questions, and I received a receipt with a stamp.

A passport and a valid visa were required to check into an international hotel in India. Without them, it was a problem to get a decent room. According to immigration officials and the police, I was supposed to stay on the boat, but I had had enough of the sailboat— with her rolling like crazy, with the lack of comfort, and with the lack of air-conditioning. I tried to get a room in local hotels where I could check in without documents, but these rooms didn't have showers or any modern comforts.

Bernard was in the same spot. Although he had his passport, he didn't have a visa. I went to the Oberoi Trident Hotel, a famous international hotel, to see if I could find a way to get a room. Bernard was trying the same at the Taj Mahal Hotel. We were both successful. I improvised and took advantage of the confusion created by a group of twenty tourists who were just checking in. I managed to get an additional room pretending to be in the group and paid cash in advance so they would never find out.

Bernard, on the other hand, was not so lucky. He hooked up with a lady—a tourist from France. She was a very nice lady, but way too old for him. Because I got lucky with my room, he didn't have to do anything he would regret later for a shower and soft bed with the lady. We ended up sharing just like we had in Dubai.

In spite of the reason we were there, Mumbai was worth the trip. Everything looked different here. It was a different world altogether— a very interesting city to visit. Misery is everywhere. It reaches out and touches you, as beggars and people with birth defects catch you by the arm to ask for money or food. If you make the mistake of giving them anything, you end up with a whole street of people after you.

The people are crazy drivers, but, curiously, in the one week I was there, I didn't see a single accident. It was better to move around in taxis than rent a car and try to drive in the incomprehensible traffic. Taking a taxi is an experience in itself. The price is a bargain, if you negotiate it. This is something I found irritating—constantly having to negotiate the price for everything. In Mumbai, you are surrounded by poverty and misery, but the price of a hotel room is outrageously expensive. I didn't see how nationals could afford it with the going wages there.

The crowds were impressive. People were everywhere, occupying every single square foot of the ground. It was a very colorful country. The traditional dress of the people is loud and bright. I could feel the history of this place, just by looking at the buildings, the stones, and the architecture. I felt peace and freedom, as if I were on a vacation. I was very happy to not see any white *khandouras* anymore. I never understood why the Emiratis never embraced variety. For all of them to dress the same blocks their minds and free will. At last in Mumbai I felt enriched, seeing people dressed in different outfits and colors.

Two days later, I returned to the French Consulate to get my new passport. I felt like I was somebody again. You don't know what it means to not have a passport until yours is taken away. You truly lose your identity and your ability to function as a human being in society. Emiratis know it well and take advantage of that to keep people hostage and off balance. Now that I had my passport, I turned to getting my exit visa. I expected that getting it from Indian immigration would take some time and involve some complex bureaucracy, but I didn't expect how much of a problem it would be.

I went to the immigration office in Mumbai Port with the police report. I presented my documents and my new passport and told them my story.

Right away I knew there was something wrong. The immigration officers were not too happy, and they had a problem with my story. They didn't accuse me of anything, but they were angry that somebody could just walk into their country, unchecked. They phoned the police, the navy, and the coast guard in front of me to question them and ask them if they had any records of my arrival. The immigration officer told me they had to check records with other agencies to put in the file; he explained to me that they could not just close the file without some explanations or a report from somebody. Bureaucracy at work. They were trying to understand how a boat could have entered into the country without being detected by any of their law enforcement.

Mumbai is not a small town on a remote shoreline. It is a big city with a major commercial, political, economic, financial and demographic influence. Mumbai has vital government buildings, a port, an international airport, a navy base, a coast guard base, and police. It is a tourist destination with travelers coming from all over the world. It is altogether a sensitive location, which has been targeted by terrorists. The worst of these attacks happened very recently, in the very same hotels where I stayed, causing the deaths of more than 200 people. I understood why they were so upset and wanting answers. My undetected arrival was a major security issue. Already the authorities were quite concerned about terrorists smuggling arms and explosives from neighboring countries, and there I was, strolling into the country, making it seem as if nobody had done his job to check me as I arrived in full view in the port.

If I managed to get to the Mumbai streets from the ocean without anyone stopping me, it's easy to see that determined terrorists with guns and bombs could do the same. We know now that the terrorists who attacked Mumbai in November 2008 came from the sea on a hijacked fishing boat; then went onshore with a dinghy. These officials were right to be concerned about my entry.

I told them it was not my fault that I had not been detected. I didn't try to evade anybody, and that I had been checked by an oil rig security crew. I told them I called on the radio when we arrived but nobody responded or understood me. That part was not true; I really didn't call on the radio, and I had no intentions of calling at the time I was out there. But this fact was unverifiable, and I knew it. They were not able to reach the security crew on the oil rig, but that didn't surprise me. I doubted they would get any report any time soon. I would be long gone before they received anything.

Before issuing my exit visa, the immigration authorities needed to sort out and understand the problem of my undetected entry. But I was not about to give them any more details. I stuck to my story. I kept it short and simple, and continued to play the tourist who innocently came through the door because it was left opened.

The officers worked on the problem for three days. They came on my boat, not really to inspect it, but rather to see how it looked. In the end they just had to let me exit the country without the verified report they were waiting for. So, they asked me to write a statement with all the details that I had already given them.

Because of their bureaucracy, I had to do it three times, in three different offices. It took me six hours. The immigration officer who acted as my escort was very nice to drive me around the city to go to the different offices. Eventually, I returned to the immigration office, they offered me tea and sweets, stamped my passport, and gave me the exit visa. They will know now the exact circumstances of my entry into India, and I hope it helps them secure their procedures.

I had done them a favor though, by exposing a hole in their security. I didn't mean them any harm. I considered myself a refugee. I didn't mean to maliciously break any Indian laws or to take advantage of its officers. They didn't try to make it hard on me. They treated me with respect and were very friendly.

My entry illustrates the difficult issue they have to resolve because it is almost impossible to control small boats and recreational vessels on the water unless you turn the country into a Big Brother regime. Nobody ever pays attention to sailboats or dinghies and their friendly appearances...except Dubai.

Dubai does pay attention to every vessel of every type. But over there it is not to prevent insertion of terrorists—it is to keep people inside the country. The government would not hesitate to put more patrol boats to watch the sea for every sailboat and dinghy increasing the already inconvenient pressure on boaters and discouraging tourism and leisure on the water. Because as much as they'd like to, they cannot put a fence in the water along the limit of the territorial waters. Even if they had an electronic fence provided by a network of radar systems, they would still need the officers and the boats to patrol the waters.

With my new passport and exit visa, I was ready to book a flight to return to the U.S. I was looking for a direct flight to New York with no chance of getting diverted to the UAE in case of an emergency. I didn't want to even think about the possibility that I could be up in the air, on my way home, and then be diverted to some Gulf country because of mechanical problems.

I would not leave any stone unturned. I had to check everything. Too much was at stake for everything to be ruined so close to the end. I have seen this happen before. It was not just my paranoid musings. A businessman from India was wanted in Dubai. One day he took a flight from India to Egypt. In mid-flight, there was a problem with the airplane, which caused the crew to make an unscheduled landing in Dubai. All the passengers were taken to a nearby five-star hotel, all expenses paid. All of them but this guy. The police took him to the central prison, and I don't know what happened to him after that—but I'll bet whatever it was, it was bad and long.

I decided to go with Air India because they had a direct flight from Bombay to New York, and it avoided GCC airspace—perfect. Given the chaos I had gone through to get here, I indulged myself with a first-class ticket. This was no ordinary flight—it was a return home after a year of nightmares, and a daring, against-all-odds escape.

Bernard booked a flight to return to France the next day. With everything in hand—my ticket, flight reservation, visa, and passport—I went back to the marina to sign a sales agreement with the local broker to sell my sailboat. There were more chances to sell it in Mumbai than in Dubai anyway. Mumbai was a larger market with more people sailing sailboats and with more freedom to buy and register a boat.

Two days later we left the hotel, six hours before my flight. Check-in was four hours before takeoff, and there was a two-hour transit through the traffic jams of Mumbai. We made it to the airport after a long tour of the colorful and populated city. I left Bernard at the lounge. We said good-bye, and I gave him a big, heartfelt thank you for his help. This is how true friendship works, and for sure I would return the favor to him—anytime, anywhere, in any way.

At the airport, my new passport and exit visa were stamped by Immigration without even one raised eyebrow; I had all the required paperwork. I boarded the plane. It was a first for me. I had never flown Air India before. I was impressed, and I would definitely recommend it. It is an excellent company, with good service, good food and very comfortable seating. The lady next to me was Indian. She worked in New York and on her way back after a vacation in India. "What about you?" she asked me after we started a conversation. "What is a Frenchman doing on an Indian plane from Mumbai to JFK?"

I looked at her with a smile on my face and told her, "You would not believe me if I told you."

Chapter 10

Back Home

I landed in New York, passed through U.S. Immigration control without a glitch, and took my connecting flight to Miami.

My wife, along with my children, picked me up at the airport. I don't have to tell you how emotional our reunion was.

At last it was all over. I was safe in the United States. I fought against the Dubai government and I won back my freedom. I had gone head-to-head against the most powerful businessman in Dubai, who used the police and his auditors against me with no chance of justice, but I had come out ahead. My escape was complete.

Ironically, my Dubai experience started and ended the same way: on a once-in-a-lifetime opportunity, so to speak. I arrived in Dubai on a red carpet, with all doors opened for me, transported by private jet, chauffeured in Porsche Cayennes, to build one-of-a-kind vessels—but I eventually wound up launching a dinghy from the beach to escape from the same people who had invited me—and left Dubai running for my life.

My experience was an adventure that needed to be told. Now that I was free and far from these people, I decided to write my story.

The title was easy; *Escape from Dubai* is self-explanatory. I didn't just flee the country, I escaped with no passport on a 1,300 mile trip across the ocean. I would also need a website to support the marketing of my book, so I reserved the domain name www.escapefromdubai.com, and started to work on its design.

Six months later, I had completed my first draft and presented it to reporters and editors. In December 2008, Greg, a reporter at Bloomberg, wanted to write an article about it. He interviewed me, and for two months he investigated my accounts. He traveled to Europe and Dubai chasing Sultan for comments, to get his side of the story. As

I warned Greg, Sultan was not keen to speak about me. He dodged meetings with Greg seven times.

But eventually, in February 2009, Greg got to talk to him and told him the subject of his interview: "Hervé Jaubert escaped the country on a boat and is writing a book." It was as if Greg had dropped a bomb. Until then, Sultan and everybody else at Dubai World thought I was still in Dubai hiding somewhere. With a copy of my documents, Greg confronted Sultan and caught him in lies several times, especially when he showed him a copy of my passport that supported some of my files. A couple of days later he saw Sultan during a press gathering, screaming in a burst of anger about how Bloomberg was trying to destroy Dubai World with negative reports. Such an outburst was unheard of from Sultan, who is a very quiet and calm man. To see him out of control shows the state of panic lying underneath.

After he completed his investigation, Greg went to the airport to fly out of Dubai, but he didn't make it through immigration. He was detained by Amn Al Dawla police officers. Sultan Bin Sulayem is a powerful man. He can unleash the secret police on anyone who wants to speak the truth about his company. For ten hours, Greg was questioned about his contacts in Dubai and the sources of his information. Eventually, Bloomberg pulled the story because of the threat of losing their wire news terminals throughout the Middle East, being barred from press releases and press gatherings, having their assets in Dubai seized, and finding their employees fined and arrested.

I warned Greg this would happened, but he thought with such a big name and reputation as Bloomberg, he would be safe. Nobody is safe in Dubai. Sheikh Mohammed, the ruling families and the top officials think they are gods—that they can get away with anything, so they use their power to coerce, blackmail and threaten people from telling the truths about Dubai.

Once the Dubai government learned I had escaped on a sailboat, officials took immediate actions to prevent that from happening again. At the time they didn't know the details on how I had done it, but they implemented new rules. Today all boat owners in Dubai must install a tracker inside their boat so the coast guard can track them on the water. Officially, they say it is for safety—in case of an accident the coast guard can be onsite more quickly. If a boat sails without the tracker, it will be spotted, stopped, searched and the owner fined. In addition, anyone who wants to buy a boat is screened by the CID to check if he is wanted by the police. If so, authorities will not allow him to register the boat, leaving him with a useless boat and no refund.

The conditions for boating in the UAE were unpleasant before—but now it's becoming more Orwellian than ever. Emiratis believe they have the best legal system. They reject claims their justice process is biased and blame problems instead on the Westerner's disobedience and free mind. So, when someone goes to the extreme to escape the country, they don't want to address why, but how—so they can put more restrictions on the expatriates.

However, it is a useless exercise. These new requirements would not have prevented me from escape because I bought my boat under somebody else's name—a foreigner visiting Dubai—for export and with a foreign registration. Furthermore, I escaped on a dinghy only to reach my sailboat in high seas.

After government officials heard that I escaped the country and was in the process of getting my book published, Dubai World started a court action against me. It was a farce of a trial, in a rush, with corrupted witnesses providing false statements and false evidence. I did not receive any notification nor any legal representation to challenge my accusers proving I could not have a fair trial. So it was no surprise I was found guilty in absentia for embezzling $4,000,000, sentenced to five years in prison, and given a $4,000,000 fine. A one, three or five year prison sentence is not relevant in the UAE. It means only that the prisoner can qualify to be released after he served his term, only "if" or "after" he pays his fines; otherwise he remains locked up until then. In my case, since I never embezzled anything nor did I have this kind of money, I would never been able to pay the fine. So in reality and make no mistake here, I received a **life in prison** term in disguise, for something I did not do. These court cases are all too familiar and not credible. This was a scare technique to shut me up, make me renounce publishing my book, and it was an attempt through Interpol to extradite me back to the UAE.

Interpol is a highly recognized organization. It facilitates cross-border police cooperation, and action is taken within the limits of existing laws in different countries. Interpol does not arrest people at the request of the Dubai government. In democratic countries, extradition procedures go through due process, hearings and court appearances where the defendant has the opportunity to defend himself, unlike in the GCC and in Dubai. However, I am looking at filing a dispute with Interpol. This organization should not put any credibility to the UAE requesting red notices on innocent people just because they want to shut them up or have them arrested for crimes they did not commit.

I found it particularly appalling for these people to accuse me of fraud when they, the government officials, are the ones who robbed me of my salary and benefits, and who commit fraud on a daily basis and in every possible way.

I am exposing, therefore, the true face of Dubai.

It is not about revenge or about liking Dubai or not. It is about straightening up the records—lifting the lid off this basket of snakes.

According to Emiratis, no one should speak negatively about the UAE. If you don't like it, you should just pack, leave and stay quiet.

But it's way too easy for them. Then what? They can screw more people, and nobody knows about the trap? No way! The right thing to do is to speak out and denounce the frauds and the hidden sides of Dubai, tell the reasons why you should not travel to Dubai and why you should not spend or invest money there. The following information is derived from verifiable facts. You don't have to believe me. But if I can only get you to ask Emiratis the right questions, seeing the expression on their faces is all the answer you'll need, and I will have fulfilled my goal.

Chapter 11

Dubai—The Fraud

Dubai, as a whole, is a bottomless pit of Emiratis who lie convincingly. They are able to entice innocent foreigners to their country, promising them a better life, only to devour them later, till they are bare to the bone. I, like many others, became part of these acquired goods. Under this unethical and tainted government, Dubai officials set out to destroy expatriates through intimidation and allegations of embezzlement. This is used to justify trial and imprisonment. Expatriates find themselves with only a snowball's chance in hell of getting out with their life and their sanity intact. I was accused of similar allegations. I could be facing life in prison for not being able to pay a fine, or death for having dared to escape and to write a book about my experience.

The Ruler—Dubai's Ruler claims he is a "beloved" ruler.

Sheikh Mohammed is the 13th Al Maktoum ruler of Dubai. One hundred seventy nine years ago, the Al-Maktoums led the Al Falasah Tribe out of their settlement in Abu Dhabi and moved north, to take Dubai by force with the help of the British. Unlike Royal families in other countries, where lineage run through centuries of generations, it is by decree that Sheikh Mohammed (Sheikh Mo) was appointed Prince of Dubai In 1995.

Sheikh Mo is at the top of the Dubai social pyramid. He owns the lands, the buildings, the air and everything in it. What he does not own, he merely permits to exist under his sponsorship. Right below him, is the nobility, the Sheikhs—numbering about 5,000 in the whole UAE. They thrive, as they are considered to be the elite of the Society. A child of a Sheikh becomes a Sheikh (male) or Sheikha (female). As these children mature and become titled adults, fictitious organizations are formed for them to chair. Upon marriage, to maintain family alliances, or as royal favors, many Sheikhs and Sheikhas are gifted with ownership of businesses. A Sheikh can never be an employee or report to anyone other than a higher-ranking Sheikh.

Within their own realm a Sheikh is excluded from the laws that apply to everybody else, he can never be arrested or prosecuted. Crimes of tortures and slavery remain undisclosed, and in the hands of these Sheikhs, are fully dismissed. "Do as I say, not as I do," is a motto highly practiced among the Emiratis of all levels.

The Ruler, the noble Emirati, does not work—he owns and rules. He appoints CEOs and CFOs to run his businesses for him, from which he collects huge revenues. If there are losses, he jails the CEO and takes his personal possessions. The Ruler gives land and local powers to his Sheikhs according to their rank. Key positions are awarded via lineage—to sons, brothers, or cousins, not via meritocracy. Look at the names of the chairmen and executive directors of all the big Emirati organizations.

If there was a Who's Who directory in Dubai, there would be only a handful of family names. From birth, any Emirati who is a relative to the ruling family is entitled to money and titles, regardless of whether he works or not. Eventually, if and when he is given a government organization to Chair, he improves his financial situation 100 times over and he does not even have to worry about the brain work because expatriates are hired for this purpose.

The goal of the ruling families is to maintain and develop their power and guarantee their cash flow. There are exceptions to the rule of keeping the power in the family, and the Sultan is one of them. He is the chairman of the biggest government company, Dubai World. He is a relative of the ruling family in the sense that he comes from the same tribe and is personally very close to Sheikh Mo. But he is not a member of a ruling family.

Just below the Sheikh's are the Emirati nationals, who represent ten percent of the population. Their obedience to the Al Maktoum dynasty is rewarded with cash, free education, free power, free water, subsidized housing, and government jobs. They make up the leisure class. Their uniform of privilege is the traditional white *khandoura* accompanied by a head scarf held in place with a black rope around the head. Most Emirati nationals are government employees as they cannot outperform expats in the private sector. Many do not work at all and they are never, ever, found in jobs requiring manual labor. They consider themselves above the expatriates whom they treat as helpers or mere guests. They are raised with the idea that working is a degrading exercise and they are above having to work for a living.

Traditional rule in the Emirates is tribal and patriarchal. Every Emirati family observes a political allegiance pretty much defined in terms of loyalty to the family or tribal leaders, then to the leaders of their individual Emirate, and ultimately to the leaders of the UAE federation. Below the Emirati nationals, are the indentured expatriates, who make up ninety percent of the population—Westerners, Middle Easterners, and Asians, working as laborers, managers, or professionals. That is where I was. Like any pyramid, the lowest level is the biggest in terms of its size, and it's the level propping up the upper levels of the pyramid. If the foreigners were to leave the country, the UAE Emiratis would go back to the dark ages.

The bottom most section of the lowest level of the pyramid is made up of the laborers from South Asia. They build and maintain the city. They are expected by the Emiratis to be grateful to their superiors for their meager living. They are forced to sign themselves into virtual slavery for years when they arrive in the UAE. The Emiratis justify this treatment by saying that these people live on dirt floors with leaves above their heads in their home countries, so when they come to Dubai they should be happy to live in a trailer.

The truth is that Emiratis prey on these impoverished people and enslave them. It is true that many immigrants in Dubai earn more there, than in their respective countries. However, for this short lived privilege, they are legally bound to a single employer. They lose their freedom, they are separated from their families for years at a time, they live in squalor, and they are subject to totalitarian social controls. They are banned from the luxury malls and hotel lobbies. They are crowded in work camps on the outskirts of the city. They are segregated and treated no better than camels. Sometimes companies who hire these desperate workers hold their checks for months to make sure they don't run away. When the workers strike, they are jailed, or deported and replaced.

Human Rights Watch in 2003 accused the Emirates of building prosperity on forced labor. Although the UAE Minister of Labor was reportedly shocked by the unbearable living conditions of the laborers, he did little to improve them. The UAE has always denied categorizing this situation as modern slavery, yet at the same time, they vehemently refuse to adopt the International Migrant Workers Convention that would protect these workers.

I remember one day, Sultan consulted me about making fiberglass tanks to hold drinking water for Sheikh Mohammed's horses. I explained to him that the chemicals and microscopic glass fibers could pass into the stored water and I didn't want to be liable if any of Sheik Mo's $10 million horses were to get sick, so he cancelled the request. But, at the same time, it was okay to make the same water tanks for the laborer workers at the camps.

The Emirati society hides its true nature behind a friendly face and artificial hospitality. In truth, the inhabitants of Dubai are living under Sheikh Mo's dictatorship in a caged country where the civil servants are accountable to him and to his vision. They do not have the right to change the government; there are no general elections and no popularly-elected representatives of any kind. Like in the middle ages, people may only express their concerns directly to their leaders through traditional but useless consultative mechanisms, such as councils, called Majlis.

It is a fraud to present the UAE as an open society, and it's laughable to describe Dubai as the Miami of the Middle East. Dubai would need some serious psychological reality checks to even come close. In reality, the Emirati Society is ruthless in its goal to get rich as quickly as possible while others do all the hard work. Dubai has been built with billions of dollars invested by foreigners, the blood and sweat of hundreds of thousands of South Asian workers, and the creativity of Westerners. All of this is to provide the materialistic comforts of the twenty-first century to the Emirati feudal society. Their mentality dates back to the medieval ages. In the privacy of their homes, they still sit on the floor and eat with their fingers. You find out, only when it is too late, how the Emirati society sets the roles and positions of everybody in Dubai. For Emirati nationals, the role begins at birth and ends at death. For expatriates, it begins at the airport arrivals and ends at the airport departures.

Interaction between Emiratis and expatriates is based on service and profit, not genuine friendship. You can be their best friend, but only if you increase their income. They might even allow you to make some money while you are helping them build a fortune, but you will never, ever be their true friend. You may have a good relationship, but it is all temporary and based on their self-interest. When the Emirati loses interest in you, the relationship snaps like a twig. The Emiratis I have met are not like other Arabs. I have long-term Lebanese, Moroccan, and Algerian friends—all great people offering durable and authentic friendships. Emiratis are not able or willing to offer friendship to people from other countries because the structure of their society is the same tribal way it was hundreds of years ago. It is a highly hierarchical society, where vassals pay homage to their lord with an oath of allegiance. In exchange for their fidelity, they keep jobs and receive rewards. This applies also to the expatriate population, where homage is paid by the employee to his sponsor. This succession of homage and its hierarchy is even reflected in public life during events, races, or contests.

Whenever there is a race or a contest involving the ruling families, the outcomes are always an exact replica of the Emirati homage pyramid. Regardless of the number of contestants, their origin, or their level of skill, the order in which they cross the finish line is the same as the hierarchy in the Emirati society. So fixing the races or doping is a normal way to ensure this order.

In January 2009, Sheikh Mohammed won an International Horse Race. Second place was awarded to his son, Sheikh Hamdam. The Crown Prince of Dubai, and Sultan finished just behind. All were celebrated with trumps and flags up in the country. Only for a short time though—because they were all disqualified after the FEI (Federation Equestre Internationale) tested their horses' positive for prohibited drugs. They received a six months suspension and a fine. They cheated and they got caught.

Of course, all three pretended not to know their horses were doped, sure—as if their trainers would take the risk on their own, inject addictive drugs in million dollar horses with no chance of profiting from it. Adding to the shame, Sheikh Mohammed's wife, Princess Haya, President of the FEI, had to step down during the investigation and the scandal. The local press, a mockery of freedom of the press, was barred from reporting the decisions of the sport tribunal. However, after his ban is expired, I doubt that Sheikh Mohammed will ever run in another horse race again if he can't have this public arena to further inflate his ego, and win from the start by doping the horses or fixing the race.

The competitions are not limited to camel or horse races. Everything is a contest or competition, including business deals. In the medieval ages, the noble would spend his time in tournaments or hunting. The same remains true for modern day Dubai. The nobility of Dubai have their tournaments in the form of exhibitions—horse racing, car shows, boat shows, aviation shows, and falconry. These are places where an observer can readily see their contempt for outsiders and their ostentatious displays of wealth.

Noble Emiratis are popular—but only because they are feared due to the unchecked power they wield over their own people and hapless visitors to their country.

In public, it's as if people bow and kiss the floor where Sheikhs have walked. I saw the same effect on my own employees during visits of Sheikhs to the factory. Expatriates are invited to constantly hail the actions of the Ruler. Dubai is not about leadership, it is about leader worship. There is not a street, or a single office in Dubai—not a room, not a meeting room or hallway in public buildings—without a portrait of Sheikh Mohammed hanging front and center. There is not a single hotel without a portrait of the Ruler in the lobby. His picture is everywhere. Even private companies are required to display a portrait of the rulers somewhere near the reception area or in the conference room, demonstrating their allegiance to the rulers. The more extreme fanatics go further in their leader worship by installing pictures of the rulers on the windshields of their cars. This is where the vision of the

Ruler is apparently more important than the vision of the drivers. The media are required to insert a picture of Sheikh Mohammed in their newspapers every day.

The Culture—There is no Emirati heritage to protect or culture to preserve.

It took 1,000 years to build my homeland, France. It took 250 years to build my adopted country; the U.S. Neighboring countries, Egypt, Iran, and Iraq have thousands of years in history. Forty years ago, the UAE didn't even exist. The first building ever constructed out of stones or concrete came out of the sands in 1956—up until that time, the entire population lived in traditional *barastri* (homes made from palm fronds) and they drew water from communal wells. There was no nation, but people washed up from neighboring countries living in poverty on borderless lands between the Persian Gulf and the desert. All attempts to show some archeological heritage of ancient civilization have failed. Hard cash may buy you legitimacy but not history. There is a museum, yes—it is the size of a two bedroom apartment.

All attempts to show an Emirati culture and history are justifications to impose rules and restrictions on the expatriate population to maintain a minority in power and to guarantee its cash flow.

After the discovery of oil, the vast flow of petrol-dollars made the Emiratis immensely rich and eager to have their share of the luxuries and comforts of modern life. They had been envying Western comfort and technology for centuries. Now that they had money they wanted everything right away, like children desperate for a new toy. But they had no roads where they could drive luxury cars, no airports where they could fly private jets and helicopters, and no fresh water to fill up their swimming pools.

So in order to enjoy their new wealth they needed to build themselves a city. The problem was they didn't know how to do that, and they didn't want to do any of the backbreaking work themselves or even use their money to pay someone else to do it. They knew that with careful planning, they could get foreign investors to pay for the development of their city. Emirati banks welcomed foreign cash and asked no questions about its origin.

The government used this influx of financial resources to fund Dubai's gigantic projects, and today, Dubai has successfully channeled cash, goods, and equipment into the city for its development. The Emiratis have achieved the ultimate funding to build their city state. They put their money in the West and had foreigners put their money in the UAE to buy properties and develop businesses which will ultimately end up under Emirati ownership and control if they are not already. As a result of the success of this master plan, we have seen a considerable transfer of wealth to the Emirates and with it access to luxury of the most superficial and conspicuous type.

In Dubai, money does not buy good taste—it seems to only buy bigger egos. The laws of Islam do not allow men to wear jewelry other than watches, so they wear the gaudiest watches they can find. In my professional field of the boat industry, I saw their profound need for extravagance. Custom built boats ended up thirty percent heavier because of the pompously rich interior decoration and useless amenities. To have a swanky looking yacht was more of a concern than the mechanical functions of their new water ride. I have met wealthy individuals with such immense disposable incomes they didn't mind buying luxury cars by the dozen, custom yachts they never sail and cargo airplanes tailored to transport their horses or to play golf. They would pay huge amounts of money for the silliest things—such as four million dollars for a license plate with the number **1** on it.

I remember one time, a friend of mine, Abdulha, invited me for a weekend at his mansion. He had fifteen cars in his garage, Mercedes, a couple of Lamborghinis, Ferraris and a Bentley. Here he was, twenty-eight years old with $5 million worth of automobiles sitting in his air conditioned, dust free garage in the desert.

As I wandered around the garage with a couple of other guys, looking at the cars, Abdullah was pulling out a large duffle bag from under kitchen sink. He seemed shocked, as if he had just remembered what it was. The bag was wet from water that had leaked from the sink, so he opened it to check if it was wet inside. Inside was bundled money. There were piles of $100 bills stuck together by the moisture. He asked us to help him separate and dry out the bills. All ten of us took the whole afternoon to lay out all the bills, and when we finished, he counted $10 million in total. How rich is rich when you don't even remember the $10 million that you stashed somewhere in your house? He probably didn't have to sweat much to earn this unchecked money. I have never seen so much cash in one place before. But compared to him, it was like I had recovered a forgotten $10 bill inside my night stand.

Sheikh Mohammed has a fortune, estimated at over $18 billion. Not too bad for somebody who lived off dates and well water in a shack forty years ago. He owns a large yacht that I know cost $500 million to refit and costs $100,000 for every day she's at sea. I heard from people who worked on the yacht, that every time Sheikh Mo visits her (about once every month); he orders changes that cost no less than $300,000. In addition to this yacht, he owns a shadow yacht, which is a supply ship that follows his yacht to provide everything from spare parts to food and toys. When I was at Exomos, Sheikh Mohammed offered a $20 million, 250 foot yacht (the Cosmos still under construction) to his son for his twenty-second birthday.

Many members of the Dubai elite have incredible wealth. They are not shy about spending it, which is reflected by what is on display in shops and behind glass windows. I was looking at marble medallions once, for my home in the U.S. The medallions were round or square geometric designs that you embed in the floor for a couple thousand dollars. I went to a shop on the side of a dusty street in an industrial zone, thinking it would be cheaper given the low labor cost and the cheap look of the shop. I saw beautiful masterpiece medallions in Lazuli, three feet in diameter, but selling for $800,000 a pop. They were lined up in rows, as if they were on sale—twenty million dollars just sitting there on the floor. I looked further down the row to a gorgeous blue marble tile sample. "Not available, sir." I understood a Sheikh had just bought the whole marble quarry to make sure that nobody else would have the same bathroom medallions.

I observed foreigners trying to get their way in with the Elite of Emiratis, by giving them gifts. Don't even think about it, there is no way you could satisfy or impress them with a present, anything you can imagine or fantasize, they already have it. I saw a Chairman give to his driver a $3,000 gold fountain pen gift he had just received, like if it was a candy bar, because he had fifty in a bucket somewhere. I saw a $20,000 custom laptop passed on to a secretary because Mr. 'the' Emirati looked at it as if it was a gift card.. I saw a Sheikh, distribute to his staff twenty keys to SUV's parked outside, as if they were company logo key chains—*that* raises the level of gift giving to a Sheikh. And last, I saw a hangar full of left over toys, brand new jet skis by the dozens, exotic cars, flat screens, electronics, still in their boxes. It is all an unbelievable display of waste and spoiled wealth, howver, what makes it more complicated to understand is that it is still never enough...

Segregation - Dubai, a cosmopolitan city?

The population of the Dubai Emirate is a mix of about 250,000 Emiratis, 250,000 Westerners, 800,000 South Asians, and 200,000 Arabs from neighboring countries. Emiratis are a minority in their own country, but they are the people of His Highness. Everyone else there is expendable, replaceable, and not even represented by his consulate.

Sheikh Mohammed likes to say that one of his proudest achievements is having introduced gated communities to Arabia—the land of nomads and tents. He is damn right about that. He grouped foreigners, who came to build his country, into gated and segregated communities, and required them to work in different clusters. These clusters and communities divided and separated, rather than worked together towards a harmonious city. He then confiscated their passports, their identity, their citizenship, and decided what they could watch and read, somehow convincing them they are happier this way. Emiratis do not live in these gated communities. They are more nomadic than ever. Only today they are no longer roaming on camels but on private jets, yachts, and personal helicopters between their properties all over the world.

Segregation is a state policy in the UAE. Every permit, license, authorization or application follows a maze of different process depending on categories in which fit the applicants. Emiratis always get preferred treatment and fast service of course. Men, women, married, single, Westerner, South Asian, graduate, unskilled, are all different categories with different rights and different customer service lines.

At the beginning, the elite of Dubai were treated as VIPs. But that got old quickly because there were too many VIP expatriates, and Emiratis don't like being on the same level, especially the Sheikhs. So they invented a new elite class of special people they call the VVIPs. (They excel in pure arrogance and complete disregard for the rest of us.)

What is unacceptable is not the fact that there are VIPs and VVIPs—that will always be the case. Rather, it is the lack of the most elementary and decent treatment of the general public. Everywhere else in the world, VIPs receive better treatment while the general public receives good treatment. Better for a few means it is good for everybody else. In Dubai it is not better and good, it is best and worst. Below the excellent treatment of VIPs and VVIPs, there is nothing but chaos.

Emiratis consider themselves the chosen people, with noble blood flowing in their veins. But at the same time, they have an inferiority complex toward Westerners. One rule to always keep in mind when dealing with Emiratis, is to remember that Middle Easterners abhor the weak and fear the strong, whether friend or foe. In the West, weakness can be an advantage. In the Middle East, if you show weakness, they will take advantage of it. They are ruthless and have no pity. Showing respect to an Emirati is not the same as being weak in front of them.

Dubai public events are just another example of the worst in Emirati arrogance and their disdain for everybody else. Because exhibitions are tailored for the local rich Emiratis, the public around them is only a necessary annoyance to bring credibility to their functions and make them appear to be popular venues. This is why nothing is done to accommodate the public. If you are not a VVIP, you will rot in the sun waiting in line, you will waste hours at entrances filling out forms, and you will walk hundreds of yards under the smoldering heat from the parking lot. It is not lack of organization or planning—it's that Emiratis just don't care about the well being of those who cannot buy. I know the difference from personal experience. I was treated like a VIP when I first came to Dubai, and when I had outstayed my usefulness, I was treated like one of the rabble.

The Dubai World cup, the most celebrated event of Dubai—the million-dollar horse race—is the worst in public discrimination. For the non-VIPs there will be three to six hours of waiting in line, dehydrating in midsummer temperatures reaching as high as 120 degrees Fahrenheit with no cover for those waiting outside the venue. For those who have the patience to wait and make it to the paddocks, it is another hassle to get out. Why bother, when in reality, everybody else is considered an accessory to this event.

Sheikh Mo leads everyone to believe it is an open venue where Western owners send their horses and jockeys all the way to Dubai to run in the races. But in truth Sheikh Mohammed pays them to participate. I have friends in Florida, horse race owners who would have never made the trip otherwise. This constitutes misrepresentation. Sheikh Mohammed buys himself legitimacy, inviting sport stars, with large money offers, to lend their names in an effort to sell the Dubai life to investors and tourists.

Equality—Women equal to Men?

Any rules, laws, or statements made by officials and from Sheikh Mohammed himself regarding women rights, are just attempts to make the rest of the world believe that, in Dubai, women are considered equal to men. But that is a blatant contradiction. The Emirati women have it the worst in many ways—starting with their dress. They are covered all in black in the searing heat, walking in groups together or five feet behind a male in white. For such arid climate, black is for sure not the color of choice to repel sunlight. Regardless of the justifications, the only reason women wear their black robes or *abayah* is because they must remain invisible. Their existence remains in silent shadows, living in hiding and remaining obedient.

In public, they cannot even recognize each other unless there are accompanied by their Indian drivers or Filipino maids. In shopping malls or public places they take pictures of themselves in groups, in front of buildings, landmarks or whatnot. But what is the point of pictures with unrecognizable black silhouettes?

The domination of men is assured and maintained by unwritten simple rules—a woman, during her life, will obey her father until she gets married to a husband who has been chosen for her. Then she will obey her husband. If she becomes a widow she will obey her sons. The ruler is the master of his people, the father is the master of his sons, and the husband is the master of his wives. Wifely disobedience is a cause for divorce. Husbands have a legal right to discipline their wives physically.

I sympathize with women in the UAE. They work really hard to improve their situation. Many confided their grief to me. They are like every other woman in the world—they like attention, and they don't want to be part of a harem. But they have no choice or they would be cast away from their families with no money.

Western influence has helped Emirati women overturn parts of their patriarchal culture and make some advances in their society, particularly in the work environment. A few more women in Dubai today are able to have a professional life, participate in economic life, and communicate in a working environment—yet there are still many restrictions. They still need permission from husbands or fathers to work. Most of them work in government agencies where contact with other men is limited. Yet, working Emirati women are present throughout the social pyramid, from the CEO level down to lower paid civil servants.

Women are paying the ultimate price for their society's reluctance to move into the modern world, with their health. Cervical cancer is the second cause of death for Emirati women and is increasing at a staggering rate. In the Western world the disease can be easily treated and even cured if diagnosed early. The problem is not the prevention and screening of women, but rather the censorship of Emirati men who don't want to expose their direct responsibility in the transmission of the disease, which is most often linked to having sex with multiple partners.

I have seen firsthand, my Emirati friends picking up the phone and ordering flowers. I soon discovered they were ordering girls for their daily pleasures—parties on their farms, entertainment on their yachts. They indulge themselves with one or two different girls every single day. I am not talking about Emiratis having one mistress or a couple of girlfriends, but hundreds of different girls per year for hired sex. Due to their abundant extracurricular activities, unknown to the wives, the husbands transmit illness. Sadly, their demise does not help prevention either, because too often, the death certificates are misrepresented and reported as heart failure. This conveniently leaves the husbands with nothing more to explain.

Women in Dubai have little access to health information relating to diseases that affect sexual organs, because any pictures of bared bodies or exposed skin is banned or blocked. When the women die from diseases they've caught from their unfaithful husbands, it is not just wives who die, but the mothers of their society, thus its future—a future that is being trampled into the dust by their own men.

With the influx of foreigners, Emirati women can observe expatriate married couples and women. They can compare them with their own situation and, as a result, they choose to marry later and sometimes they try to marry foreigners.

Seduction, romance, thrill of the chase is nonexistent to the Emirati men. They rely on their families to arrange marriages and I was shocked to discover that forty percent of Emirati marriages are consanguine. Almost one out of every two Emiratis marry their relatives—most often their first cousin. And guess who is a prime example: Sheikh Mohammed himself, whose senior wife is his first cousin. Like father like son, Sheikh Hamdan is engaged to his cousin Sheikha bin Saeed bin Thani Al Maktoum.

There cannot be any interaction in public with eligible young Emirati women when they are covered from head to toe and are not allowed to go out unless accompanied by a male family member. But at the same time Emirati men can easily socialize with weak foreign women looking for a rich husband. With the greater interaction between foreign women and Emirati men, there results a naturally higher probability of an Emirati man getting to know more foreign women and therefore end up marrying one, even if it doesn't last long.

I witnessed many Emirati's version of attempts at romance. One of them was at the Dubai International Boat Show. I was talking to one of my hostesses. She and a few other girls worked at the boat show, answering questions about our vessels and Exomos. They were very cute girls that everyone loved to look at. An Emirati friend of mine, Mohammed, walked up with a smug look on his face, interrupted our conversation, and boldly suggested that she go home with him after the day. She was offended by his rudeness and presumptuousness, rightfully so, and politely turned him down. He responded in an even ruder tone than before, expressing his confusion as to why she was resisting him when he could buy her anything she wanted.

This is seduction, Middle Eastern style. Emirati men don't seduce women with affection and compliments—they buy them, bargaining with money, family, camels, tribal favors, watches and whatever else their society values or once valued. They consume women, treating them as a commodity. And when they are finished with them they change them. At least my hostess could say no—the Emirati woman, she can say nothing, not even yes.

Once the Emirati woman is installed in the home as a wife, she has to stay there to take care of her husband, take care of his children, and take care of his house while he entertains girlfriends elsewhere. If she was caught doing the same—having an extramarital affair, she would suffer the direst consequences. This is not to say that Emirati women do not have affairs—they do have them. Many times I received text messages on my mobile phone in public places through a blue tooth connection, from married and obviously neglected Emirati women seeking out men, broadcasting the deal in plain sight but anonymously under their *abayahs*. When they seek out a match, they always make sure the man does not speak Arabic, in an attempt to avoid traps or problems with her husband. If they find a match, they meet somewhere else with a signal to identify each other. They never exchange phone numbers for fear that their husbands might find out when checking their wives' mobile phones.

In the evenings, on the Jumeirah beach road, Emirati women drive their cars with their tinted windows down just enough to show their eyes through the veil, again seeking the attention of other men. If she rolls the window down farther, she is indicating that she has found a match, and both cars drive off somewhere else so their occupants can meet in person. Again, no phone calls or words are exchanged in that first meeting. I know because I had a couple of expatriate friends who admitted to having a sexual relationship with a married Emirati woman. I knew some of them did it because they liked the excitement and playing with fire. It is a very dangerous game indeed, where prison could be the least of their problems—for both of them, if caught.

The double standards between Emirati men and women abound. The Emirati society is drowning in its own contradictions and hypocrisy, and it is creating more problems by not evolving towards modern standards. Emirati women are frustrated, and their men don't care. They blame it on Westerners for contaminating their wives' minds with our ideas of romance and love. It is becoming more common that Emirati women are staying in school, studying longer, and avoiding arranged marriages. More Emirati men are reluctant to marry Emirati woman too, because they prefer the freedom of the luxurious materialistic life that Dubai has brought to them and easy access to expatriate women. The cost of living and inflation have increased the dowry that a bridegroom's family has to pay to the Emirati bride to seal the marriage. With a foreign woman, there is no bride price. They can divorce them with a text message and keep the children, if they have any. Inevitably we are seeing fewer marriages between Emiratis, and little-by-little their society loses its identity.

Eight years ago, UAE ruler Sheikh Zayed launched a $68 million Marriage Fund to encourage Emirati men to marry Emirati women. The incentive was a $20,000 gift for the couple. It didn't work. There have been cases of couples marrying to collect the money, who then split the cash and part ways. It shows that the leaders of the UAE have missed the point entirely. Emirati women are tired of being married to their cousins, traded for camels, and being treated like chattel. Money is the motivator for any of these youths to enter into an Emirati marriage. It appears these veiled beauties find considerate men from the Western world much better marriage material. The government of Dubai considers this a grave situation and a threat to their culture. So it is implementing programs to ban marriages with foreign nationals or penalize young men who marry foreign women, and continues to make it overwhelmingly difficult for an Emirati woman to marry a foreigner.

As long as an Emirati is a member of the royal family, no matter how distant, he is entitled to live at government expense. These families keep their daughters under lock and key to ensure they marry a member within the royal family to keep the cash flowing, another reason for consanguine marriages. The children of an Emirati man and his foreign wife get UAE citizenship, but the children of an Emirati woman and her foreign husband are not entitled to UAE citizenship. This negatively impacts the woman's situation and that of her children if the couple divorces later. If the father is an Emirati and the mother is foreign, she cannot leave the country with her children without the permission of the father. Even if she has full custody, she must remain in the country if she wants to raise her children.

Wait, it gets worse for foreign women with foreign husbands. If they give birth in Dubai and do not qualify to sponsor their baby for a visa, due to salary requirement or job category, their baby can and will be deported with or without the mother. And if a woman gives birth without being married she goes to prison.

Divorce has a greater stigma for women in Emirati culture. They usually prefer to suffer silently, being married rather than live in misery as a divorced woman. It is always considerably easier for a husband to divorce his wife than for a wife to divorce her husband.

Oral divorce is still in effect for men in the UAE. A man just has to say it out loud three times. A man can just declare that his wife is not obedient, and he is off the hook—the marriage is over. A woman, on the other hand, has to show abuse and mistreatment to justify a divorce and go to court. The general assumption is that a woman wants to divorce only for frivolous reasons.

Even though divorce is easy for an Emirati man, many of them will not divorce their wives. They are allowed to have up to four wives. So they keep them on the side and provide for them. The man always keeps custody of his children, especially his sons when they are older than thirteen. My Emirati friends had three or four wives, but these wives didn't live together in the same house. The Emirati are rich enough to retire their senior wives in different houses and pay them an allowance while they live with the junior ones and they never, ever talk about their wives.

The senior or divorced wives are not allowed to see any another men. If by chance you see an Emirati with his wife, it is always with the newest one. You do not get introduced, and there is no handshake for the wife—the most you can do is say hello from a distance, and only if you are invited to do so by her husband.

Most Emirati women are forced by traditions and their families to wear the *abayah*, to be modest, they say. There is no modesty in the hearts of the Emirati women. They have spirit and the desire to look sexy, just like every other woman in the world—but that is only for their husband to enjoy. Under the veils, many of them wear makeup, dress in modern style, with fancy, tight jeans, sexy shoes, and sometimes, absolutely nothing. I saw it once with a married Emirati woman. I knew her from work, where she was always talking to me flirtatiously. I was surprised by her behavior and a bit afraid of her, too. If her husband knew she was talking to me like that, I would be in big trouble. I told her that her just being dressed like that was an impediment for any man to even talk to her in public. In return she told me it was actually a good cover, a good way to hide from her family and husband. She could be with people without being recognized, and she could even be naked under her *abayah* and nobody would know. That I didn't want to believe, so she caught me by surprise when she quickly opened her *abayah* and revealed her nude body underneath. Wow, I didn't expect that move. There was nobody around, but we were out in the open. I told her that I could be arrested, and she just laughed at me. I rushed off to an appointment that I had just made up in my head.

The purpose of the veil is supposedly to prevent temptation in men. Frustrated single men can easily be tempted at the sight of a beautiful woman, especially if he is a South Asian expatriate worker who has not been with a woman for two years. But it goes both ways;

the woman must be faithful to her husband. The veil prevents her from making moves to be seductive to other men—the Arab woman must be attractive to her husband only.

My Emirati friends told me that in Islam, when looking at a woman, the thought of temptation alone was a sin. If it's a sin to think of women, then they are the worst sinners I have ever seen. They gawk as they covet foreign women, with both desire and hate. Women visiting Dubai should not fool themselves. Emirati men consider all Western women whores. Many of them said this to me, from the highest government officials on down. But it does not stop them from running after these women in a disgusting, rude, selfish and arrogant way. There is a fundamental difference between the Middle East and the rest of the world. Women in the free world are worshiped, seduced and romanced, but in the Middle East they are mere sexual commodities forced into silence and obedience. It is against the law to have sexual relations with a girlfriend, in essence a free-minded woman, but men openly indulge themselves with prostitutes, because they are seen as sex objects—not women.

During private social occasions women are completely segregated from the men. I have been invited to weddings split in two separate parties, in time and in location—one for the men and the other for the women. No men get to see or even know the name of the bride. Men dance and socialize with each other. I could never go to a wedding with my wife because she would be segregated away from me. People can always be polite and pretend, but the truth is, these segregated parties are totally boring. After one or two invitations, many expats just don't respond anymore.

During public social occasions, women and men are mixed. However you can never directly address a woman draped in the black robe unless you are invited to. A woman with her face covered can never be acknowledged, unless she is a government employee behind a counter. In public she is a ghost to be ignored. There are a lot of Arab professional woman involved in public events which requires that they interact with others, including men. One can easily be confused when trying to follow the rules regarding female etiquette in the Emirati society.

These covered women are not insensitive to foreign women. They turn their heads at passing miniskirts and tight jeans or strappy heels. One way or the other they are frustrated—they cannot be neutral— either they hate them, or they envy them. Being completely covered, they cannot show off jewelry for people to see and envy, so they find other ways to display their wealth and style and to provide an outlet for their egos. For instance, they use the canvas provided by their mobile phones, they bling it out with accessories in the most conspicuous fashion. Mac book Pros are embossed in eighteen karat gold and the Apple icon in pure white paved diamonds—some of them $50,000 or more in price.

The first time I walked into a salon for a haircut, I almost got arrested. I felt like a clumsy child in a china shop. In the UAE hair salons for woman and men are segregated. Once I stepped over the threshold, everyone inside went into a panic, women were uncovered pointing fingers at me, and the Filipino hairdressers rushed me out. After four years in Dubai, when I returned to a hair salon in the U.S., I felt a bizarre sensation when I saw only women. In the men's hair salons in Dubai, the whole staff is male even if they sometimes look like females. There is similar segregation with doctors, where Muslims women are not likely to be examined by male doctors, because their husbands and fathers feel extremely embarrassed, which is a problem because of the shortage of female doctors. Sometimes they are prevented from going to the hospital. The unfortunate result is that when an Emirati woman becomes ill, she is likely to suffer silently and die, or seek delayed treatment and hiding in a foreign country. The segregation of women extends to the roads, with only seven percent of the driver licenses held by women. Numbers don't lie.

The stunning Dubai architecture?
A catastrophe waiting to happen.

As you drive through the city you don't see real transitions—it is either the old Dubai or the modern one, the desert or the city. The expression Old Dubai is overrated since there is no part of Dubai that is actually old, compared to other cities where old means at least 200 years. Old Dubai is a mere thirty years old, and it is gradually being demolished and replaced by more modern structures. Most of the buildings in modern Dubai are less than ten years old. The city has been built up in a hurry and is artificially sustained against the desert, waiting to claim its sands back.

Dubai has created its own style. It is luxurious modernity built with the best that money can buy. But there is nothing in the architecture that makes it an iconic city for the Middle East, it is not even a mix of Arabian culture as one might expect. All of the towers and buildings are inspired by a Western mind—not Emirati and not even Arab, with the exception of a few hotels that have a gorgeous Middle Eastern theme such as the Madinat Jumeirah, or the Royal Mirage. But even these are merely imitations of foreign Arab traditional architecture without essence. The Image of the Burj El Arab Hotel, shaped like a sailboat sitting on an artificial island, became Dubai's trademark logo and is on every license plate. The seven star rating was issued by only one judge, its owner, Sheikh Mohammed.

The mosques in Dubai are the only buildings of genuine Arab architecture. Some are really beautiful and rich in detail. A majority of the population is of the Muslim faith, so it is not surprising to see a mosque every ten blocks. As new buildings, condos, and gated communities are being erected, so are new mosques to accommodate the Muslim population.

Almost none of the buildings in Dubai are actually designed or built by Emiratis or in the Emirati style of architecture, simply because there is no Emirati architectural style in existence. The few Emirati architects are younger than thirty, with no experience. This is not the case for Arabs in general, who have an extensive architectural history. Many Western construction projects are inspired by ancient Arab designs. Many prominent Arabs work in architectural teams who design and build extraordinary buildings all over the world. The Dancing Towers in Dubai was designed by an Iraqi architect. The first city built with a concentration of high-rise buildings, Manhattan-style, was Samarra, a city in Yemen built in the sixteenth century.

The designs used for buildings and towers in Dubai are picked from the concepts of architectural contest or from borrowed foreign ideas. They must be designs that no one has ever done before, and the credit for the beauty or innovation for a building's design must always go to Sheikh Mohammed and his vision. Thanks to investor's money, Dubai hires the best architects in the world, who seize the opportunity to express themselves with stunning designs and daring construction— and then enslaves engineers and workers from foreign countries to build them by working round the clock. This achievement looks extraordinary, but it is a materialistic achievement and an illusion. There is no emerging architectural trend in Dubai. The city is a collection of different modern towers with unique yet uncoordinated features sitting next to one another.

Dubai couldn't hold a candle to the likes of Miami, Las Vegas, Monaco or Singapore. Dubai took inspiration from what these places had already built, by making things bigger and more flamboyant. Unlike other large cities in the world, Dubai lacks character, a soul, an atmosphere, and a culture. The fact that extraordinary buildings are being built in Dubai does not make Dubai extraordinary.

However there is no *faux décor* or flimsy fakes in Dubai—it is all solid concrete, steel, glass and stone. The quality of the materials is definitely there. But with sorely underpaid workers and engineers, the buildings are completed too fast with too many hidden defects and poor workmanship. Behind the walls and underneath the floors, problems are waiting to happen. The outlandish mega-projects such as the artificial Palm Islands and the Atlantis Hotel have seen their openings tarnished (despite the cover-ups) by sewage drainage failures, water supply shortages, rotten mud beaches, flooding in the underground parking lots and frequent power outages.

Dubai was trying to do in five years what it would take twenty years for any other country to achieve. There is not a place in Dubai that is not, somehow, under construction. The disturbance is all over the place and construction is not limited to real estate and five-star hotels. Dubai is building a metro system, a new airport, a new port, new hospitals, and new government buildings.

The government has rushed to develop Dubai with no reflection on the long-term socio-cultural or environmental consequences. There has been no land-use or infrastructure planning, other than building the city into clusters of specialized activities and identities. Clusters are not new—many countries use them as a part of their overall development, but not to make up the entire city like Dubai has done.

The clusters of Dubai are cities within cities, with security cameras and guards scrutinize every move of everyday life activity of their populations—like in George Orwell's *1984*. The monorail connecting these clusters will not solve the transportation problem, because it does not address the ethnic differences between the people and the half-mile walking distances that still need to be traversed through the 105 degree Fahrenheit heat. No disrespect here, but many people don't use soap because they cannot afford it. The resulting body smell and the heat outside make traveling in these metros and buses a very unpleasant olfactory experience.

Today, half of all major real estate projects are now on hold. They are running out of cash. In the desert, on the outskirts of Dubai, Dubailand is still a desert. No more money is finding its way to fund this mega project. The project would have employed 300,000 workers to build a venue to entertain the planned 15 million visitors per year, with world-class projects, global landmarks, and history theme parks. However, with the economic turmoil shaking the world and the truth revealed about Dubai, this is not ever going to happen. Cranes, once all over the landscape, are now receding. Eventually clusters and business hubs will turn into enclaves. Advertising this unfriendly and segregated environment for an efficient business place will no longer fool anyone.

The environment—a Dubai Priority?

Environmental considerations are just an irritation and a hindrance to the rapid development of Dubai. With 335 days a year of excellent sun exposure, Dubai has not done anything to install solar panels to produce electricity, which would reduce their power plant fuel consumption and greenhouse gases significantly. In this most arid region nothing is done to recycle the condensed water from the air conditioning units and millions of gallons of fresh water are wasted. There has been no planning for the waste being generated by Dubai's explosive population growth. With the increasing number of workers, tourists and the development of commercial and industrial activities, sewage output was rising at twenty-five percent per year—which triggered a chain reaction creating an environmental disaster and closing the beaches. Sure, most visible parts of Dubai are spotless and clean, but it is typical for Emiratis to embellish what is visible on the surface and to ignore what is hidden beneath. The hidden truths are coming out, and recently, one of them surfaced on the beaches, in a most disgusting way.

Most residential and industrial areas are not connected to a sewage system, and the existing thirty-year-old sewage system does not have the capacity to absorb the rising level of human waste. Instead there are hundreds of sewage trucks collecting vast amounts of human waste. The drivers have to spend up to ten hours waiting in line before they can discharge their raw sewage at the one and only treatment plant in Dubai. The tank drivers are paid per load, not by the hour. In order to avoid loss of money because of the wait in the dumping line, many drivers don't go to the treatment plants at all. Instead, they dump their foul load anywhere around the city—in parking lots, deserted streets, or even in storm drains, so that they can pickup more loads. The wastewater has to go somewhere and that somewhere is in the sea. Storm drains spews human waste into the harbor of Jumeirah's sailing club, ruining Dubai's reputation for cleanliness and shamefully causing the postponement of yachting events.

Adding to the problem is the way the government is attempting to deal with the issue. Rather than focus on building the much needed waste treatment plants, the government chases after these truckers to catch them in the act of dumping, in order to fine them. In response, to compensate for the lost revenue and the fines, the truckers charge more for waste pickup. At the same time, building contractors and residential management companies, who face higher charges for waste pickup, skip septic tank purges, which cause those tanks to overflow into the streets and create stagnant sewage ponds in parking lots. Again, the raw sewage water finds its way to the sea through the storm drains, which is causing the closure of marinas and beaches to avoid public contamination. The municipality cannot cover up the problem, because the stench is unbearable and the sight of floating feces, unmistakable. The government of Dubai does not seem to understand this simple equation: bigger city equals more people, equals more shit. Blaming or fining sewage truckers will not stop people from going to the bathroom. The flow of shit has to be treated, but the one and only plant is not big enough to manage all that Dubai generates.

The lack of capacity of the sewage treatment is bad enough, but it's not the end of the story. The government built the sewage treatment plant without planning for future growth and population trends, and as a result, it is now very close to the residential areas. A friend of mine lives in a community near the sewage plant and the stench is unbearable. Unbelievably, the municipality does nothing to remedy the problem. Instead, they make positive statements and congratulate each other with awards and certificates of excellence. They use water from the sewage plant to irrigate and water the lawns of million dollar housing developments. Parents whisk children inside when the sprinkler systems kick in, because of the smell and the fear of catching an E. coli infection.

When the Palm Islands were built, the sewage system was standard. They forgot one thing though—the topography of the ocean is dead flat. With no slopes, nothing could flow down and away from the houses there. The pipes would get clogged. When the houses were delivered, this is exactly what happened, so the last I heard they were putting a vacuum sewage system in place to compensate for the lack of gravity. Imagine all those people who invested their money in those supposed luxury homes to find sewage backing up onto their floors. Gross!

The last government decision to deal with the problem was to dig huge pits in the desert the size of three football fields so that sewage trucks could dump their loads into them and let it rot there. They gave them a pretty name: sewage lagoons, as if there was something exotic in it. It doesn't hide the fact that they are nothing but huge shit holes—and I am looking forward to seeing them on the next Google Earth update.

Adding to the sewage infrastructure issues is the problem with the pleasure boats berthed in marinas. Most of the boats are locally built and have no holding tanks for the toilets. In Europe or in the U.S., holding tanks are mandatory. In the UAE it is common to dump wastewater from the toilet directly into the surrounding water. Even worse are the old *Dhows* or traditional boats in the old port, hundreds of them. Their bathroom is an open platform rigged on the back of the boat just above the water with a hole in it. The crew can squat and dump, vertical, and in plain view. I appreciate tradition, but what happened to evolution?

Not only are floating feces discouraging swimmers, but the sea water itself is a soup saturated with sediment, sand, particles, chemicals, and leftover sludge from the desalinization plant a few miles away. That plant, along with the work on the artificial islands, the dredging, and the reclamation, is contributing to the destruction of ALL marine life along the Dubai shoreline. Without marine life, the water turns foul and contaminates the beaches.

Dubai needs astronomical amounts of fresh water for human consumption and landscaping, to fill swimming pools, for horses and, irrigation systems for golf courses. As machinery dig trenches and excavate the land, the projects under construction also need huge quantities of water to wet the sand to keep the dust on the ground, reducing air pollution. There is no natural flow of fresh water in the UAE, so Dubai built one of the largest desalinization plants in the world. It is located near the artificial Palm Islands in Jebel Ali. Without the water plant, Dubai as we know it would not exist. The plant has only one week of fresh water reserve. A desalinization plant produces drinking water by extracting fresh water from seawater. Presented, without all the facts about desalinization, the plant in Jebel Ali does not seem harmful—but knowing how the process works, sheds new light on this dangerous situation.

A desalinization plant processes a tremendous flow of seawater through huge pumps and electro-chemical systems that extract the fresh water and dumps the remains back in the ocean, a few hundred yards away. The remains consist of highly concentrated saltwater residue, with added chlorine and heat from the process. This wreaks havoc on marine ecosystems along the shore.

For every gallon of fresh water produced, there is another gallon of doubly concentrated saltwater byproduct, in effect the Jebel Ali plant dumps 1.5 billion barrels of salty sludge per year, and this sludge contaminates the water near beaches and resorts where tourists stay—but it is illegal to mention it.

In addition, the plant intake pipes vacuum up and inadvertently kill millions of plankton, fish eggs, fish larvae, and other microbial organisms that constitute the base layer of the marine food chain. It also costs more than petrol to produce, and belches vast amounts of carbon dioxide into the atmosphere. As a result, the residents of Dubai have the biggest average carbon footprint of any human being on earth.

Trust me when I say, you don't want to swim in the water around Dubai. Not only do you have to worry about severe contamination from a variety of sources, but also the water is way too murky and too hot on the surface—100 degrees Fahrenheit in the summer. You cannot swim any more than 100 feet before exhaustion sets in. The water is so warm that it does not cool off your body as you burn calories.

Nakheel executives are lying through their teeth. They buy off friendly, positive reports from marine biologists who perform faulty analyses and studies, to convince the public that marine life around its projects is improving. First, they deny any claims that coral reefs are being destroyed or that the water is contaminated. Then they blame any destruction that is brought to their attention on red algae or sea stars. But I have seen the destruction first-hand.

I dove around the islands for three years. I could not stand getting sea water in my eyes because of the burning sensation brought on by the high concentration of salt in the water. The fish are dying; the sediment is clogging their gills. Coral reefs, sea grasses, and oyster beds that were once part of protected marine lands lie choked under a barrage of dredged up sea sand. Fish float to the surface—dead.

I once had Exomos participate in a program to re-populate Jebel Ali waters by releasing hundreds of fish into the water behind my building. Only one month later, all the fish had disappeared or washed up dead on the beach. And it is not only the fish that suffer in the waters of Dubai. Sometimes I would find hundreds of dead birds on the beach, dead from poisoning of some sort.

Sultan, who is the first to claim that diving around Jumeirah is fantastic, never dives there himself—he dives in the pristine waters of the Maldives, from his hotel or in Djibouti, where he owns a house. He called me once at 1:00 in the morning to invite me, the same day, for a weekend of diving. Later in the morning we jumped in his private jet, and four hours later we were diving in Djibouti. There are so many fish there you can practically walk on them.

The best proof of my claims regarding the terrible water quality and harm to marine life in Dubai, was provided by Nakheel itself. I had to service many of its boats used for security, delivery, worker transportation, inspection, and whatever needs to go through the water. Their propulsion units and antifouling paint were wearing out in just three months due to corrosion and high speed sediment abrasion. Antifouling paint on boats is good for two years anywhere in Europe or in the U.S. In Dubai you are lucky if you can keep it for six months. But this is something they don't want you to know. These facts are swept under the rug and misreported in the news by self-censoring reporters or other self-interested parties.

The Hotels? Don't fall for the illusion …

If you like the hotel lifestyle, Dubai has the best money can buy—beautiful designs, stunning buildings, and unique architecture. From the lobbies down to the bathrooms, everything is focused on providing complete guest satisfaction. You will pay four times the price for a shirt or a watch in the hotel gift shop, but you will get free valet drivers, maids, concierges, doormen in traditional costumes, and other servants—even in the bathrooms, butlers place hand towels right in your palms and in some cases dry them for you.

But this illusion of a fancy life in these luxury hotels stops right at the doors. There is no great vacation outside. There is not much to do—dust and contaminated beaches, heat and bad behavior will ruin your vacation.

Some hotels that are advertised do not even exist. Many have heard of the Hydropolis underwater hotel. The guys running the marketing were good. They managed to put the hotel on the map and even on street signs, but it has not even been built yet and never will be. At least with this project they could always pretend the reason you don't see it is because it is under the water. At one point Sultan wanted to build a hotel on the Palm Islands with the lower floor and a couple of rooms under the water. It would have been a good idea in any other place, but not for the Palm where there is nothing to see.

Hotel valet parking areas are the location of choice for sighting luxury sports cars. It seems as if Emiratis own Lamborghinis and Ferraris only to drive them to park in front of the hotel to use as eye candy and to quench their egos from onlooking tourists.

Health care—Dubai is a health trap.

Medical facilities in Dubai are far from equivalent to those in Western countries because infrastructure and equipment are only part of the equation. Surgeons and medical staff are young. They come from south Asia or the Middle East with little experience and no motivation. I never heard of top scholars from Harvard or Oxford going to work in medical facilities there. Although medical costs are relatively low, it does not translate into good health care.

Health reporting is intentionally inaccurate, the statistics are censored and the medical staff lacks the motivation to make the efforts to save lives. Most believe that life is a mere transition into eternity, so they have a very fatalistic attitude about death and disease. Many, if not all, believe destiny is controlled by God, not the hospital, and if God wills there will be an accident, death, or disease, then so be it.

Emergency response teams in Europe and in the U.S. literally fight for the life of the patient. But in Dubai, paramedics take a back seat. They show up after twenty minutes at best, and what are supposed to be emergency life-sustaining procedures merely end in transportation to the hospital. Car fatalities always make front page of the Gulf News and, in some cases, I have seen pictures of a rescue team transporting dead victims from a crash with smiles on their faces. Overall the emergency response time sucks and if you find yourself in a life and death situation more than likely you will die.

"Patient: beware." Whomever you pick or wherever you go for medical care, always get a second opinion. If you have a critical condition, go back to your home country, even the elite of Emiratis do not use the UAE medical care. They prefer to go to the UK or the U.S. to be treated for serious illnesses because they don't trust their own system.

Health care like everything else in the UAE is a business. Most hospitals will try to get as much money as possible from you by providing treatment or lab work that you may not even need. You might find yourself getting a prescribed treatment plan that requires many repeat visits to the same doctor.

Many of the immigrants, who come to Dubai from South Asia, carry harmful germs past the screening at the airport because they are either immune to these germs themselves, or show no symptoms yet. These germs spread and expose everybody else. Westerners who have not built up the same resistance to these germs can fall gravely ill. Respiratory, skin, and blood diseases are common. A friend of mine, a French doctor in a clinic in Dubai, confirmed the high rate of respiratory diseases in Dubai is due to airborne germs, dust and pollution. This especially affects the children.

Tuberculosis is common in Dubai. Many patients affected by TB think it is a simple disease, like a cold, and treat it with cold syrup. It is only after long months of coughing blood and weight loss that they show up at the hospital for real treatment, but by then they've contaminated countless other people.

Once, my son had a sore throat. To play it safe and because infection or suspicion of infection in children in Dubai must be treated immediately, I took my son to the American Hospital. "American" sounded civilized, legitimate and professional – but it wasn't. The doctor was Syrian and suggested surgery to remove his tonsils, after one sore throat? I was concerned about the use of general anesthesia and a surgical procedure on my seven-year-old so I decided to get a second opinion. I went to another hospital, this time with a French doctor, who told me that my son didn't need any surgery or removal of his tonsils. He just had a common throat infection found in children in Dubai. The second opinion was a relief and an eye opener for me. I could have put my son through with an unnecessary intrusive procedure.

Medicines are available in Dubai, but not like in Europe or the U.S. Most medicines that I saw were expired and delivered over the counter without prescriptions, except the hypnotics and mind-altering drugs. When I came back to the U.S., I had some medicines I had brought from Dubai. I showed them to my doctor. He was surprised to see these medicines were still being prescribed and used. He told me they were outdated by at least five years. All kinds of sex stimulants are banned of course, but they are available on the black market. Some medications, those for sexually transmitted diseases, may get reported to the Department of Health and can get the person who bought them deported.

Dubai claims to be the safest place on earth to live; another lie to lure you in. It is actually one of the most dangerous cities in the world. It may be true that there is little chance of becoming a victim of a violent crime; however there are many other ways to lose your life. The leading cause of death in Dubai is heart disease. The government covers up the death rates to hide the fact that the way of life in Dubai is directly responsible for the higher rate; and to not scare off expatriates who could realize that there is a much greater chance of dying in Dubai than there would be if they stayed in their home countries.

The Dubai Statistic Center states the death rate in Dubai at 1.4 per 1,000 inhabitants. The United States' CIA website puts the death rate in Dubai at 4.2 per 1,000. Already this is three times the UAE official rate. The government manipulates the statistics to hide the true high death rate. When they report their numbers, they purposely avoid the use of adjusted rates that take into consideration the age of the population. At first glance, the rate of 4.2 deaths per 1,000 in Dubai looks good, compared to 8.2 in the U.S., but it does not take into consideration that in the U.S., eighty percent of the total deaths occur in the sixty and older age group. But in Dubai, there are **no** expatriates over the age of sixty and only 12,500 Emiratis according to their census. A country with this few elders should have a much lower death rate than average, because young people die in lesser numbers than old people. The median age in Dubai is twenty-eight years old, yet the leading cause of death is heart failure, that is a very worrisome sign. Taking this into consideration brings the adjusted death rate for the UAE in the range of twenty per 1,000, which is one of the highest death rates in the world. If foreigners knew that their risk of death went from four to twenty, I doubt they would be in such a hurry to work in Dubai – and that is exactly what Dubai is trying to keep the world from finding out. All together, expatriates and Emiratis have a higher risk of dying on the road or from stress, bad diet, or lack of exercise than anywhere else.

The public perception of preservation of traditional values and vitalization is the key reason for biased and fallacious healthcare reports. Sadly, this will only lead to the Emiratis own demise because when an expatriate dies, he may be replaced, but when an Emirati dies, it is a loss for the country and a threat to their survival. Because Emiratis are sorely outnumbered they will find themselves totally absorbed by foreigners in the near future. Without proper and genuine reporting, it proves an impossible task to curb these entirely preventable causes of death in the UAE. The government faces a dilemma—does it acknowledge the causes of death and admit to the world its people's lifestyle is killing them or does it allow them to continue on until extinction?

Emiratis blame the causes of deaths and diseases on exposure to the West's decadent culture, as if they have been forced into it. Yet it is their government that brought the world to its doorstep. And the Emiratis don't fight the changes; they welcome them with open arms. Money brought them something they didn't have before—diversity. With wealth comes complacency, arrogance, and an apathetic lifestyle. You can see obese men walking around in *kandourahs*. They're young, but they don't even walk anymore, not even to the mall. They have drivers, valet parking, electric cars to use inside the malls, and personal maids that run errands for them so they don't have to move. They go to bed at four o'clock in the morning, wake up at noon, talk all day on their mobile phones, work a couple of hours, and eat a lot of cheap and high fat food.

The UAE has the second highest number of diabetics in the world on a per capita basis. According to a study published in Arabian Business in October 2008, seventy-five percent of the Emiratis are obese. One Emirati out of four has diabetes. The waistlines they are trying to hide underneath their immaculate *kandourahs* are unmistakable proof of their lack of exercise and rich diet. HIV is a big problem in the UAE. There are 800 reported cases of HIV among 900,000 Emiratis. There are no statistics on how many expatriates have the virus, because anyone who is found to be infected is immediately deported. Hence the number of people infected is eighty-eight out of 100,000. In the U.S., the number of people infected is twenty out of 100,000. Emiratis like to say that America is decaying due to decadence and lust, but with an HIV rate contamination almost five times higher than in the U.S., it sounds a lot like the pot calling the kettle black. Knowing how the statistics are misreported in the UAE, the contamination rate is probably even higher.

Another manipulated use of statistics in Dubai relates to the death rate on the roads. According to the police, the road alone kills 330 people every year, putting the official rate at twenty-two deaths per 100,000 inhabitants. This too, is a misrepresentation since at least two-thirds of the population does not drive. A more accurate number of deaths should be quantified per 100,000 vehicles, not people. If you use this measure, the rate is eighty-two deaths per 100,000 cars. In the U.S., the death rate under the same criteria is fifteen, so in Dubai you have five times the risk of dying in a car accident than you do in the U.S.

The government can manipulate the numbers and the wording as much as it wants, but the fact remains that Emiratis are dying at a much higher rate from heart attacks, cancer, HIV, and car accidents than people in other areas of the world. This is a direct result of them practicing the seven deadly sins—lust, gluttony, greed, sloth, envy, wrath and pride. They have a lot of nerve, lecturing the so-called decadent West.

Housing—Housing in Dubai or Dante's inferno

Finding a place to live is one of the biggest problems every expatriate faces, unless he is an expert in demand, and is provided with accommodation based on his position. Everybody else is left on their own. Rents are typically half their salary, so many share villas or apartments with others. This only adds to the chaos since sharing housing was made illegal by the Government. Only direct relatives can live in the same house or apartment. The majority of workers and helpers live together in camps and dormitories.

Services and operations, requiring highly qualified employees, are priced through the roof—because, one way or another, housing costs end up in the payroll. There are no justifications for the high rents. It is not that there is a lack of housing. But rather, what is available, is artificially maintained as very expensive or kept vacant for speculation. Also Dubai is one of the only cities in the world to require a rent deposit of six months, one year in advance.

There cannot be stability in the housing market because Dubai is a transient society. People wade through very restrictive housing regulations, and they risk eviction, fines, or deportation if they are caught sharing, and prison if they are unmarried couples. There is no sanctity of the home or rights to privacy because police officers have the right to inspect any property at any time. Those who get evicted lose not only their homes but their six months deposit.

The housing problems are aggravated by segregation; people are not free to look for housing wherever they want. Singles or bachelors are not allowed to live in just any community. They have to live in gender-segregated buildings. Single women buildings are guarded, not to protect them, but to make sure they don't have male visitors.

The official reason the government gives for these rules is to maintain a safe and clean environment. What does that mean anyway—that singles are criminal and dirty?

Visas and residency, a permanent probation

Many people think they can make plans for their lives, but how can anyone have a feeling of stability in a place where there is no possible citizenship and not even a permanent residency. There is no other option than to live on a temporary visa that can be terminated at any time and without reason. There are no unemployed in Dubai, and there is no visa for the retired either. An expatriate can only be a working guest or a visitor.

You cannot make a ten or twenty year plan. My plans were ruined after two years. Thus, investing in a house, vehicle, boat or a business is a high risk decision.

The ruling families will never let foreigners become citizens, or let them gain an identity, respect, or representation. Because then, there would no longer be any differences between immigrants and nationals. The rulers are too concerned with keeping their power and their lineage with the life term benefits they carry. The President of the UAE said, in an official declaration in 2007, as published in the Gulf News, that all expatriates are merely guest workers and cannot be considered migrants. So if they want to blame people for going to Dubai only to make a quick buck, it is not the fault of the expats—it's the fault of the Dubai government who will never consider expatriates equals to UAE nationals. They are welcome in Dubai only as long as they serve the Emiratis, to build and maintain their country.

Many job candidates go to Dubai on a visitor's visa and then solicit a job position on site. They call on companies and offer their resumes, go to interviews, and often get hired. I hired several employees this way. They start with an entry-level salary and remain on probation for three months before getting a raise and a permanent position. This probationary period is the law, but, in effect, people are on probation permanently, as it is easy to get fired or deported.

Applying for a visa does not follow standard rules. In the UAE, segregation is official. The process that one must go through to apply for a work visa varies, depending on many factors. For example: it depends on whether the person is a man or woman, whether the applicant is young or old (because anyone older than fifty-nine will be denied), where the person is from, what skill level the person has, and whether the applicant is married or single. If a woman is under twenty-five she gets maximum scrutiny at the airport and almost has to prove she's not a sex worker, even if she is married. Her husband may ask approval of the Director General of Naturalization and Residency Department to sponsor her visa. Even with this scrutiny, there are still tens of thousands of prostitutes in Dubai.

There are many categories of people in certain professions who are banned from sponsoring their direct relatives. Housemaids, drivers, cooks, mechanics, and nurses are among the people who do not have the right to bring their families to Dubai. For the groups who are permitted to bring in and sponsor family members, they still must meet a minimum salary requirement before family visas are approved.

Applying for a visa is always a costly, restrictive, and painful experience. Many times, visas are denied for no reason. Sanil, my assistant, with his fifteen years of experience in Dubai, was an expert in understanding these processes, and he greatly facilitated the development of the company through securing visas for the employees, or should I say his friends and relatives. He knew all about government agencies, and being Indian, he had the connections and relatives to facilitate the process.

Most foreigners, applying for a work permit and temporary residency visa, are attracted by a better salary, better living conditions and the high life publicized by Dubai. Even years later, many lock themselves into believing that their life is better than anywhere else, and brush off any negative comparisons by friends and visitors who have traveled to other countries and can see the differences.

Dubai has created restrictions on visas for family members, to avoid the demand for lower-end apartments, (favoring instead high-priced residences) and to keep the number of foreigners' relatives as low as possible. It is better to house 100 single people segregated by gender in camps, docile, with nothing to do but work, than to have twenty working couples with their children living in private homes.

What the government of Dubai and the Emirati don't seem to understand is there cannot be an upper class if there are no middle or labor classes. The wealthy need people to service their cars, take care of their children, and clean their houses. There will be a time when people making up the lower class of Dubai will want to live somewhere other than in camps. Since there is no affordable housing for middle or labor classes, nor any projects to build in the near future, eventually these people will return to their countries, leaving the rich alone—who in turn will leave as well. Investors and owners of properties will probably sell and go, not only because of the mass exodus of the workers and upper class, but because real estate contracts cannot be trusted.

Dubai real estate: the scam

Dealing with the real estate developers in Dubai is risky and an exercise in frustration. Many owners, who buy a property from plans, receive something that looks much different than the brochure. They end up with other buildings and pass over's cropping up around their property that were never depicted or disclosed. I've seen people end up with a major roadway interchange right outside their living room windows and people with their beach views blocked by a tower.

A friend of mine bought an apartment on the fourteenth floor of a tower at Dubai Marina—the top floor. He wanted the penthouse and paid the price for a penthouse. When his apartment was handed over to him, he didn't get the penthouse because they had built an extra six stories on top of his floor. As for his neighbors in the higher tower behind, they thought they were going to have a unique ocean view but they were wrong; they have now six new stories blocking their view. For my friend and everybody else that also meant less parking, although they kept adding floors, the underground parking garage remained the same size.

I also heard many complaints from people who bought properties from Nakheel that were supposed to have golf course views. When the villas were handed over, they discovered that their golf course views had been replaced by a new batch of 350 villas.

The same thing happened with the villa I lived in for three years in Jebel Ali. There was to be a park behind my house with trees, plants, and flowers, just below my living room window. As I was leaving the house one day, Nakheel was leveling the grounds of the park to turn it into a site for an extra 150 villas. Too bad for my neighbors who purchased or rented these villas and were told the land would remain a park. Not only was it a misrepresentation of what they were purchasing, but also, as a result of the new construction, they will be eating dust for the next two years.

The Palm Jumeirah Island design has changed at least three times. You can see on the brochures and conceptual drawings how it was first presented to the media, investors, and home buyers. Now it looks completely different. The changes have greed written all over them. Nakheel tripled the number of villas on the branches, razed parks, reduced lots, and doubled the number of stories on the condominiums on the trunk of the island. In such cases of misrepresentations and breach of contracts you are left with no recourse against the contractors. Any complaint, lawsuit, or court proceedings will turn against you—you cannot win.

I don't believe Nakheel when he says that David Beckham, Christina Aguilera, or any other stars have bought properties on the Palm—they would certainly not live there. As a matter of fact, I met one celebrity that Nakheel had advertised had bought an island on the World Island Archipelago. He later confided in me that he didn't buy anything. Nakheel made it up, using his name to attract buyers. It may be fine to do that in Dubai, but in the west, it constitutes fraud. I don't believe Donald Trump invested in a tower on the Palm Jumeirah Island either. It is just another scam to lure investors.

Many foreign executives bought freehold homes in Dubai. Freehold properties are the only properties in the UAE that can be acquired by an expatriate. They cannot own the land on which the property is raised though. And these homes are located in designated areas or have been built on reclaimed land. Acquiring property anywhere else in the Federation requires citizenship of a Gulf Country.

I bought a house in freehold shortly after arriving in Dubai, in 2004—two years after Sheikh Mohammed opened the Emirate's property sector to foreign investors. I trusted Nakheel, the developer, that upon completion and handover, I would get a permanent residency visa attached to the property and not to my job—which would have given me some feeling of stability. But that was a lie. Dubai lured investors with promises of residency visas and then, when the property was purchased, the government of Dubai changed the laws and the people were stuck owning property without a residency visa. Marwan Bin Galita, of Dubai's Real Estate Regulatory Authority made statements in the *Gulf News* that people who bought houses thinking they were going to get a residency visa were just confused. He said they misunderstood, too bad for all those expatriates who misunderstood. They now own property they will have to leave and sell cheap when their visas expire or when they lose their job.

More than 20,000 families moved into their freehold homes under false pretense. One of the reasons why Dubai has witnessed its economic boom is because of this residency visa real estate law. Now in order to get a residency visa after you purchase a house, you must work for a sponsor. But if you are older than sixty, you cannot have a work visa. Farewell to any kind of retirement for expatriates in Dubai. These housing and residency visa issues are typical scenarios. It's always about the bait and switch in Dubai.

In the U.S., buying a property does not grant the buyer an automatic residency visa, but at least buyers know that in advance. They are not lured into purchasing properties with the promise of residency only to have that promise withdrawn after they've spent their money on million dollar homes.

Due to the large amount of new properties (about 300,000) recently handed over, there is only about a thirty percent occupancy rate. I predict that Dubai is going to be a ghost town soon—with poor workers crowded in camps on one side of the city, and empty apartments on the other. The financial crisis has reached Dubai, despite the messages from the government claiming that Dubai is booming and real estate values are on the rise. When investors lose money in Europe, China, or the U.S., this is money they no longer have for their property installment payments. A lot of these buyers will default on their mortgage payments or installments. They will lose their deposits, and they will be charged a thirty percent penalty. And if they go to Dubai to complain, they will be arrested at the airport. In Dubai these penalties are legal, and few people realize it. Anyone trying to fight them in court will lose. In Dubai, when you don't pay your debts you go to prison.

Initial investors of property purchased in Dubai multiplied their gains. Many of these properties have since changed hands, sometime three times—but in the end, the final owners will have problems selling their properties, when property values take a nose dive and nobody will buy them. Sales have already declined. There's been a fifty percent drop in value of Dubai properties. The housing problems got worse and worse during my time in Dubai—and, from what I've read, they are no better now.

I know what happened to two properties purchased by foreigners who lost them. Two of my Emirati friends, Humaid and Hussein received a free villa from the Government. They didn't even try to hide the fact they had gotten these villas from expatriates who had been pushed out, or in other words: ripped off.

The lifestyle—The Dubai rich lifestyle is an illusion

In the beginning, living in Dubai works well under the illusion of a new life in an exotic country. Numbers are presented so people think they can make good money. But soon, they realize they don't make that much—because they work at least forty-eight hours a week, they have no retirement plan, the cost of living in Dubai is very expensive, and the inflation rate is upwards of twenty percent.

The local economy is tied to the European market, and most Western workers convert their salary into Euros, but the local currency is pegged to the U.S. Dollar. So every time the dollar loses value, expatriates see their incomes shrink. All together with the ongoing inflation, it's like getting a twenty percent salary cut every year. The only employees to receive salary raises are the Emiratis—not only do they get a paycheck, but if they don't work it is okay. They cannot be fired.

In its efforts to attract workers, businessmen, and investors, Dubai advertises itself as a tax-free environment, with no import or export duties, no restrictions on maximum imports, no personal income or capital gains taxes, no corporate taxes, and 100 percent repatriation of capital and profits. Is Dubai a fiscal heaven? Not quite. Their laws are misleading. Once again they perpetrate the bait and switch. This is how it really works...

The income tax free environment is limited to the free trade zones and to business conducted outside Dubai only. There is a five percent custom duty for all imports, applicable in the free zones. Since everything is imported, every consumer and company pays five percent tax on everything.

At one point I wanted to start a boat charter company, buy a passenger boat, and get a license to offer offshore tours to tourists and hotel guests. I found out that a boat charter company cannot operate or be established from the free zone. It must be operated from Dubai, for which I needed an Emirati sponsor. When I inquired about the whole process, the cash investment represented about $500,000 for a boat, $50,000 "fee" for a UAE National to sponsor me (a ten percent fee which turned out to be a bribe in disguise), another $50,000 to maintain the bank account and $50,000 in government fees. Already that is twenty percent out of the bank account before getting the business running. The UAE national and sponsor, would invest nothing of course, would get a salary for doing nothing, and would own fifty-one percent of everything including the bank account and my boat, which had to be registered in his name. My charter company would have been taxed at ten percent for revenues above $280,000 and up to fifty percent for higher revenues.

Of course I had many Emirati friends who were more than happy to volunteer to help me with my boat charter company. One of them was already making $300,000 per year just sponsoring other companies. What a great job! He didn't even need an office. In the event of a conflict against my sponsor, I would have had no hope of recovering anything. I could have found myself in limbo, blackmailed or caught in legal loopholes forever with no way of winning against a National. Emiratis always say the fifty-one percent Emirati ownership can be reversed back to the foreign investor with a contract. They promise the Emirati sponsorship is just a front. During disputes between a foreign national business owner and his sponsor, no back door contract will save the foreign national whose passport may be held by the police, and whose court proceedings could last years and be very costly.

When I saw that, I just walked away. It's nothing but racketeering to me. The UAE National doesn't bring any added value to the company, does not know anything about the business—yet he owns it. How good is it, to not pay personal income taxes when you lose fifty-one percent ownership and end up paying more than fifty percent of the company incomes to the Emirates, to the sponsor, to the government, to inflation, or to the tollgates—they just don't call it taxes.

To find out whether any tax savings affects your cost of living, you need to know how much your earnings are worth and what you can buy with them. The only way to compare Dubai to the rest of the world is to look at a measure like the Purchasing Power Per Capita (PPP), which is more reliable than statements or statistics from the biased Dubai government. The PPP takes into consideration all economic factors in a given country and divides it by the population. It compares country to country how much you can buy with your money.

On the world PPP list, Dubai ranks eighteenth, proof that Dubai overstates its position. Singapore, a place often compared to Dubai, is ranked fifth. The U.S. is ranked sixth. This means it is less expensive to live in seventeen countries than it is to live in Dubai, and these are seventeen nice places to live. So it is certainly not a bargain to live in Dubai.

The cost of living just keeps getting greater and greater. When I was in Dubai, school fees increased ninety-seven percent in two years. The government had to put a cap on rents because of a twenty-five percent increase per year. However, many landlords find other ways to increase rent. In Dubai you may make money, at the beginning, but you can easily lose it, because of the lifestyle and debts. In the end, many expatriates find themselves leaving the UAE bankrupt and ripped off.

The risks, or how you can lose everything.

The risks you face in Dubai are serious. Risks include becoming the victim of an investor state scam, a business rip off, or a debt (real or alleged) that you cannot pay. Civil matters in the UAE are crimes. An executive, a CEO, or manager of a company can be accused of mismanagement or breach of trust by the owner and be imprisoned indefinitely without charges or evidences. This is Sharia law, applicable to everyone—including non-Muslims.

I am not talking about illegal enrichment or embezzlement here, but normal expenses that occur in doing regular, day-to-day business. These expenses can be turned around suddenly by the Emirati and made to look like money has been lost. This is done as a pretext, for him to turn it into a debt and claim monies from his partners or employees. Things that would amount to nothing illegal in the West, or at most, a civil cause of action—take a dramatic turn in Dubai with prospects of life in prison. Once in prison, the person's term is extended indefinitely by a judge until the incarcerated person pays the money claimed by the Emirati party.

This means you face life in prison unless you reimburse monies you are accused of owing—even if you were just doing your job and running the company using standard, normal business practices. Had I known this before going to Dubai, I would have taken precautions before accepting a CEO position. I would have left my family back home, moved to Dubai with just a briefcase and been prepared to pack and take off as soon as a conflict rises, that is the red flag.

The more you wait and think things can get better, the closer you get to the call from the police—and, when you get the call, it is too late. They ask you to come to the police station right way for questioning because of an on going investigation.

Even if you have your passport handy, you already have a travel ban on your name, only you don't know it. When you get to the police station, you are under investigation, your passport is confiscated and you may be arrested. From there—whatever problem there is, it will only get worse. It is too late, and you are trapped.

Under this ready to pack and leave situation, it is always a risk to own anything or do business there. It does not matter if you can leave your doors unlocked or walk the streets without the risk of getting assaulted. That is not where the dangers are. You can lose money at the very same place you earned it—at work. Anyone considering living and working in Dubai should know that in the UAE, any employee, from the lowest paid worker to the CEO can be held personally and financially responsible for business losses or involuntary damages. It doesn't matter if it is written in an employment contract that a person cannot be held personally financially responsible for any losses in the company, because such a clause is against UAE law. Emiratis want it to work only one way—their way. They want it set up so that if they lose, you pay.

Already you can lose money on the little things of everyday life, like getting ripped off for anything from car repairs to household items. There is no customer satisfaction in Dubai, and there is never a refund when you buy a defective item. At best, you might get lucky and get a replacement with a used model.

You can lose your assets fairly easily because ownership can be affected by divorce, death, departure from the country, the loss of a job, the termination of a visa, an order of deportation, or a conflict with an Emirati national. In the event of deportation, property must be sold in a hurry through a third party, with major losses.

Unlike anywhere else in the world, there are many, many ways in Dubai that you can end up being deported with a mandatory one way flight out of the country. Even if you live like a Trappist monk, you can be prosecuted and deported for the silliest reason.

Any criminal offense carries a deportation, but you don't have to be a criminal in the normal sense of the word to be deported. A French kiss at sunset on the beach, a bottle of whiskey in the trunk of your car, a liaison with a girlfriend, flipping your middle finger, or car pooling with a friend to work could each make you a criminal. Deportation takes place thirty days after the end of employment, twenty-four hours after a judgment that carries a deportation order, or immediately after your release if you have been jailed or diagnosed with a STD, and that is, if you can pay for your flight ticket. Otherwise, you stay jailed until someone comes up with the plane ticket; the UAE does not pay for the deportations.

In the case of inheritance or divorce, title to property or ownership doesn't mean anything either. It is important to know, as it is not clearly advertised by the government, that everything a foreigner owns falls under the Sharia law, or Islamic law, whether they are Muslim or not.

The government of Dubai advertises that its employees can take risks to promote innovations and new ideas. It is nothing but a lie, a trap, and a fraud. They do encourage taking risks, and if anybody promotes an idea which actually works, he gets a reward—a small financial bonus and the usual, useless crystal trophy. The whole idea is highly advertised so that everybody knows and can get motivated. The trap is when the risk does not pay off. Those who tried new ideas at the company's expense and didn't succeed were forced to reimburse the company out of their own pockets, were accused of embezzlement and their passports were taken away until they reimbursed the company for everything.

The last time I attended a conference at Dubai World Group, Sultan himself promoted taking risks by the employees of the Group without fear of any personal liability. One year before, Sultan had authorized me to buy and try a new propulsion system for one of our boats. Six months later, after I concluded that this was not working for applications, he sent auditors to ask me to personally reimburse the costs. I refused and everything went downhill from there. You don't have to believe me, but anyone who trusts the word of an Emirati will be in for a world of hurt.

I know of about ten executives of Dubai World companies who are currently locked up in prison in Dubai with no charges against them. They have been set up by their Emirati partners. The police themselves admit these people are in prison for further investigation, to determine if charges can be pressed, and to see if their cases can be referred to the court. In other words, they are guilty until proven guilty. If they are kept in prison, it is only to force them to pay, it is not about guilt. It is about money. If they are guilty of anything, it is for having run their businesses and becoming the scapegoat for their employers' mismanagement. Or, if the company didn't make the money their Emirati bosses wanted, they are now in jail until they pay back millions they don't have.

I came to Dubai because they asked me to. I trusted everything and, in the end, I was betrayed by His Excellency Sultan Ahmed bin Sulayem, the Chairman of Dubai World who has over $200 billion dollars in assets.

The government advertises the benefits of traveling and working in Dubai, but does not disclose the restrictions that can land people in jail or get them deported—for fear that people might get scared and decide to go somewhere else. They're right to fear this. If people knew they risked up to six years in prison for something that is normal in Miami or Rio de Janeiro, they would probably re-book their trip to South Beach instead and spend their money there.

The Emirates actually never changed their laws. They pretended to be more liberal and open by western standards, but the laws are the same as in Saudi Arabia. Instead, they hid them temporarily to attract foreigners and their money. They waited until the foreigners with their businesses and money were established and until they were used to traveling to Dubai. And then, little by little, the Emirati government went backwards and began to enforce their existing laws. Again, it's the oldest game in the book—the bait and switch.

Driving in Dubai, where discrimination meets death toll

With people from so many different countries, Dubai has imported every bad driving habit that exists in the world. But what is unique about driving there is the high death toll, the segregation, and the arrogance. Nationals have the worst road manners I've ever seen, only promoted by the most unbalanced traffic laws in the world. If only the police would pull drivers over for their traffic violations regardless of who they are, maybe Dubai would be a safer place to drive. Not surprisingly, the problems with traffic and congestion feed most of the table conversations and chatting in the workplaces.

The most irritating and common problem is while driving in the far left lane of the road you are being harassed by someone coming from behind at high speed who wants to overtake you. He incessantly flashes his headlights and dangerously tailgates. These drivers, mostly locals, act as if they own the roads and as if the speed limit only applies to you. I overheard arguments where Emiratis yelled at other drivers, that it is their country and that as mere guests, foreigners should give priority to nationals. I have been a passenger with Emirati drivers. I heard them discussing the useless lives of other people who should be somewhere else other than driving in front of their cars.

Picking up students at school is the same in every country. When you have a large number of parents showing up in a very narrow time frame, you can expect lines and sometimes chaos and frustration. But what makes it worse in Dubai is the arrogance of the Emirati parents who force their Maserati's or Bentley's in the way, cutting everyone off because they feel more important than anybody else.

It is not that Emiratis forget that foreigners built their schools and the roads to get there—they just don't care. They act as if they threw some money away and the expatriates should feel privileged to have been able to pick it up and leave when they are finished building their country.

Many have found there is no point in fighting back—that can just get a person in trouble in Dubai. Don't dare give them the middle finger, it can land you in jail for a month, and all it takes is a phone call from an Emirati to report you. A friend of mine lost his temper once while driving. He flipped his middle finger at the other driver, and drove off. The offended driver called the police to complain about this grave offense, and it didn't take more than ten minutes for my friend to receive a call on his mobile phone, requesting him to stop immediately at the nearest police station to report for this complaint. If you don't report when ordered, it is like resisting arrest, worsening your offense when they catch you later. He denied it, and without a confession or witnesses, the police confiscated his passport for three months, pending the investigation and in the end, he got a one month jail suspended sentence.

Causing an accidental death on the road carries a mandatory payment of $55,000 to the victim's family (half if the victim is a woman—equality?) whether you are responsible for the accident or not, even if the victim threw himself under the car to commit suicide. This actually happens in Dubai. Destitute and desperate laborers have been known to do this so that their families could receive the blood money equivalent to twenty years of their salary. The victim's family does not have to sue to get the money because a judge automatically grants this compensation. If the driver who killed the person doesn't have the money to pay, he will sit in jail until he can pay. Some, but not all insurance companies provide coverage that includes this blood money payment, but they don't pay if the accident is declared criminal—due to drunk driving or a faulty car for example. Because of the high rate of accidents, insurance is very expensive; four to five times the cost in the U.S.

A French lady I knew hit a pedestrian who had decided to cross the highway. The pedestrian tried to avoid a vehicle ahead of her, lost his balance, and ended up just throwing himself on her car. The guy was taken to the local hospital and died later that night. At three o'clock in the morning, the police knocked on the door of her house to arrest her. Her husband was on a business trip at the time, so she had to leave her two children alone in the house for three days before she could get bailed out.

In four years I was lucky never to have an accident—near accidents don't count, as they are a normal way of life in Dubai. Accidents, when they occur, are horrific and deadly. No doubt this is exacerbated by the prevalence of powerful cars with inexperienced drivers behind the wheels.

Finding yourself on foot in Dubai is not a pleasant experience because of the heat and the lack of pedestrian bridges. Emiratis don't care about the lack of infrastructure because they're never on foot. They have drivers and multiple cars. Traffic is already crazy enough—trying to cross the roads can be a fatal experience.

The police are almost invisible, but they are everywhere, mostly undercover in plain clothes. The only visible police are the ones in police cars. You don't see a lot of them on the roads, but they drive BMWs and Mercedes, and are actually quite helpful to distressed motorists. They don't seem to spend much time enforcing traffic laws other than to pull over cars with tinted windows. Enforcement is handled mostly by a system of live cameras and radar. They are everywhere, at major intersections and every 1.5 miles on highways—sometimes fifty yards after a speed limit signal just to make sure that you won't get away with speeding even after hitting the brakes. Many other traffic violations are never caught, such as changing lanes without signaling—a normal trend in Dubai—or driving the opposite direction around a traffic circle to avoid the full three quarters of a turnaround to go left.

Traffic fines range from $30 to $500. For the most serious offenses the car can be impounded. There is jail time for drunk driving, or even drunk walking. Fines are paid upon license renewal.

Although it is true that high-paced development has a tendency to confuse traffic, I do believe that previously permissive road laws in Dubai were in place temporarily to lure foreigners into the country. Now that the flow of expatriates has been established, in just four years I saw drastic changes in road laws. They became increasingly restrictive by the month: toll gates, driver license eligibility, car resale restrictions.

The government deems them necessary to cope with the rapid development of Dubai, when the true reason is to throw people off the roads, so the local elite can drive with less traffic. But it doesn't work. Drivers who cannot afford the tolls are still driving because there is no adequate public transportation system. The traffic has not been reduced—it has only been rerouted onto no-toll secondary roads where the congestion has become even worse than it was before. Ultimately the congestion spreads and gridlocks, blocking access to the toll roads. The government is pushing the public to use public transportation by implementing all sorts of laws and rules. But using the limited public transportation is impractical, and the infrastructure is not in place for this to be a reality. Users of public transportation end up walking for miles in heat over 100 degrees from the stations.

To own a vehicle, you must be a resident with a valid working visa. If your vehicle is financed, you own nothing, not even your freedom. Miss two monthly payments and you end up in jail.

In the end when you try to resell your car, you will not get any more than twenty percent of the price you listed it for. The law there prohibits the transfer of ownership of any car older than ten years. Who's going to buy a car that's five years old knowing they're going to have to junk it when their visa expires after two years? The import of vehicles that are more than five years old is forbidden. I don't know any other place on earth with such drastic limitations. It is not justified from what I saw there—the vehicles on the roads in Dubai were in pretty good condition compared to cars in Western countries. Emiratis are not concerned. They don't have a visa that will expire. And they keep their cars for three years maximum, and then sell them to expatriates. They buy cars like you and I buy shirts.

Because the traffic is still jamming the roads in Dubai, the government took traffic control one step further with the use of segregation. They banned the issuance of driver licenses for people in over 100 professional categories—people like nurses, carpenters, mechanics, and cooks are no longer authorized to have driver licenses. They are only granted to people who work in jobs where a university degree is required. Everybody else must be crammed in buses.

As a result and because of so many loan defaults, the market is already swamped with used cars, forcing owners to sell their cars cheap for export or just dump them at the airport and leave the country before the banks report them to the police. There are so many of them that banks have found a name for them—they call them skips. This is why they arrest people who miss just two car payments. When people are behind on their payments, the banks think their borrowers are going to skip the country and they want to stop them before they can leave behind an unpaid debt and a car in the airport parking lot. Once a person is jailed he can only be released after all the car payments are brought current and fines paid.

Once you buy a car, you need to register it. It takes two hours of waiting at three different counters, or thirty minutes and two counters if you pay the fast lane service charge of $50. VIP's or Emirati's don't even bother to stand in line for a driver's license—somebody else does it for them.

The drive to work for most people is along the thirty-five-mile Dubai stretch. The main road, the Sheikh Zayed Road, or SZR, is parallel to the shoreline. It's a ten-lane highway with automatic tollgates. You cannot miss the huge signs with portraits worshipping the ruler of Dubai and his sons. Street signs are written in Arab and English but are useless if you don't know the city.

Grass, palm trees, and flowers are maintained on the main roads, crossings, and around buildings. Armies of municipal employees in jump suits keep the side roads immaculate. The roads appear to have been designed overnight with no oversight. Miss a turn, and you'll likely end up on the other side of town before you are able to make a U-turn and go back. Don't even think about asking for directions either or you will also end up on the other side of town. Maps and GPS are useless because the road network changes every three months. New circles and intersections appear in one week without notice.

Given the cost per square foot of built-out space, developers prefer to build towers one against another, instead of parking lots, and there are no laws like in other countries requiring a certain number of parking spaces per square foot. Developers build one parking space per apartment—but with four or five adults living in the same apartment, obviously somebody is going to park on the sidewalks or between trash bins. Parking spots are also way too small. Lots of people drive SUVs in Dubai, but the spaces are more suited to Smart cars. With my big Hummer I always had a problem trying to get out of the car without leaving a shoe stuck in the door because I could not open it completely.

When expatriates complain about discrimination in the traffic laws, Emiratis don't even deny the existence of double standards. There's no reason to—really. They are not shy about doing what they want in their country—their attitude is, if you don't like it, you should leave. They admit the laws governing the roadways and driving are different for citizens than they are for expatriates. Officially, they say there is merely some flexibility toward the application of road rules. But what I observed throughout my personal experience in Dubai was that the higher the Emirati is in the social pyramid, the less likely he is going to be fined or even blamed for a traffic violation. If there is an accident between an Emirati and a foreigner, it is almost certain that the foreigners will be found at fault. The police officer who responds to the scene of the accident, usually a Yemeni on a government sponsored visa, would rather believe the Emirati who can extend the flexibility of the law to changing the color of intersection lights from red to green. Many officials and other powerful Emiratis in Dubai have their license plate numbers listed in the police system as ineligible for fines and for inclusion in police reports. They can flash past radar systems everywhere they go, or park anywhere, and they'll never get a ticket for it.

When Emiratis crash their cars all by themselves, and they are such good drivers that it happens quite often, they just walk away, call someone to pick them up, and abandon the wreck on the side of the road like a bag of trash. They don't care, the next day they just drive another one of their many cars. I witnessed a handful of these accidents, with expensive cars left abandoned on the side of the roads.

As a result of their bad road behavior, locals don't get any sympathy from other motorists when they trash their cars. Rather, they make faces that say, "Well done, you moron." Once, I saw a red BMW, the latest model fully loaded, being driven by an Emirati driver wearing a *khandoura*. He was forcing his way through dozens of cars, beeping his horn, flashing his headlights, and being obnoxious. At the end of the line of cars, a bus crammed full of Indian laborers was blocking his way, so he tried to go around them. It was such a tight turn that, even though he was not going really fast, he managed to flip his car over and slide down the grassy side of the road. He got out of his car in front of a crowd that was silently mocking him. I was laughing my head off. I will never forget his face; it turned purple with the rage and hatred boiling inside him, while he attempted to feign indifference. "After all it was the fault of these foreign imbeciles who got in his way and caused him to have this accident."

Twice, I was pulled over because of my tinted car windows. I mentioned to one of the police officers that I had seen many other cars with much darker windows than mine, and they didn't seem to have a problem. His response was a monument to the ridiculousness of their road laws—those with the dark windows have permission from the Road Authority, but according to the cop I would not qualify for that permission because I was not an Emirati.

I come from a democratic country and such blatant inequality just infuriates me. So I asked him politely to enlighten me. I wanted to understand what made me so different from an Emirati driver. How is it that he can get permission, and I cannot? He explained to me that the difference is because of his women—his wives and daughters. The law provides privacy to Muslim women so that other men cannot stare at them. So I asked him—what about my wife? Does she not deserve the same respect as a non-Muslim woman? He had no answers for me.

One day I vented my frustrations over being discriminated against by playing a trick on an Emirati with dark windows. One evening, I picked out a car that had tinted windows that was in an outdoor parking lot in town. I slipped over to it unnoticed, checked for surveillance cameras and covered the whole windshield with a large, black, vinyl sticker I purchased from the local craft store. Then I went to dinner in a bar across from the parking lot to watch my prank unfold. What I saw still makes me laugh to this day. It felt good to make an arrogant Emirati look like a fool. This guy came out of the nearby building all dressed in his *khandoura* as I expected he would be, got into his car, and turned on the engine. The headlights turned on automatically, but of course he could not see the light in front of his car through the windshield because my big, black, vinyl sheet was simulating darkness. So he got out of the car and went to the front of it and wiped the headlights off, as if dirt was the reason he could not see his lights. Then he got back into the car. After a minute, he pulled down the window and stuck his head out, saw the light ahead and stared at his black windshield, wondering what was happening. Damn—where did the light go? Finally he realized that the windshield was darkened, and he'd been duped. The whole scene lasted a good three minutes. I watched him grab his phone to call for help. The police came with some Indian worker. I saw the whole drama unfold—the police looking at the windshield and the Indian worker trying to peel off the sticker. I should have filmed the prank and put the video on You Tube. It was a classic. Don't play tricks like that in Dubai, especially on an Emirati— you might end up in jail. Emiratis have a very short sense of humor and an oversized sense of pride.

When you read the statistics put out by the Dubai government about cars and traffic, everything seems normal, like most other modern countries. But the numbers don't add up. For instance, their statistics show that there is one car for every two people in Dubai. But given the fact that the immense majority of those working in Dubai, laborers and many other employees do not even have a drivers license, the real statistics show an average of seven cars per driver—ten cars per Emirati and the expatriates who only have one car, two at the most. My friend Abdullah had fifteen cars; Sheikh Mohammed has more than 100.

With all the traffic and congestion in Dubai, you might think that people would be car pooling. Well, you would be wrong, because

Dubai is the only place on earth where car pooling is illegal. It's called passenger smuggling. If you take your neighbor to work with you, you can be fined $1,500. There is no appeal for this charge, and if you are a repeat car pooling offender, you can be deported. The government says you can always apply for a car pooling license, but the process to get a car pooling license is so stringent that most people will never qualify. The whole idea seems crazy to me—getting permission for something that should be a basic right—something that is good for the environment, in a very traffic-congested city. These charges are the government's way of convincing people to get out of their cars and onto public transportation that is owned by the Road Transport department. It's also another ill-disguised measure to prevent non-married couples from driving together.

This makes it even more frustrating to drive in Dubai, because with this law being enforced against expatriates, officers will be pulling drivers over to check if they are legally car pooling. If they find something else, like an unmarried couple or a Johnny Walker in the car, these people will go to jail.

Emiratis don't limit their rude driving to the roads. They are also menaces on the ocean. Jet skis have been banned mostly because people drive them like morons. Emiratis drive their watercraft or boats like they drive their cars—after all, they own the water too! Locals have absolutely no clue of the rules of the sea and sail. They have only one rule, and it's 'Get the *@#$% Out of My Way.' Unfortunately that rule doesn't work, especially if the other boater is another arrogant Emirati. Believe it or not, even though the ocean is a big place, Emiratis crash their boats out there frequently. If the collision involves an expatriate, he will always be wrong, and will have to pay the blood money for any deaths or go to jail.

I heard about this poor guy, a German citizen, who was sleeping at night on his sailboat, moored to a buoy. A crazy, drunk boater was speeding in the darkness of the night and slammed into the immobile sailboat. The crazy boater was a sheikh who died on impact. The German was lucky to be alive but found himself in prison for having been in the way of His Highness and being the cause of his death. When I heard about him, he had been in prison for six months already because he could not pay the blood money, as he was not insured while moored. He lost his boat and everything else. Overall, there have been a lot of accidents, and some young sheikhs have died on their powerful jet skis where there was nobody but them to blame. So in response the government banned the use of these watercrafts for everyone.

Food and dining in Dubai, good but imported

Cuisine and dining in Dubai is excellent and can be rated five stars only because it is imported. That is certainly not a good reason in itself to travel there, because you can find good food many places in the world. After my escape to India, I enjoyed fabulous food in Mumbai's hotels that rivaled any Dubai cuisine.

You will not find the best cuisine in the world because top chefs cannot own their restaurant, like in every other major city in the world. Opening a restaurant in Dubai is like opening any other business there. It means that an Emirati must own fifty-one percent of the business. The Chef would have to invest all the money of course, put up his name and have his residency visa sponsored by an Emirati national who would become the actual owner of his restaurant with zero investment. I doubt that a world-class, top chef, someone who has already made a name for himself, would accept this deal in trade for a temporary guest status. It's different for the young chef who needs Dubai as a proving ground, a place to get exposure and make some money quickly to return home after three years with prestigious Dubai on his resume. After doing his stint in Dubai, he could open his own restaurant in Rome, New York, or Paris where his invested money means he owns the restaurant.

The night life? Yes—reserved and restrained.

The night life offers a lot of smoke-filled bars and nightclubs. Again, everything in Dubai is imported and copied. Nothing is typical of Dubai, including the popular belly dancing. It is the oldest form of social dancing in human history, with its origins deep in ancient Egypt; it is definitely not part of Emirati traditions. Belly dancing is as much out of place in Dubai as in Beijing. It is entirely too sultry for their puritanical sensibilities. The profoundly Islamic Emiratis reconcile this contradictory practice of allowing women in Dubai to expose their skin and dance in suggestive ways in public only for marketing reasons. If a western woman did the same in a bikini at the beach she would be arrested. Hypocritical Emiratis enjoy the dancing as well, but again, it's the do-as-I-say not do-what-I-do rule so frequently followed by the Emirati nationals.

The entertainment is not limited to nightclubs. Most hotels offer outdoor and indoor salons with all types of different atmospheres and events imported from all over the world—like the Arabian Nights atmosphere where locals and tourists sit around on couches smoking *sisha*, a form of tobacco. The tobacco is burned with charcoal. Fumes are circulating and bubbling in water mixed with other flavors from fruits and leaves to be inhaled through a hookah pipe. It may look like an exotic or friendly thing to do, but this bad habit will kill five times quicker than cigarettes. Tourists either don't realize this or don't care since they are just on vacation, enjoying something different they will leave behind when they go back home. The Emiratis on the pipe are something else altogether. They display a lot of arrogance, they enjoy two or three slaves to prepare and serve the glass tower. They look pathetic showing their false confidence and importance.

The heat is suffocating during the day, but the weather at night is cool. It is nice to have a drink with friends on a terrace at the hotel, but there is no culture café or walks along the creek in the city. People for the most part are nice and seem to enjoy each other, and I never saw any fights or felt as if there were any risks of getting mugged or attacked. It is the expatriates themselves who fuel and maintain the night life in Dubai, finding ways to go around the police restrictions and codes imposed by the government. There is always something happening, like a party or an event. The city stays open very late into the night. Yet bars are regularly closed down because of Western behavior having gone too far for the Emiratis' comfort level. Alcohol, loud music, and women in miniskirts eventually wear down Emirati acceptance.

Dubai is absolutely not the Miami of the Middle East. There's no way it could be with so many restrictions that are sanctioned by prison. We are not talking about fines here, but hard time behind bars in crowded cells, toe to head bunks. Outdoor entertainment is no longer allowed, unless sponsored by the government for the purpose of advertising Dubai.

As time goes by, there are more and more restrictions placed on entertainment for the visitors. Little by little, Emiratis forbid what was allowed previously, believing that expatriates, once installed in their routines, will just accept these new restrictions and not complain. The mix between Arabian and western culture is an illusion. The reality is a constant confrontation between two cultures—one requiring a docile population, obedient and anesthetized—the other wanting to have fun, to be loud and free.

Bars and nightclubs reveal rampant prostitution, exposing a disturbing contradiction in Dubai. Prostitution is illegal and punishable by one year in prison. The government supposedly enforces very strict immigration rules to prevent these girls from coming into the country, but they are in nightclubs all over the city. The police know it and just look the other way, apparently with the permission of the government. Girls come from all over the world, to make ends meet, or as a result of being forced into it. There are many stories about the human trafficking that goes on in Dubai. Sadly, expatriates and tourists unknowingly support it when they pay for this type of entertainment.

Looking closely at other forms of entertainment available in Dubai, other events and shows, reveals more of Dubai's public relation illusions. The government of Dubai pays a great deal to advertise its city. It systematically funds all performances put on by international superstars. Almost all events are corrupted. No one seems to question how it is that celebrity pop artists are going to Dubai to give concerts for the couple of thousand expatriates who show up. The numbers don't add up. This is show business and these top performers only move for big money. They don't come for the price of 2,000 tickets. They come because the Government paid them to come.

What's the big deal? Well, the point is, it is part of the whole big scam perpetrated by Dubai on the world. This is marketing, designed to sell Dubai to the tourists and business people who have money to invest. You read the papers and see how stars come to Dubai to perform to a packed audience, and you assume Dubai is this cosmopolitan, modern, forward thinking place, where even your favorite pop stars want to be. It is all an illusion. To top it off, these performances are never as good as they would be in London, Los Angeles, or Rio. There is no chemistry between the performers and the audience. The government censors the performers' acts, and the audience looks like a group of students listening to a lecture in a classroom.

What they don't put in the papers is what happens at the concert. For most of the concerts being organized in Dubai, the CID shows up to turn down the volume, lecture the organizers, and warn the performers about behavior that does not comport with Emirati tradition. I was backstage once for a famous New York rapper's concert. This guy was a big shot and a talented artist. I watched two CID officers lecturing him about his inappropriate clothing and his indecent moves. They also threatened the arrest of participants and members of the audience for indecent exposure or uncontrolled behavior. I have to confess this put a smile on my face. What I saw there was nothing less than time travel. I saw a group of people talking to each other who could not understand one another because 400 years separated them. In the end, the volume was turned down, and the rapper accommodated the police under threat of cancellation of the concert. I don't think he will return.

There is no way, artists from London, New York, or Los Angeles would ever live in Dubai under such anachronistic restrictions imposed from a ten percent minority upon ninety percent of the population, for traditions that go back to when tribes were running around in the desert. Artists could never be creative in such a mind-binding environment. I challenged Emiratis, asking them where are their Mozart, Beatles, James Brown, or Madonna. They told me that our artists are decadent and perverted and the UAE doesn't produce that type of deviant—as if they had no interest in that kind of artist. So why do they invite them to Dubai? It's to trick the Western world into buying into Dubai.

I was not impressed by Emirati artists. It is always the same litany, and the musicians playing their instruments look like over-the-counter government employees. Their performances are not even snappy or engaging. Artists from Egypt, Morocco, or Lebanon are much more entertaining—with them you will enjoy the real Arabian Nights.

Emirati music is deeply attached to Muslim culture, and it therefore obligates women to modesty. This means there cannot be any female Emirati entertainer. How could they? No entertainer can hide behind a veil, never revealing her body and never using evocative gestures.

After thirty years of traveling and listening to music, I've found that creativity, talent and emotion are borderless. African culture has produced rhythm and blues and Spanish tradition has produced Latin music—what else comes from the Gulf Countries. The only artists, who can accept living in Dubai to make a living, are the less talented. The owner of a jazz club in Dubai could never meet the requirements of a jazz band from New York City, nor would the musicians accept living, packed in a two-bedroom apartment, on a "kick in the ass anytime" visa and a free ticket to jail for their little extras. So, you are left with the Chinese jazz bands that may sound a little like jazz, but it is never the real deal. It does not matter; the tourists don't have the time to mind this lack of talent in Dubai.

I went to one of the *Cirque du Soleil's* spectacles in Dubai—an awesome presentation, and again sponsored by the government through Nakheel. There were lots of expatriates under the tents who were really enjoying the show. But I could see embarrassment on the faces of the few Emiratis who were there, accompanied by their wives in black veils, looking at the young female athletes with only skin suits stretched over their bare skin. They were trying to compose themselves for this indecent exposure, but I have seen the same Emirati men being very, shall we say, enthusiastic in strip clubs in West Palm Beach, Florida, when they were visiting me.

There are plenty of people in Dubai who will vouch for the fantastic night life there, saying it's the best in the world. The people making these statements are either Emiratis advertising their city with the hope of luring more people there, people who have not traveled anywhere else, or singles, away from their families in shared housing. Going out is better than sitting home, watching sterilized television alone. Without the expatriate-fueled night life, Dubai would be quite boring. The truth is there is much better night life in any other countries.

The risk of Dubai Night life is not about being mugged—it is about being arrested by the police. Consumption of alcohol is forbidden in Islam and can only be consumed in hotels and in a handful of private clubs—and only by non-Muslims. Drunkenness in public carries a mandatory prison term. The purchase, possession, and transport of alcohol is illegal unless you have a license, which you can apply for with an approval letter from your sponsor. The license is like a credit card, and it allows you to purchase no more than two percent of your salary per month.

Liquor stores are out of sight behind steel doors with no advertisements, insignias, or other indications. The first time I was looking to buy some French wine, it took me a while to locate a liquor store. And once inside, I was surprised to see Emiratis in *khandoura* lining up to buy alcohol—hypocrisy again. The quantity you can buy is not much, and if you throw a party you better plan it in advance to stock bottles. Every time friends or family would come to Dubai to visit me, I would ask them to bring me wine and liquors. Airline travelers are authorized to carry up to seven bottles into Dubai.

Dubai beaches—rot, fry, eat dust and E coli, and go to jail.

Advertising Dubai for its beaches is another fraud. With the frenzied construction and real estate development greed, there is no longer any natural beach in Dubai—all along the thirty-five mile shoreline.

I remember when I first came to Dubai; people were going to the beach for picnics or kite surfing. Nobody can do that anymore—anywhere. The beaches are all private or require payment of a toll. They look immaculate because the sands are sifted daily by workers who are paid $200 a month, but the illusion doesn't pass the sands though.

Due to the contamination associated with sewage dumping and the sludge spewed out of the desalinization plant, a stay at the beach could put a person in the hospital for a skin rash or a gastroenteritis let alone the nasty picture of floating feces.

Nights at the beach are not so good either, especially if you are there as a couple. Police officers have nothing better to do than sit on roofs with binoculars to spot illegal kissing. There is a good chance, any couple walking or sitting on the beach at night will be stopped by a police officer who will want to check the lady's ID—to see if they are married. They are very rude in their approach, asking very indecent and offensive questions, obviously making the assumption that the woman is not the man's wife.

In 2006, the Dubai official police reports said there were 1,500 arrests for lewd behavior at the beach, they made it sound like they were mostly men stalking women in swimsuits, what the official report didn't say was that in reality 1,450 of them were to women for wearing indecent bikinis. The other fifty were the guys caught staring at them. I don't think there was ever a ticket issued in Miami for a wearing a thong.

Boating—forget it.

I have been sailing since I was eighteen. I've spent quite a bit of time on the waters around the world, so I was looking forward to boating in Dubai. But again, the advertising of boating in Dubai is a fraud. There cannot be boating. I tried. First, there is not much to see—second, there are too many restrictions—and third, there is too much bureaucracy.

Dubai does not have the scenery. The beach is a long stretch of sands with buildings and curtains of towers. Deep sea fishing is a joke, and after you have satisfied your urge to see the outskirts of the artificial islands, you have seen it all. There are some small islands in Abu Dhabi, but they are private and owned by the royal family—the police will stop you if you get too close.

Nakheel has planned to open its new marina on the Palm Jumeirah, I doubt they will, but if they do they are going to create the same problems as the other marinas in Dubai. There will be severe live onboard restrictions, because local boaters flush their toilet outboard. As a result marina managements forbid owners to live on their yachts. But how good is it to have a boat if you cannot spend nights onboard. It will be even worse on the Palm Islands because they built marinas less than 100 yards away from the beaches.

Everyone bought these beachside homes, never realizing they were going to be swimming in a huge saltwater toilet when they take a dip in the ocean off their private muddy beaches. So boating becomes boring quickly. You have to sail at least eighty miles out to find something worth the trip. But then you have to cope with the administrative hassles. Anytime you want to go out on your boat, for every single trip of any duration, you need to file a sailing permit with the Coast Guard and provide a list of your passengers with a copy of their passports. If you want to go past the territorial waters at twelve miles you need two sailing permits, your passport stamped at immigration, and to apply for a visa if you enter any neighboring country waters—Iran, Saudi, or Oman.

The Government discovered this open-door to freedom through my escape and implemented new rules that restrict boating even more. Now, people who own a sailboat must install a tracking device onboard—and anyone who buys a boat must get an approval from the CID before registering her. This insane regulation is for only one reason—to prevent anyone, filed in the police system, from using a boat in case he had the funny idea of escaping by ocean. Expatriates who own a boat are not very happy. The tracking device costs $2,000 to install, it drains the batteries of the boat, and it is a serious restriction to the freedom of boating.

Of course these rules do not apply to Emirati boat owners. They use their boats to show off and to bring prostitutes onboard to sail around with. There is no chance of them wanting to flee. Only the expatriates need to be repressed and tracked at all times. Boats are berthed in dedicated marinas that are managed like apartment complexes. There are no vacant spaces for visitors. So if a new boat arrives, it is unwanted and must leave immediately.

Boating in Dubai is not like boating in the Mediterranean or the Caribbean where boats can sail from one place to another, stay a week or two and continue. You cannot just jump in your boat and go. Failure to comply with the regulations can get you in serious trouble. My advice is, if you like yachting, go somewhere else. Yachting in Dubai can also be a waste of money due to the risk of losing your boat. If you ever had to leave the country due to a canceled visa, you would have to sell it in a hurry. Buying a boat and retiring in Dubai is not possible.

Shopping, Dubai, or Do buy?

One of the big advertisements for Dubai is shopping—and it has the beautiful malls to support it—absolutely stunning. There is high-end marble everywhere, pristine bathrooms, gold accents, stone columns, decorated and high ceilings, and billions of dollars of goods from all over the world waiting to be purchased. The malls are all built after a theme, like in a theme park. Sometimes they have attractions, like Ski Dubai at the Emirates Mall—an artificial, refrigerated ski slope. On weekends, the malls are packed, but not necessarily with shoppers but with people because it is cool inside. There are always events or attractions inside the mall—it is a nice meeting place with bars and terraces and a lot of good things to see. People go there to spend the day and eat at the fast food restaurants.

Shopping for anything out of the ordinary, or against Emirati traditions, must be ordered through Internet, with the accompanying risk of confiscation by Emirati Customs. This is conducted at their discretion with what seems like no justification and with no appeal. Many Internet retailers do not ship to the Middle East, so it is best to keep friends back home as freight forwarders for your packages.

Besides the malls there are other exhibitions that run throughout the year, including car shows, air shows, boat shows, and real estate displays. They are all displaying luxurious items of course, but these exhibitions are nothing more than advertising for Dubai and marketplaces tailored for the Emiratis and Arabs from neighboring countries, not for the tourists or expatriates.

Take a car show for instance—you will see mostly high-end, luxury cars. Most expatriates cannot afford to buy any of them, but they sure enjoy visiting the show and seeing the cars and hostesses up close. The buyers of the cars are local Emiratis. It's the same with the air shows which, every year, gross more and more sales. There are a lot of expatriate visitors, but they are not the ones buying private helicopters or jumbo jets to transport their families. Exhibitors themselves admit in interviews that they come to Dubai to generate sales from the local rich Arabs, with no mention of the expatriate population. Tourists and expatriates are merely guests, invited to watch.

The Dubai Government always claims tremendous successes after the shows are over. They are nothing but false reports passed to the media to lure people into believing that they should come, sell and buy. It is corrupted. I saw this happen firsthand.

After I left my company, the press announced that Exomos had netted $3 million in yacht orders that were allegedly placed during the boat show. Six months later they fired the CEO who had replaced me. No orders had ever been secured and no down payment was ever received—that was a lie to lure buyers. What happened there happened 100 times over with other companies in Dubai. The UAE exhibitors make false reports about their sales to create an illusion of business success to lure real buyers to their companies.

When I received a $150 million order from an Asian Navy, I wanted to keep it confidential because of its sensitivity. However, the order made it to the papers to advertise Dubai.

Expatriates have many other interests that are not shared by the Emiratis due to their Islamic laws and Government restrictions—so there will never be events or exhibitions that cater to them. You can forget about lingerie or swimwear fashion shows, or a beer festival—they are illegal. Same with comics, stamps, toys, agriculture, antiques or gun shows—these are events that you will never see take place in Dubai. Art and movie events are censored and thus, without interest.

Dubai: a police state

It is common to see employees at the mall filling up the ATM machines with cash. The money is piled up on the floor in plain view as if it they were reloading a candy bar machine. Million dollar jewelry is on display with no armed guards or armored glass. Armed robberies are less likely, because Dubai is a trap for hard criminals, also. The very simple reason why violent crime rate is so low is because Big Brother is alive and watching.

The whole country is completely under surveillance. Everybody is standardized; filed, identified, and linked to his passport and mobile phone which can be tracked by the police, like a homing device. The police have live access to an extensive electronic network with centralized data from immigration records, hotel guest check-ins, rental car records, car registration records, utility records, phone records, road toll gate cameras, company employee lists. They also have an extensive network of informants who get rewards for information leading to the arrest of suspects. It is true that career criminals cannot prey and survive in this police state. The perpetrators of the rare burglaries and bank robberies are quickly apprehended and jailed because of the drastic restrictions of the police system, but it is at the cost of everyone else's freedom.

There is only one way to live in Dubai and it is through a work visa and working forty-eight hours a week. Anyone who does not show up for work more than three times, without a good reason, gets fired and deported. Tourists cannot overstay a visitor's visa without being flagged in the police system. They get caught when they try to rent a car, get a hotel room, use a phone, use a computer, get cable service, or go through a toll booth.

In four years, I heard of only one armed robbery—in a jewelry store inside a luxury mall. The criminals forced their entry inside the mall with two cars, bursting the glass doors. They robbed the jewelry store at gunpoint. They were disguised like Arab women, covered completely in black robes. They got away with a million dollars in jewelry in less than two minutes, and then drove out of the mall. The stolen cars were found the next day, burning somewhere in the desert. Because people in Dubai are exposed to so many cultures, store employees were able to tell the police that the robbers were talking to each other in Serbo Croat. The police went into their system to check for passports and visas and pulled out about 100 people who were in

Dubai from Central Europe. They traced them all to their hotels or residences and searched them. They were all taken to the police station and interrogated. They pulled over and seized all the vehicles. The police found the stolen jewelry hidden in one of the cars, and from there they narrowed down their suspects to five perpetrators. They released everybody else and jailed the criminals. They found the guns—they were plastic toy guns. They also found the women's clothing. I heard about another mass arrest after a series of robberies that were committed by men on bicycles. The police response was to impound 1,000 bicycles and question their owners without explaining their reasoning. I cannot see mass arrests and mass seizures like this in a free country, for the single reason that criminals were using a certain type of vehicle or were speaking a foreign language. How many innocent people were swept up into this investigation for no good reason?

Because they are never confronted by hardened criminals, security guards and police officers in Dubai are soft, under-armed, and unprepared. Most of the police officers are expatriates from Yemen or other GCC countries, on Government sponsorship. They are underpaid, lazy, and not willing to take any risks. They have no real police experience. When criminals show up with plastic guns, they don't know the difference and everybody ducks or runs away like a chicken—including them.

Most crimes are perpetrated by petty criminals trying to cash in on small-time crimes or smuggling, home burglaries and sex crimes—but nothing compared to Paris' suburbs, Los Angeles, or Cape Town.

Censorship

Sheikh Mohammed claims freedom of the press exists in Dubai, but his government practices extensive censorship in all areas of journalism, media, movies, literary works, art and other forms of expression. All major media and news agencies, international or local, that have offices and assets in Dubai, fall under the Dubai media law that allows for the fining of journalists, editors, and publishers for articles that offend the government, in addition to being banned from Dubai. The local media is restrained from reporting negatively on the rulers, the image of Dubai, and its economy. The UAE ranks a dismal 137th on the global Press Freedom Index.

The authorities are in complete denial. They pretend there is no censorship, yet they decide what people can read and watch in the privacy of their homes. I could not complain about it. Like everybody else, I had to accept the censorship or leave.

Under international pressure the UAE drafted a new law towards more freedom and international standards. It is a lie and a trick. The new laws regarding fines for reporters, editors, and publishers are actually worse than before. Dubai claims that instead of imprisonment, journalists and media are now only subject to fines up to $272,000 for publishing anything that damages the reputation of the UAE or harms the national economy. But this new law now applies to everyone, like printing companies and wire services—not just reporters like before. In effect, the media can lose its license or fire the reporter over a controversial article. What the new law does not say is that the reporter may be jailed indefinitely—not for the article, but for failing to pay the fine that no one will pay for him.

When Arabian Business published an article about me being convicted for fraud, I wrote to the reporter for a right to respond. They agreed and published a more balanced article in which I strongly denied any embezzlement. Two days later Dubai Media Council ordered the editors to pull the article out of Arabian Business—proof that you can never have a fair hearing or challenged accusations.

As a result, self-censorship in Dubai is very effective. Anyone who lives and works in Dubai needs sponsorship for a visa. As a result everybody practices self-censorship, by keeping anything negative or disparaging to himself, so as not to risk deportation, regardless of whether he speaks the truth.

Reporters covering the world markets from Dubai, or who want to be able to travel to Dubai for their stories, must be very careful about what they say regarding the government or the members of the royal family. They could find themselves turned away at the border, detained for hours at the airport police station for threats to State Security, or trapped inside the borders if they owe a fine. Not being allowed into the place where the news is happening, is a career ending event for a reporter.

The UAE government exerts severe and strict censorship over Internet access through its sole Internet service provider, Etisalat. It monitors, filters, controls, and blocks web sites and email providers that feature poker, adult content, blog sites, forums, American TV, Flicker, YouTube, Skype, dating sites and more. Only Muslim dating sites are accessible and for Muslims only. Again, the double standards rise up in favor of the Emirati. However, Sheikh Mohammed, his family, his executives, and the Emirati Elite have full and unrestricted access to anything they want through their own private ISP, because they are above the laws they create.

In my early days in Dubai, while browsing through a bookstore at a shopping mall, I laughed at how much trouble the local authorities took to use black markers to mask every bit of women's cleavage, shown on every single page, on every single magazine. I joked with a friend and customs official once, telling him that I wanted to be the guy with the marker, because he was the only one to have unrestricted access. The official was not embarrassed to tell me that he had access to uncensored magazines too, but was not looking at them, and that suggestive pictures had to be blackened because people were not capable of controlling their thoughts by themselves, George Orwell in action.

Even satellite TV is censored in Dubai. You can receive HBO and Showtime, but the shows are edited and censored. You will never see a commercial with a woman shaving her legs or showing her bare feet—all of this is cut out by the censors.

They have the latest technologies to achieve the best censorship and make it appear as if there is none. For awhile there were pirate tuners available so people could watch racy shows without blocks. But the government found out and blocked them too. Later I would find Chinese vendors knocking at my door at 10:00, trying to sell me dirty movies on pirated DVDs.

Some movies don't even make it to Dubai. It is only after I returned to the U.S. that I realized I missed *V for Vendetta*, a great movie. Censors don't just reject movies with adult content; they also reject movies about mind control over an obedient populace and movies that worship women.

George Orwell and Fritz Lang movies and books are banned. I can see why the government of Dubai would not want those movies around—they might give funny ideas to the people. *Charlie's Angels* was banned in Dubai. They couldn't have all those beautiful, independent, capable women running around getting the people of Dubai all excited. The movie *300* was banned, as if these half-nude, muscled male bodies could give funny ideas to their wives and daughters. The movie *Syrianna* was censored.

I had at least twenty French movies that I ordered through Amazon.com confiscated by Customs. Half of them were children's movies that still didn't meet Emirati censorship standards, for some unknown reasons. There have been so many complaints from consumers that Amazon no longer ships to the UAE. For some reason my wife was on the postal blacklist. Every single package she received was opened by Customs before it came to us. Perhaps it was because Customs confiscated my collection of comic books, a very rare and valuable erotic limited edition of *Tintin* I received under her name. Or maybe it was because of her Victoria Secret catalogs. I can only speculate because no one is ever given a reason for the confiscation of his or her property in Dubai.

Even at the Virgin Mega Store in Dubai you are not getting what you think. Sometimes you get home and play what you bought and find that you have some crazy edited and censored version, and they don't even bother to let you know that with a label or anything.

A friend visited an art expo in Dubai in 2008 and told me pictures of statues and renaissance paintings were covered with black stickers— or should I say desecrated. It is ridiculous for anyone in Dubai to proclaim the city a place of the arts. How can Sheikh Mohammed consider himself a patron of the arts, and then support censorship stickers on great works of art? One of the reasons despots can rule in the region quite successfully is because it is forbidden to criticize them. The UAE constitution states that freedom of opinion and expressing it verbally, in writing, or by other means of expression, shall be guaranteed within limits of law. They put freedom and limit in the same phrase. There is essentially no freedom of speech in Dubai at all.

Dubai is trying to buy itself legitimacy with Western-like free thinking events such as the Dubai International Film Festival where they hand out awards for best film and so forth. But the only award they should be handing out to themselves is the award for most hypocritical society. How can a country that condones and practices strict censorship host an international film festival of all things and have the audacity to proclaim itself the new cultural hub for the world. The Dubai Film Festival is the most pathetic event I have ever had the shame to see. In an effort to show some legitimacy, the government pays international movie stars to come to Dubai to promote their movies and incidentally, endorse the festival.

I am no longer based in Dubai, I am out of their jurisdiction and out of their reach—I am free to tell the truth, loud and clear. And frankly, I don't give a damn about UAE censorship. They shoot themselves in the foot with it. Let them stay in the Middle Ages if that is where they want to be.

Sheikh Mohammed preaches about the benefits of censorship as if it will save his people from the ruin of Western influence. What it's really about is maintaining and guaranteeing the power of his family over the Emirate—forever. He does not want his people to wake up one day and ask for general elections and a share of the country's wealth. He does not want inconvenient truths and contradictions to be exposed.

Independent thinking is discouraged and condemned. He does not want his people to make their own judgments. Instead, he gives them the judgment the government deems proper, to keep his people docile and accepting of the government's control. Free access to media is a factor that influences young women's expectations—but young Emirati men and their fathers do not want women who challenge their dictates. French author De Beaumarchais once said, "Without the right to criticize, praise cannot exist. Only small men fear the words of small pens."

In the UAE, flattery for the ruling families is omnipresent—and they actually believe it is genuine and true. Huge panels on Sheikh Zayed Road depict the benefits of Sheikh Mohammed's accomplishments and gifts to Mankind. A gift? For Mankind? Anywhere else in the world, people would laugh at his megalomania. In Dubai, not only will nobody say a word, but they'll also act as if they approve and support it.

However, censorship is harmful to the people of the UAE. It is slowly eroding the fabric of their people. Sheikh Mohammed likes to claim he's a change for Dubai. Instead, I see him as the man responsible for exploiting an entire people through ignorance and refusal to see the forest for the trees.

It is not exaggerating to say that some people die as a direct consequence of censorship. Emirati women die of breast and cervical cancer at a much higher rate than women anywhere else in the world because of their family environment and restricted access to information. Anything that shows or talks about a woman's breast is considered pornographic. Doctors and surgeons can practice medicine and surgery on women only if they are women doctors and the chances for a woman in the UAE to become a surgeon are close to none—given the fact they do not have full access to education. Many of the Emirati husbands would rather see their wives die than go through, what they perceive to be, a shameful disease or to be touched by a male doctor.

Emiratis are even going so far as trying to ban Valentine's Day celebrations—or at least inconvenience those who want to celebrate. Valentine's Day is a very bothersome day in the Emirati household because the women watch and envy foreign women being gifted with flowers and poetry about everlasting love. I remember I had to rush to the mall late after work, so I could get in line to buy my wife Helen some roses. For the third year I noticed that roses were very scarce so I spotted a giant red heart that was four feet tall, all embroidered with artificial roses and flowers, almost as big as a highway sign. It was a perfect demonstration of the big love I have for my dear wife, so I bought it. Here I was walking through the mall with this gigantic heart, an obvious object of affection for this beloved celebration that Westerners observe every year—and all I could see around me were angry stares from Arab men because of the frustration I was causing in their women.

In many Gulf Countries, such as Qatar, they are trying to make the celebration of Saint Valentine illegal. Dubai is split between wanting to attract the Westerners and the constraints of their feudal mind. They have found a smarter way to limit the damage of Valentine's Day on their doomed culture—the Customs authorities just limit or stop the import of roses during the week of Valentine's Day. No florist is going to risk his money by importing roses after having received implied threats by Customs authorities that his load of roses might be held at customs for agricultural inspections and analysis. Limiting the import of roses is a poor attempt at censorship, which ultimately does not work anyway. Emiratis do not understand that the affection is not in the flowers—it is in the attention.

Valentine's Day is a more profound cultural conflict for Emiratis than Christmas. With Christmas, in the eyes of Muslims, we just celebrate the birth of a different prophet, and it is a family-oriented holiday. I guess they figure we Westerners are all going to hell anyway for this mistake. But Valentine's Day is something more insidious and destructive to their culture, because it affects the relationships between Emirati men and their women. Middle Eastern women see that Western women have many more rights. They have the right to look sexy and dress pretty, wear makeup, and show themselves to the world and receive compliments. I'm sure it should go without saying that when roses are off limits, sex toys are in outer space for these people. Ahmed Butti, the director of Dubai Customs told me about the number of a sex toys his officers were confiscating every year, hence I learned straight from Emirati women why the electric toothbrush is a very popular item in Dubai.

Again numbers speak for themselves. The divorce rate in Dubai is higher than the divorce rate in the U.S. One of the reasons is Emiratis are shielded from reality through censorship, and they are forbidden from expressing themselves freely and clearly. Censorship cannot generate genuine commitments, or conditions that support living with love and stability.

Censorship takes many forms in the UAE. Not only is it the blocking of information or restricting access to information, it is also providing an environment where groups are encouraged to report false data to entice others to invest in Dubai. Professionals can actually pass their own stories on to the media, and those stories will be published without fact-checking—as if they were unbiased reports.

In Dubai, you can have articles published that are never called releases so they look like some reporter wrote them from an unbiased perspective. News-marketing representatives publish companies' news releases as articles, after the companies agree to buy ad space in the publication. Often the publication does not even edit what is submitted. Many companies in Dubai take part in this type of news reporting. Many times news agencies came to Exomos, asking us to write a news story that they would print as their news release.

I have seen Nakheel use this media in a dishonest way, claiming imaginary sales of its islands to celebrities that never occurred and publishing reports by paid-off environmentalists, claiming that marine life has been preserved during the reclamation of Dubai's artificial islands. This is the evil of the news for sale that goes on in Dubai. You cannot trust anything you read or hear in Dubai because the sources are biased or corrupt.

Emiratis are not very enthusiastic about seeing the success of expatriates in the news. The only reason I can ever come up with to understand that reaction from Emiratis is ego and jealousy. It bothers them to see a foreigner getting credit, when they feel it is their money that brought him there. At Exomos, whenever top management knew the press was going to interview me, I was directed to state that all of the submarine ideas coming out of Exomos were due to Sheikh Mohammed's vision and forward thinking.

Emirati Hypocrisy, the biggest sham ever.

In trying to convince the world that Dubai is an open and liberal city where people can live under Western standards in harmony with Emirati heritage, Emiratis and Sheikh Mohammed have brought their hypocrisy to a whole new level. They have used fabricated images, a manufactured life style, and distorted truths—paid for by the very same people who invest there—to perpetrate the biggest sham the world has ever known.

They have built a city of superlatives, the best, the biggest, and the tallest—but they can now also claim the biggest hypocrisy in the world. Emirati profess qualities and virtues they do not have, to mask their depraved behavior and anachronistic laws in order to lure investors and visitors for their money—and to blame the decadent Western influence for losing their identity and mounting cultural losses.

Dubai is not an open society. The most barbaric punishments are still rampant—like death by stoning, flogging, female genital mutilation and many others. Disturbing rumors of women kept prisoner by their employer are never investigated because Emiratis condone such practices. They are sadly confirmed by news reports when fires erupt in apartment complexes and burn the occupants who are locked up inside.

On one end, a Westerner caught drinking or with another woman, gets a mandatory prison sentence followed by deportation, but on the other end everybody looks the other way when Emirati men drink alcohol and enjoy hired prostitutes in the privacy of their farms or yachts. If you happen to look around in the marinas you will see limousines and drivers dropping off Russian or Arab girls for on-board Emirati entertainment.

At the Dubai Yacht Club they couldn't even use the excuse that they were just going out for a ride on the boat, since the construction of the new bridge on the creek blocked the access to the ocean. Sheikh Mohammed enjoys this tradition as well. It is a well-known fact in Dubai that every month he takes his 500 foot yacht out and hires up to fifty girls for the occasion. They get paid $10,000 each for the weekend. So while he puts anyone caught in an illicit affair in jail, he parties on the weekends with prostitutes and spends half a million dollars to accommodate himself and his guests.

The hypocrisy of Dubai starts at the top of the pyramid. I was on Sheikh Mohammed's yacht with Sultan and his wife once, and I was having a conversation with her as she was showing me the bedroom next to the discothèque. (Yes, the boat is big enough to accommodate a disco.) I could not help but ask her who in the world would have this strange idea to build a bedroom next to a discothèque. How could anyone sleep with dancing and music going on right next door? She turned to me with resignation on her face, as if I should have figured out the answer for myself, and she explained that the owner of the boat wants to keep the sanctity of his wife's bedroom when he has company onboard. I quickly figured this was the bedroom for girlfriends. The Emirati's wives must live with the facts that their husbands sleep around and have their boats to accommodate their affairs. I am not here to judge what is right and what is wrong between wives and husbands, but I know for sure that in a democracy, when a head of state is caught with his pants down, he takes a hit for it. It is especially bad if he is the one to speak in support of laws against extramarital affairs and to jail those who get caught—yet he acts as though these laws do not apply to him.

Sheikh Mohammed has nineteen children that he fathered through four women—two of which have never been married to him. It is in the public records, and so is the UAE law that sends to prison anyone having a baby out of marriage. But no one would dare to speak out against Sheikh Mo or launch an investigation. He owns the courts, the judges, and the prosecutors.

Once I was invited to an Emirati party on a dinner boat for a business event. I was amazed to discover the completely hypocritical organization they have. We were on the boat in the middle of the creek, when later that night an Emirati transferred a group of Iraqi girls and cases of alcohol onboard from another boat out of nowhere. It is less the fact that Emiratis imbibed themselves and indulged with women that shocked me, but the fact that every other day they lecture Westerners against the same.

Every society has its own standards regarding what is socially acceptable. Without these standards a society would collapse. Many standards are universal and recognized internationally, especially terrible things like crimes of murder and theft. However Dubai has double standards, as laws do not apply the same way to all the people living there. Emiratis do not see international norms as norms they must adopt. Emiratis get away with torture and sometimes even murder. Amnesty International has made several findings to support this contention. A brother of the President of the UAE was caught on tape, torturing a Pakistani, and got away with it. What Emiratis consider police procedure, is clearly seen by the rest of the world as torture. In some cases of murder and manslaughter, the court can drop the charges if the victim's family accepts financial compensation from the defendant's family.

It is a mistake to think of Dubai in terms of a Constitution, civil or human rights, or justice. None of these concepts carry any meaning or value there. Under the despotism of Sheikh Mohammed, Dubai is a corporation governed with a business plan—where its inhabitants are expendable employees, or valued visitors, not citizens.

When the UAE gets called out by the media or the international community, they don't change their rules. They just change the way information is disclosed. They censor and cover up even more, so next time they don't get caught. For instance when the world discovered in 2006 that the UAE police were forcibly injecting detained foreigners, accused of being homosexuals and cross-dressers, with drugs, Colonel Al Sayar, the UAE Ministry of the Interior, responded to the public outrage—not by saying that they would stop injecting drugs, or by saying they would amend the laws. Instead he said it was normal to recommend psychological and hormone therapy to homosexuals in order to address the immoral and unacceptable behavior of these individuals, but the drug treatments would be made optional in the future. They dressed up the law by rewording it to make it sound friendlier—but they're still injecting these people with these drugs. The UAE is not only Orwellian—it is also strangely reminiscent of *This Perfect Day* by Ira Levin, where people are injected with drugs to control certain behaviors. These stories actually depict what is currently happening in Dubai.

The UAE signed international treaties to abolish slavery in 1963. But in 2005, the U.S. State Department revealed, that children as young as four, were still being trafficked into the UAE and forced into being jockeys for camel racing. They and their families alleged that, along with other abuses, they were subjected to injections of hormones designed to keep them small and light.

When Sheikh Mohammed made child slavery illegal, it could not have been because he felt slavery is wrong. How could it? He was part of the offensive practice of the camel racing industry. Are we to believe that he saw those little people on those camels and didn't know they were children taken from their parents from neighboring countries? He made it illegal because he got caught by the rest of the world with the worst form of slavery, going on right in his front yard—the enslavement of 30,000 children working as camel jockeys for the Emirati Elite and their million dollar camel races. In 2006 Sheikh Mohammed was served with legal papers at the door of his private 747 aircraft during a trip in the U.S. He was sued for these acts of slavery.

Later in 2007 he launched Dubai Cares, a campaign to raise money for needy children worldwide. He used someone else's money, obviously to draw attention away from him as the perpetrator of modern day child slavery and towards the new spin of him being a savior. The $900 million raised brought praise for Sheikh Mohammed's generosity, and supported his newfound self-righteousness. He sent a letter to the President of the United States, George W. Bush, to request the dismissal of the entire case. And on July 30, 2007, a Federal Judge in the Southern District of Florida dismissed the case. That dismissal effectively sent all of these abused child slaves into oblivion, and the sad thing is—the U.S. government supported it. They had filed a brief with the court, suggesting that Sheikh Mohammed be given diplomatic immunity for his crimes.

The Emiratis have not turned away from the enslavement of people, if recent news reports are to be believed. Last July there was a story in the news of seven family members of deceased Sheikh Muhammed Khalid Al Nahyan from the UAE who were charged with exploiting servants while living in the Conrad Hotel, Brussels, Belgium. This case was brought to light when a thirty-two-year-old Moroccan woman managed to escape this family and went to the Belgian police. She said the family had exploited her and many others and their passports had been taken away.

The widow of the Sheikh had been living in the hotel for the past year, together with her four daughter-princesses. They paid for the entire fourth floor of fifty-three rooms for a year. They had a total of fourteen servant girls and three body guards, from the Philippines,

Morocco, India, Egypt, Turkey, Iraq, and Syria. The girl who escaped was paid 500 Euros a month, while the other servant girls were paid less—some as little as 150 Euros. Belgian officials called it human trafficking and slavery. If slavery were truly outlawed in Dubai, Emiratis would stop doing these things to foreigners. But they know they can keep on doing what they've always done because no one is going to stop them.

Dubai's constitution states, social justice applies to all, and that before the law, women are equal to men. They are supposed to enjoy the same legal status, claim to titles, access to education, and rights to practice their chosen professions. This Constitution also guarantees them the same access to employment, health, and family welfare facilities. In accordance with Islamic principles upon which the Constitution is based, the rights of women to inherit property are also guaranteed and insured.

All of these Constitutional rights for women are outright lies. Judge for yourself—under Sharia law, oral divorce is still legal in the UAE, but only for men. Emirati women need permission from a male relative to work, travel, and receive treatment at the hospital. An Emirati woman is not entitled to any monetary inheritance, unless a male relative has been assigned to dictate how she can spend it. The man in return can use his inheritance any way he wants, without oversight.

Emirati men can be married to four wives at one time—and can marry more if they divorce any of their first four. In addition most of them enjoy extramarital sexual relations. I can only imagine what would happen to a woman who would even try to marry more than one man, claiming equal rights. She would probably end up in a mental institution or a prison. Take for instance, contraception—every woman in the UAE, not just Muslims, must get the husband's consent for doctors to prescribe contraception. Also if a woman does not have a husband, she cannot get contraception at all.

The Emirati Society is articulated around hypocrisy, flattery, and worship of the ruler. However, flattery does not work to achieve quality and improve business. Flattery only promotes incompetence. I attended many of Emirati awards ceremonies because I was directed to go by the top management of Exomos, and I even received a couple of awards.

Everybody was standing around congratulating each other for their great accomplishments, and I felt uncomfortable. Everything looked so fake and cold. It came off as a pathetic attempt to indulge one's ego and imitate awards ceremony they have seen on Western television— but without the genuine joy, pride, or cheers one normally sees at those events. There is not a week that goes by in Dubai where the rulers are not praised and awards are not distributed. Almost all businesses are forced to enter into these awards programs and pay fees to participate.

Fear and denial

Hypocrisy leads to fear, and fear is the most dynamic component moving Dubai. There is a near-constant fear of job loss, deportation, missing deadlines, fear of the police, fear of the justice system, fear of getting caught with a girlfriend, fear for your life when driving, fear of catching an infectious disease. Nothing in Dubai can be taken for granted—no gift, no position, and no promises. A deal is good only as long as it is a good deal for an Emirati.

The problem is that a person has no control over his life because he is trapped in a visa sponsored situation that can be ended for no reason, and without appeal. Nationals of course, but truly anyone can exert pressure on somebody to threaten his job, his income, and his freedom. The fear of losing money in Dubai is not the same as the fear of losing money in London or another Western city. In Dubai if you lose money, there is no way you can get it back because the justice system is corrupt and biased toward Emirati nationals.

Fear is omnipresent in Dubai, even though it is a paradise of personal and corporate security. Laws to guarantee financial secrecy, armies of concierges, watchmen, and bodyguards, electronic surveillance, high walls, and guarded perimeters, serve only the interests of Emiratis. If you are part of their interests you are protected. If you are against their interests, you are a sheep among wolves. When I was in Dubai, I not only felt fear but anger—anger for these people who functioned within the government, taking advantage of their closed borders, medieval and hypocritical laws, and Orwellian justice system to try and swindle money from me.

Nobody living in Dubai will ever get rid of all of their fear. It is a part of our human physical and psychological makeup to react with fear to the things going on there. At best, people can learn to live with it and become anesthetized to it—coerced into conformity and managing side effects with limited success. Most expatriates live in complete denial and refuse to admit the conditions they live in.

Conclusion

If one day you foresee yourself doing business with the Emirates, or traveling there, keep *Caveat emptor* in mind. Because, if you're not careful, you may find yourself robotized, to fulfill the despotic ruler's vision, or worse—be scammed, ripped off, interrogated, scolded, threatened, accused and thrown in a crowded cell—and you won't even know why.

The liberal outlook of Dubai is designed to attract investors, visitors and workers, while hiding a truth they can't advertise—a ruthless society imposing anachronistic laws on its inhabitants under the pretense of a nonexistent heritage. All the while, Emiratis are above the rules they expect you to follow. A small message for the tourists—why waste time and money when you can find other genuine places for your dream vacations, rather than looking at concrete buildings, breathing dust and risking first degree burns on polluted beaches?

All the reports and images of Dubai are false and misleading ploys to capture your money. It's a game of bait and switch designed to lure you in. Do business at your own risk and expect no recourse. This is a land where unbalanced laws, censorship, and hypocrisy are in place, not to pay homage to their Emirati identity, but to maintain the ruling families in their dictatorship posts and sustain their cash flow.

Do not believe people in Dubai get into trouble of their own making. They are the victims of opportunistic tribal members who have no integrity, honesty, class or honor. They care nothing for human or civil rights or for people they consider infidels and outsiders. You can never be a friend with an Emirati—he can only pretend while you serve him.

Everything I initiated at Sultan's request has all turned to a wasteland, decaying under the smoldering sun, and blown away by the harsh sand-filled winds. He lured me with his friendship, and then turned on me when money dried up.

The infamous Ahmed Butti ordered dismantling of everything I ever created and replaced me with incompetent managers who, after just ten months, failed miserably. Thirty million dollars wasted in the sands. Sultan, Butti, Abdul Qader and their associates created their own reality to suit their purposes. The only remedy, for their own money mistakes, was to blame me for everything. They always blame foreigners. Today, Dubai World is on the edge of collapse. Sultan Bin Sulayem is being scrutinized and will be sent to oblivion for his poor senseless judgments and mismanagement.

I pay my respects to Greg who risked his career by doing his job. There is no freedom of the press in Dubai. All other reporters are complacently bending to the rulers to serve their truth.

Despite the Emiratis, the harassment and the financial losses I endured, I made my Dubai experience a success. I know that Sultan, Butti and Abdul Qader are enraged that I slipped through their claws. I came out of the fight with a black eye, but it was still better than coming out on a stretcher.

I have tried to write about what I saw and experienced in Dubai as an everyday citizen. You can draw your own conclusions or investigate for yourself. I expect you to disagree with me and brush off my comments. You may even think I'm two bricks shy of a load, but don't be so quick to dismiss my warnings...or think you can weasel your way out of a sticky situation. Because the bright lights you first came to see will start to look dim. You'll see uglier sides of this pretty city and of its people without even wanting to.

My special thanks to Google for Google Earth, the Indian Immigration, the French Consulates, "Bernard," and "Robert."

For More Information Visit:

Wikipedia: en.wikipedia.org/wiki/Politics_of_the_United_Arab_Emirates
UAE censorship agency, National Media Council:
  http://www.uaeinteract.com
Road and Transport Authorities Dubai: http://www.rta.ae/wpsv5/wps/portal
Dubai Real Estate Agency: http://rpdubai.ae/rpdubai/welcome?lang=0
US State Department Info: travel.state.gov/travel/cis_pa_tw/cis/cis_1050.html
US Embassy in the UAE: uae.usembassy.gov
CIA Info on the UAE:
  cia.gov/library/publications/the-world-factbook/geos/ae.html
UAE Statistics:lcweb2.loc.gov/frd/cs/profiles/UAE.pdf
Dubai info: http://www.dubaifaqs.com
en.wikipedia.org/wiki/Dubai
Dubai Policehttp://www.dubaipolice.gov.ae/dp/english/main.jsp
Boatingand policewww.sail-world.com/Australia/E-passports-for-yacht-
  safety——is-Emirates-leading-the-world%3f/58188
Horse racing and doping http://www.fei.org/Athletes_AND_Horses/
  Medication_Control_AND_Antidoping/Horses/Documents/03%20-
  %20BEBABELOULA%20-
  %20Final%20Tribunal%20Decision%20dated%2022%20July%202009.pdf
Dubai health stats: www.ameinfo.com/169878.html,
www.xpress4me.com/news/uae/dubai/20014054.html
Women health Dubai: www.gulfnews.com/nation/Health/10313458.html
www.ArabMedicare.com
thenational.ae/article/20090204/NATIONAL/646822481/-1/NEWS
HIV in Dubai: www.arabianbusiness.com/9840
Desalination:thenational.ae/apps/pbcs.dll/article?AID=/20090831/.../LIFE
Life in Dubai Blogshttp://dubaithoughts.blogspot.com
www.grapeshisha.com
Driving in Dubaiwww.dubaifaqs.com/driving-in-dubai.php
Beach Gardens, Florida www.sba facts.com
VPN networkshttp://compnetworking.about.com/library/weekly/
  aa010701a.htm
Consanguinity in the UAE: www.cags.org.ae/cbc03uae.pdf
Cervical cancerhttp://www.cancerarchive.com
www.cancer.org/downloads/PRO/CervicalCancer.pdf
www.scielosp.org/pdf/spm/v45s3/v45s3a08.pdf
Death rates in the UAEgulfnews.com/opinion/editorial_opinion/nation/
  10258640.html
www.uaeincorp.com/dubai_population.html
Family lawhttp://www.international-divorce.com/uae_child_abduction.htm